*J.K. LASSER'S*

# PICK
# WINNING
# STOCKS

## Also by Edward F. Mrkvicka, Jr.

*Your Bank Is Ripping You Off*

*The Bank Book: How to Revoke Your Bank's License to Steal*

*1,037 Ways to Make or Save Up to $100,000 This Year Alone*

*The Rational Investor*

*Moving Up*

*Battle Your Bank—and Win!*

*J.K. LASSER'S*™

# PICK WINNING STOCKS

### Edward F. Mrkvicka, Jr.

**John Wiley & Sons, Inc.**
New York • Chichester • Weinheim • Brisbane • Singapore • Toronto

This publication is designed to provide accurate and authoritative information in regard to
the subject matter covered. It is sold with the understanding that the publisher is not
engaged in rendering professional services. If professional advice or other expert assistance
is required, the services of a competent professional person should be sought.

This book offers only general observations based on the author's experience. It makes no
specific recommendations, and the author cannot be held responsible for any loss incurred
as a result of the application of any information in this publication.

*Library of Congress Cataloging-in-Publication Data:*
Mrkvicka, Edward F.
    J.K. Lasser's pick winning stocks / Edward F. Mrkvicka, Jr.
      p.  cm.
    Includes index.
    ISBN 0-471-39357-6 (pbk. : alk. paper)
    1. Stocks.  2. Investment analysis.  I. Title: J.K. Lasser's pick winning
stocks.  II. Title.
HG4661.M75  2000
332.63'22—dc21                               00-033005

Printed in the United States of America.

10  9  8  7  6  5  4  3  2  1

To Eddie and Kelly—my children, my best friends

# Preface

To be successful in the stock market you have to trade a system. What I mean is that you must trade not on emotion, the latest hot tip from your broker, or Internet rumor, but on a series of rules based on past performance of not only a given stock but the market as well.

Of course, when the stock market is roaring, everyone makes money, which is to be expected. However, investment success is ultimately predicated on a long-term perspective, because the market's averaged yearly historical return since the early 1900s is under 10 percent, which means while some investors can and do make a short-term killing, the majority have to be in for the long haul to realize a sizable dollar return. Adding weight to the point regarding long-term investment dedication, the *Wall Street Journal* states that since 1926 the odds of losing money in the stock market over a one-year span are 30 percent. That is an alarming figure. However, the odds drop to just 4 percent over a 10-year span. Couple this with the fact that the market has experienced two down years for every three up years, and you can see that the market of the 1990s is not typical—and because it is not typical one should not see this market as a representation of what you are likely to face in the future. While you may have made money recently—even a lot of money—things will change, and when they do you had better be trading a system that can make money in both a bull and a bear market, because you can lose money in the market just as fast, if not faster, than you made it.

The Trinity Trading System (TTS), described herein, is the result of years of following various markets, seeing how they worked, discovering their sameness, and exploring how they are different. More specifically, it is the result of decades of following the stock market and seeing its metamorphosis from a market based on earnings to a market based on selling hype and investor frenzy. So much has happened in and to the market, and there is more to follow. Change, constant change, is what we will see in the stock market from now on, which is why you need the TTS. It has found the one continuing winning constant, the market's hidden code if you will, and has distilled it down to its absolute simplest form whereby you will earn more in any bull market than you would have without it and a fortune in even the worst bear market—and you will do so with very little money to start and only 10 minutes to a half hour of your time per day.

EDWARD F. MRKVICKA, JR.

*Marengo, Illinois*
*July 2000*

# Acknowledgments

Many thanks to my editor, Bob Shuman, and associate managing editor, Mary Daniello, at John Wiley & Sons; my agent, Denise Marcil of the Denise Marcil Literary Agency; and the staff at Cape Cod Compositors.

# Contents

# CHAPTER 1

# The Market As It Really Is

On December 5, 1996, Alan Greenspan, the respected and in many circles revered Federal Reserve Board chairman and (some believe) behind-the-scenes architect of the 1990s economic boom, said in a pointed reference to the stock market, "How do we know when irrational exuberance has unduly escalated asset values?" The market had closed earlier that day with the Dow Jones Industrial Average at 6,437.

Simply put, Greenspan was warning, in no uncertain terms, that he believed the market was overvalued at 6,437. That's not just *my* parsing of his statement. Bill Dudley, director of U.S. economic research at Goldman Sachs, said in January of 1999, "From the Fed's perspective, the stock market was overvalued two years ago."

Since Greenspan's original statement, he has continued his dire warning. On October 8, 1997, he said that the "stock market boom may be unsustainable." On July 21, 1998, he testified to the Senate Banking Committee that current values in the stock market may be "difficult to sustain." In January 1999 in testimony to the House Ways and Means Committee he stated that the recent performance of the equity markets will have difficulty in being sustained. These warnings from the reserved and soft-spoken Fed chairman are like anyone else shouting from the rooftop.

If, as Mr. Greenspan warned in 1996, the stock market was overvalued at 6,437, it is not inappropriate to suggest that it is grossly overvalued at its as-of-this-writing value of over 11,500. Since he first raised the specter of overvaluation just three years ago, the stock market has increased over 70 percent. That rate of growth is alarming, as you can see in Figure 1.1. It took the Dow over 100 years to reach 5,000. It took only four years to more than double its first hundred years. Not concerned? Let's look at this another way. Turn the chart upside down. If the Dow had dropped at the same rate as it rose

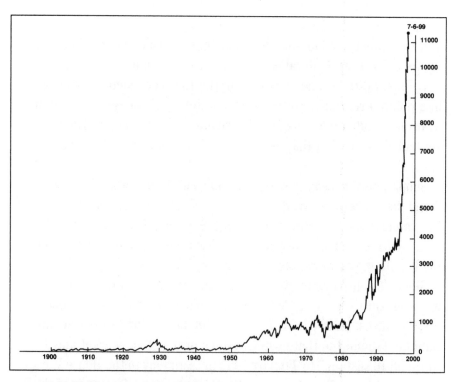

**FIGURE 1.1** The Dow Jones Industrial Average.
*Source:* John R. Mrkvicka.

you'd be concerned, right? An aberrational rise such as we've had is just as alarming, as it strongly suggests overvaluation. Nothing else can completely explain the dramatic rise and the wild daily fluctuations. A market based on corporate earnings, as the stock market once was, is considerably more stable.

Of course, it is not just Mr. Greenspan that sees troubled waters ahead. The respected *Economist* magazine said in April 1998, "It is quite possible that economic changes have merely masked the growth of a stock market bubble that may now be bursting. So there is no telling how low prices could go." The market increased approximately 30 percent in the next 12 months. Does that mean the *Economist* was wrong? Not necessarily—reversals, as you will shortly see, can be finessed by insiders and big money interests.

The stock market has been a lifelong study of mine. Sadly, based on that study, I concluded long before Greenspan's remarks that the market is no longer what it once was, an investment reflection of a free market. No, what the stock market has become is a victim of hyperkinetic overselling by market insiders (brokers, floor traders, big traders, mutual funds, brokerage houses, etc.). Why? Because insiders make more money in a bull market. How do they create overvaluation? By talking individual investors into buying stocks they shouldn't necessarily be buying. For example, brokerage houses have touted stocks for years—in fact, they are often paid for doing so by the corporations whose stocks they push on unsuspecting investors. It's this kind of selling behavior that creates a bull market for a stock or stocks out of thin air.

## Overbought—Oversold

It's not that there is an overt conspiracy to defraud the investor; it's just that "priming the pump" (creating a positive market regardless of actual market value) is what Wall Street salespeople do, and they have become extremely adept at it. Unfortunately, in the process they are overinflating the market balloon past the point where it has to burst. Whether it will burst is no longer the question—the only question is when. It could be next week, next month, next year, or many years in the future, but it will burst. Consequently, depending on when you read this, the unprecedented bullish stock market of the mid and late 1990s has either collapsed or will collapse (this warning is being penned in the fall of 1999). Also note, although most references to the "market" throughout this book will be references to the Dow or the New York Stock Exchange (NYSE), that's a convenience. I am talking about all stocks, especially those on the Nasdaq, as it is likewise at risk. In fact, it may be considerably more exposed, since "new market" stocks are, in a general sense, far more overvalued/oversold than stocks of the "old market" economy. It must also be said that the NYSE and the Nasdaq may yo-yo occasionally; that is, one may go up while the other goes down as investor faith swings from traditional stocks to high-tech, from high-tech to traditional.

Economic conditions in the 1990s made the general public a much easier target for market insiders. Bank savings interest rates fell to a pathetically low 2 to 3 percent and were no longer competitive with the rising return on stocks. Couple that with higher employment and higher wages, and you had people looking for a more rewarding place to put their money. Market insiders preyed on their desire for higher returns. Then, too, once people, especially new entrants to the market, started buying, the buying spree took on a life of its own. What everyone forgot was that the stock market is, for all intents and purposes, a reflection of supply and demand. When more and more people were enticed into the market, they upped the demand for the semistatic supply of existing stocks. So the market took off, not based on true valuation, but rather on artificially created demand of the aggressive Wall Street sales community and the willing consumer.

This is nothing more than a parallel to the Hunt brothers' attempt to take over the silver market 20 years ago. The Hunt brothers (from Texas) tried to buy up all the silver reserves in the world, knowing that if they did, a by-product of the fallout would be that the cost of silver would dramatically rise as it became harder to obtain; they were shorting the supply. By the time everyone woke up, they had driven the price of silver to over $10, $20, $30, $40, and more an ounce. In truth, silver was no more valuable then than it had been prior to the Hunts entering the silver market. And once they were caught by the authorities, silver prices retreated to the previous value level of approximately $4 an ounce in a fairly short amount of time. Of course, our current stock market overvaluation isn't being driven up by just one or two people. It's millions of individual investors spurred on by vested-interest market insiders. Today, the same false, oversold demand has been created in the stock market— which is why the results will parallel the Hunt brothers' silver scam. The market will, if it hasn't already, retreat to a realistic valuation of stock market prices. If it already has, hopefully you have figured out that the collapse was for one reason: because of overselling, it had turned into a quasi pyramid scheme where the continuation of the bull run depended on adding new investors to the mix, and for all pyramid schemes there comes a day of reckoning. If it hasn't collapsed yet, you'll soon learn the truth the hard way.

The sales goal of market insiders, especially brokers and their houses, is to accomplish one thing—drive up prices well beyond their actual worth through overselling. For brokers, this creates more billable trades and increases the value of their personal or fund holdings. This wasn't always the case, but today companies listed on the exchanges, mutual funds, the government, investors, and brokers don't want a based-on-earnings valuation of stocks. No, they want just the opposite, because they (and their clients) make the most money when reality takes a holiday and overvaluation becomes the currency of the realm. This simple statement of fact is not debatable.

One reason corporations want stock overvaluation is that many corporate executives have the majority of their potential wealth tied up in stock holdings and options rather than salary earnings. Therefore, corporate profitability often takes a backseat to the vested interest and valuation of officer stock positions. Corporate managers make tens of millions of dollars, not by taking their company to the top of their industry or by making their company a leader in technology: No, they often make money, obscene amounts of money, by manipulating the company's stock valuation to higher and higher levels, which makes their personal stock holdings and options worth more and more. Management of many exchange-listed companies will sell out the firms long-term in a heartbeat to increase the immediate value of their stock holdings and options.

Mutual fund managers are no better. They, too, want overvaluation. Making profits for their companies by selling—not investing for consumers—is their true agenda, as a manager typically receives compensation based on a percentage of the fund's assets. The bigger the fund, the bigger the fund manager's income—even if the fund loses money. And certainly portfolio managers aren't going to make money by saying that the market is overvalued, even if they know it is. Making such a truthful statement would be very costly, because the average investor, the kind who purchases mutual funds, doesn't understand and/or isn't capable of making money in a bear or bearish market. So, to keep selling their funds, the managers have to keep everything positive and upbeat. The market has to keep going up.

A perfect example of fund managers' dedication to ensure that the market continues to escalate occurred in late 1997 when the market dropped over 500 points. Based on all previous market absolutes, it should have continued to decline, but it didn't. Investors rejoiced and the market recovered its loss and more. To the average investor the fact that the market withstood the drop and rallied was a sure sign of the market's strength. It wasn't. What happened was that fund managers, realizing that the pyramid was about to come crashing down, poured every dollar they could get their hands on into buying more shares of stocks in their portfolios, thereby propping up falling prices and ultimately driving the values of fallen stocks even higher than they had been prior to the 500-point loss (similar to the Hunt brothers). Fund managers protected their positions by convincing an uneducated and trusting public of an untruth based on blatant, yet perfectly legal, price manipulation.

There is also the real possibility that there was additional manipulation by the very secretive group known as the Working Group on Financial Markets, made up of investment industry and government people, who would be in just the right position to rescue the market whenever it is poised to retreat substantially or collapse. Insiders on Wall Street call this group the "Plunge Protection Team." The *Washington Post* did an article on the group in February 1997 for those that question its existence. Some of you may read about this and take comfort, believing that it is good news that "someone" will step in and not let the market crash as it was most assuredly in the process of doing. For those of you with that mind-set, I ask you to consider this—it really only proves that the market, once thought to be free, can be manipulated. And if it can be manipulated on the way down, just think of the manipulation that has occurred on the way up.

More importantly, manipulation can be terminated or no longer viable in near-death market circumstances, meaning the ultimate fall, when it occurs, will likely be very long and very hard, because there is no longer a foundational safety net. No matter what you think of my analysis, you must start to consider, as time reveals more and more of the smoke and mirrors of the stock market, that you're playing in a game that is not as aboveboard as you'd like to believe, and one day, someday, unless you protect yourself, that's going to cost you a bundle.

There is no bigger player in market overvaluation than the government, because no one benefits more than politicians when the market is strong, or at least appears strong. The Clinton administration is brought to mind. Based on the number of independent counsels alone, there has probably been no administration more corrupt, but even when matters were at their worst and the president was impeached, no one seemed to care. In fact, with each new revelation regarding him and/or his staff, or when another former friend went to jail, his approval poll numbers increased. The more corruption, the more people seemed to have wanted to keep him in office. Why? "It's the economy, stupid" was a brilliant campaign slogan. Who realized then that it would become the Clinton administration's eight-year mantra to remain in office despite embarrassing revelation after embarrassing revelation? Apparently, as long as everyone makes money, the public has little interest in who is doing what to whom and what laws may have been broken in the process. This is important, as during President Clinton's terms the country experienced one of the most massive monetary expansions in history—money that fueled the stock overselling, overbuying frenzy.

But, in fairness to Clinton, in principle he is no worse in this regard than most other politicians; he's just played the short-term game well. No one wants to see the stock market (the economy) crash on their watch. It's hard on your political party. It makes it too difficult to be reelected, which, of course, politicians believe is their number one priority. That's why they're players in the overvaluation deception.

Everyone in the market, from the individual investor to government regulatory agencies, has a vested interest in one thing: ensuring that the market gets more and more overvalued every day. Consequently, as of this writing, people are investing without knowing anything about the companies or the true nature of the market they are investing in, because it really doesn't matter. They're making a 30 percent, 40 percent, or more return and it's completely safe, or at least that's what the so-called experts say. People are seeing the stock values of the companies they are investing in double every two to three years when company profits dictate that they should do so every 30 years. Those with personal vested interests and the ability strongly to influence the market (with the sanction of the government—even those watchdog agencies, such as the Securities and Exchange Commission, that are supposed to guard against stock manipulation abuses) have, based on the overvaluation of their stock, crammed 30 years' worth of earnings into a year or two. And individual investors believe that false valuation doesn't matter because they trust those perpetuating the untruth.

If you think I am overstating my case and/or am being an alarmist, I ask you to consider one example of extreme overvaluation. Amazon.com, one of the hot Internet stocks, opened its original issue at a few dollars a share. Almost overnight it was selling at $199+ per share—despite the fact that the company was at that time little more than a warehouse. But more importantly, projections stated that the company wouldn't be profitable for at least another two years! That's the craziness of the market that millions of small investors are trusting. An unprofitable company, with no immediate end to its losses in sight, sees its stock increase in price almost 5,000 percent within months. Alan Greenspan has said that Internet stocks are a "lottery." That's a sad and scary commentary on the market and its fastest growing stock genre.

The problem is that investments based on continuing overvaluation have always collapsed, as they did in 1929 and 1987. It's just a matter of when and how much damage is wrought. Sadly, as I'm writing this, I believe the damage is going to be severe, because the stock market now is as overvalued as the market prior to the crash that led to the Great Depression. Stocks should realistically sell at perhaps 14 times earnings (the average price/earnings ratio of the S&P 500 for the past 100 years), instead of 50 times earnings or more, which is what many are selling for now. Here again, this is happening because the stock market has turned into an overvaluation pyramid-type scheme where insiders profit the most when the market is overvalued the most.

But wait a minute—don't individual investors get rich, too, when the market soars? Again, I don't know when you are reading this, but no matter, you either know or shortly will know that individual investors almost always give back (lose) their paper profits when things turn sour because they aren't privy to inside information. Investors cannot anticipate when the overvaluation balloon will burst and then, even when it does, they hold on in the belief that things will turn around. Brokerage houses, brokers, floor traders, large traders, mutual funds, and other insiders, on the other hand, sell their positions prior to a collapse, because they know it's coming; they know when the jig is up, that the overvaluation can no longer be sustained because investors are leaving the market and prices are about to stagnate or drop.

How do they know? It's simple. They know because they are the ones that created the overvaluation. They are pulling all the important strings. Historically, the way a collapse works is that insiders pump the market up until the balloon explodes—and then the process starts all over again. Sadly, in this regard, the stock market is a lot like Las Vegas. Ultimately, no matter how much you make in the short run, the house (insiders) always wins and nonprofessionals (individual investors) almost always go home broke.

If you still doubt that the government-controlled money supply and insiders unduly influence the market, consider Black Monday, 1987, one of the worst days in market history. Millions of people lost small fortunes, and some lost large fortunes. And what about insiders? Most got out of the market before—right before—the crash. Their clients got·burned, but they got out virtually unscathed. Subsequent independent studies of Black Monday prove this fact conclusively. The majority of the people who actually suffered were innocent, trusting individual investors. Such is the power of market insiders. They profit from market run-ups generated in large part by their salesmanship—and when the run-up can no longer be sustained, they get out of the market before the reversal. They let the people they duped—for lack of better terminology—pay the price. This is now a cycle of the market.

Wall Street, because of the profit incentive based not on real value but on sales, not only allows companies to sell/promote their "product" (stock) for more than it's worth, it encourages this. Insiders know the companies are not worth what their stocks are selling for, but it doesn't matter, because they make money regardless. No matter what, they can sell their holdings for more money, because almost everyone believes the 1990s myth that the market is so strong that no one will ever lose money in the market again. Make no mistake, money will be lost. Individual investors will lose money. Sadly, much of it will be retirement money.

When you strip away all the tinsel, the once proud and rightfully respected Wall Street has become little more than a used car lot. Like the used car salesperson, the broker's and fund manager's job is to sell you a broken-down (overpriced) product for more than it's worth. Brokers call it "The Greater Fool Theory." It means that they see their job as selling stock, good or bad, overpriced or not, to a "fool" by convincing him or her that a bigger "fool" will buy it from them at a higher price than they paid.

This might be a good time to discuss the economy, as many have believed that the market will never really turn bad because the economy is too strong to let that happen. Market "experts" with undisclosed vested interests have been saying that for years. Politicians, too, have parroted the lie, especially the Clinton administration. That's not to say that we haven't been on an amazing bull run, because we obviously have. However, it ultimately can't last because economies are cyclical. History is stronger than any present-day economic model, and it is foolish for anyone to believe that America has flatlined the financial cycles that take an economy up and down. More importantly, the stock market run can't continue infinitely because the economy isn't as strong as we've been led to believe. And the inevitable economic reversal will either trigger or exacerbate the market's decline.

The current economic good news is largely smoke and mirrors propagated to keep politicians in power. And the press—well, they keep reporting the "good" economic news without an in-depth analysis to determine whether the news is accurate. It's not. For example, any housewife or husband who shops for groceries can tell you that inflation is in excess of what the government reports. If inflation were really approximately 3 percent, it would mean that inflation was under 10 percent the past three cumulative years. Nonsense. Although the government basically ignores it, a family's cost of food has gone up over 10 percent in just the past six months.

## America: Running on Empty and Heading for Recession

I think the best way to make this point of our overexaggerated so-called strong economy is to use a respected financial analysis. Fortunately, in an article entitled "America: Running on Empty and Heading for Recession" and published in the *New Australian*, Gerard Jackson provides us with just that. This was published in December 1998; the premise is entirely accurate.

> First the bad news: America will go into recession. Now for the good news: I expect this to happen under Clinton (I don't hold him responsible, I just consider it ironic justice). The editorial in issue No. 92 (19–25 October 1998) predicted, using Austrian analysis, that the U.S. economy would slide into recession and that symptoms were already emerging. Despite claims to the contrary, Greenspan's rate cuts can do nothing to reverse the situation.
>
> Let us first look at received economic wisdom (otherwise known as Keynesian fallacies).* According to this, Greenspan's interest rate cuts will stimulate the economy by increasing the level of spending through credit expansion. That the US has been on a spending binge which has helped fuel the stock market is certainly clear. What is not clear to these

---

*Author's note:* Keynesian economics is an economic theory of John Maynard Keynes that states in its simplest form that an economy can be controlled by government policy, and, in fact, is a function of government. This theory was first set forth in his 1936 book entitled *The General Theory of Employment, Interest and Money.*

economists is that this policy laid the foundations for the coming recession. That most economists are unable to detect the true link between the stock market and consumer spending was made apparent when they expected the 20 percent drop in the Dow Jones between July and December to curb consumer spending. The reason it did not is because both are fueled by the same source—the Fed. Consumer spending is not, never has been and never will be, a function of stock market prices.

Unable to free themselves of Keynesian thinking, the failure of the Dow drop to check consumption was interpreted as meaning that consumers are convinced that the good times will keep on rolling and so maintained their optimism and spending. Consumers never noticed the Dow. So long as their incomes appear secure they will just keep on spending. In fact, American consumers are spending so much the savings ratio has turned negative, something that has not happened since the depths of the Great Depression: for this you can thank Lord Keynes and his disciples. Without savings the American economy—or any other economy for that matter— cannot accumulate capital. And it is capital that raises living standards, not Federal manipulation of interest rates. In other words, the American economy is running on empty. Concentrating on consumption spending is a fatal mistake. Consumption does not drive economics and is only a small part of total economic activity.* This gross error has led some economic observers to speculate that the booming service sector will be the "powerhouse" that will offset slowdowns in any other part of the economy. Austrian analysis completely explodes this myth and we shall now see why.

The Austrians show that by forcing down the rate of interest the Federal Reserve misleads businesses, especially into the higher stages of production, into thinking that the fund of real capital has expanded. They therefore embark on projects for which the capital goods necessary for their completion do not exist. This makes itself felt through various shortages and bottlenecks. As these start to appear many businesses begin to suffer a cost-price squeeze as prices are no longer sufficient to maintain expansion or even cover factor costs. Nevertheless, the so-called service sector, the one closest to consumption, undergoes a boom with rising demand and employment. There is no paradox here.

---

*The problem is that gross domestic product figures leave out an enormous amount of economic activity on the fallacious grounds that it would be double counting to include it. In fact, the GDP is a value-added concept and is not really gross at all.

Factors must be paid. Companies that respond to the low interest rates used the additional funds to bid up the prices of capital goods and specific types of labor, which obviously raised their cost of production. This additional expenditure translated into factor incomes which were then spent on consumption goods. This in turn raised demand at the consumption end of the production structure. The increased demand made itself felt throughout the structure by bidding factors away from the higher stages. To aggravate the situation savings actually became negative, meaning that the social rate of time preference was leaving nothing for investment. The pool of real funds had run dry. These higher stage investments will now turn out to be malinvestments, unsound investments that will have to be liquidated. But before these investments are abandoned they will start bleeding financially. Unable to cover their costs of production they will have to cut outlays, sell their inventories for what they can get, and institute lay-offs.

This is exactly what is happening: manufacturing and mining are beginning to suffer a profit squeeze. Corporate profits are falling, lay-offs are on the rise, inventories are beginning to run down, and outlays are being cut. Some financial commentators are claiming that the slowdown is already as bad as the 1990–91 recession. All of this without even a credit squeeze. (The Austrians have always stressed that even without a credit squeeze this crisis stage will emerge.) Astute observers realize that the crisis has nothing to do with Asia. However, unable to explain it, especially in Keynesian terms, they are reduced to making statements about the inevitable end of the investment cycle, trade cycles, etc. In other words, they do not know. Even so, many still think cutting interest rates, i.e., expanding the money supply, is the cure. It ain't. It's the disease.

America is a dynamic and inventive country with a vibrant entrepreneurial culture. What it needs is lower taxes, less regulation and litigation, fewer meddling politicians, and a healthy savings culture. What it does not need—and this goes for any other country—is Keynesianism.

Being a true free market advocate, I reject, in almost its entirety, Keynesian theory. It has merit as a means to explain the intertwining of the private and public sectors and the role government can and should take economically during a financial crisis. However, if followed during normal times, it guts the free market and makes it a slave to the capricious whims of our political leaders, some of whom, like Mr. Greenspan, are not even elected. I object to, for example, Mr. Greenspan, by his sole determination, making millions of Americans pay a higher mortgage payment (assuming they have an Adjustable Rate Mortgage) because he raises interest rates. That is not a free market function of government (some would say that the Fed and its chairman are not "government," and in principle they would be right—but, sadly, the chairman is one of the biggest political players in Washington). Without belaboring this point, the United States should not give up what has made us great economically (a free market) because in the short run we can manipulate the economy and, therefore, positively influence the stock market.

But enough of this esoteric discussion. I felt it was necessary for two reasons: (1) to lay waste to the myth that the stock market is too strong to fail because the economy is too strong to fail, and (2) so I can discuss the real truth of our economy, which is that the federal government is broke and if it were a corporate entity would be forced to declare bankruptcy.

Is there anyone left who still believes our national debt will be paid? If there is, here's a fact of financial life: It won't. The stated debt of trillions of dollars, and countless trillions more of additional government guarantees and contingent liabilities, has, notwithstanding recent reductions, eclipsed our ability to pay. Sadly, the problem grows exponentially worse every day, because government spends even surpluses real or imagined.

And there is no solution in sight. Even the much touted Clinton balanced budget was an exercise in futility (but most assuredly better than continuing huge deficits). Balancing the budget, while certainly something that needs to be done, hasn't solved the problem. Reduced it, yes; solved it, no. Clearly, Washington is incapable of solving this problem that it alone created by spending money it didn't have. Anyone with an eighth-grade economic course under his or her belt knows, notwithstanding bait-and-switch tactics and the clever use of euphemisms, the federal government, by any reputable accounting standard used in corporate America, is insolvent.

But wait a minute! Didn't President Clinton tell us (July 1999) that we have an additional revenue (tax) surplus of a trillion dollars with trillions more on the horizon? If that's true, what are we talking about?—we're headed in the right direction. Why all the doom and gloom?

First of all, as the ensuing years will prove conclusively, there is no surplus. Does that mean the president was not being truthful? While I won't say he lied, I will repeat, there is no surplus. The president and Congress know that, yet they all started working on ways to spend the "surplus" on new social programs, tax cuts, and so on that would help them get reelected. But that's what reelection politics is all about. Clinton would, of course, be an advocate for a Democratic presidency after him (in addition to adding to his own legacy), and congressmen and -women and senators want to be reelected, so they go along.

The government's record on this subject is not good. For example, about three months prior to the administration finding another trillion dollars of surplus, it had made another prediction of the surplus—meaning that just prior to the good news of another surplus trillion dollars it was projected that there had already been a surplus of a trillion dollars. At this rate, it won't be very long until the United States can retire the national debt and buy every American a new home and car of their choosing; at a trillion dollars every three months this is facetiously possible. I ask rhetorically why, when the government's Congressional Budget Office (CBO) employs accountants that missed (just three months earlier) in their original projection by a trillion dollars, should anyone believe projections into the next century? Let me show you what a trillion dollars looks like: $1,000,000,000,000.00. Believe it or not, government accountants missed it. They missed a trillion dollars or, in easier-to-understand terms, a thousand billion dollars.

Even if there actually was, in a technical sense, a trillion-dollar surplus, looking for ways to spend it, as both parties have done, is like a poor family with pressing past-due bills going on a thousand-dollar spending spree when they win $100 in a lottery. It just doesn't make sense. The money can and should be put to better use. Only in American politics would a "surplus" of a trillion dollars be called a surplus while the national debt is still many times that.

Let me give you another example of why you can't believe the numbers that are bandied about in the never-never land we call Washington. When the savings and loan industry collapsed in 1987 we were at first told that no taxpayer monies would be required for a bailout. Within weeks the number had risen to $5 billion. Every week thereafter, for months, the number escalated until it finally got to tens of billions of dollars of our tax money being used to bail out incompetent and in some cases criminal savings and loan operators. Worse yet, they were supervised by the Federal Savings and Loan Insurance Corporation (FSLIC) and Congress. So now we have another example of government waste and accounting irregularities.

One last example. We are repeatedly told that Social Security is solvent well into the next century. In fact, the government says, there is a tremendous Social Security surplus. Sadly, that's untrue. There's a trick involved. Technically there is a surplus in the Social Security trust fund, but—and here's where you had better pay attention—the surplus isn't made up of cash; it's made up of IOUs from the government. Why IOUs? Because Social Security revenues were previously taken into and used in the current general revenue fund. In short, the government has been robbing Peter (the future) to pay Paul (the present). By talking about surpluses, the government can give us, the public, the false impression that there is nothing to worry about: The economy is strong; the future looks bright! Folks, I've said this a hundred times if I've said it once—if any publicly held company conducted its business in the same manner as the government, if it used the same accounting procedures, prepared the same misleading statements to its shareholders as the government prepares for voters/taxpayers, its board of directors and officers would be doing jail time.

This issue of trust in the economy is imperative when discussing the stock market, because the two are intertwined. More importantly, the market is a balloon of investors' trust waiting to explode. As of this writing, the market continues to be bullish—but, when the economic lies and misstatements are exposed, the market, because it's no longer based on a true earnings valuation of individual stocks, could collapse. It is this combination that is so dangerous: overvalued stocks and a false economy.

## Still Partying on the Deck of the *Titanic*

As time progresses I am somewhat gratified, yet saddened, that more and more financial realists are starting to come to my way of thinking regarding the market as it truly is and the potential consequences of it being manipulated. One such person is Don McAlvany, editor of the *McAlvany Intelligence Advisor,* who wrote the following in a special January 2000 edition of his newsletter, entitled "Still Partying on the Deck of the *Titanic*: Perspective on the New Millennium."

### INTRODUCTION

1999 was the most prosperous year ever especially in the financial markets in U.S. history. The stock market and other financial assets set new records and enormous wealth was created literally overnight out of thin air. Is the U.S. economy really that strong? Are corporate earnings and fundamentals really that good? Do they even matter anymore? Have we finally reached that "new era," that financial Nirvana whereby asset values, like Jack's beanstalk, will grow to the sky overnight and keep on growing forever?

Are hard work and 8 to 5 jobs now outdated anachronisms of the "old era" to be replaced by a "new era" of day trading, instant riches and prosperity, and overwhelming financial wealth, affluence, and prosperity? Has the Internet, unlike Ponce de León's elusive "fountain of youth," become our perpetual "fountain of wealth" satisfying our every personal or financial whim or need?

This is now becoming the dream (or is it the delusion) of tens of millions of Americans many of whom have concluded that instant, pain-free wealth from "playing the market" is better than working for a living. We have finally found (like the "perpetual motion machine") a "perpetual money machine." All the old rules have been repealed. We are in a "new era" of perpetual wealth creation.

**QUESTION:** What is wrong with that picture?

**ANSWER:** *It is a delusional psychology that emerges only once in many decades or even centuries at the peak of a speculative boom and blowoff. It is driven by rampant greed, a rampant something-for-nothing philosophy, and the very arrogant belief on the part of the masses that they are invincible, bulletproof, invulnerable to financial loss.* It is a delusion and defies 6,000 years of financial history. It *always* ends in a crash and financial disaster for its participants.

### THE MOST MASSIVE MONETARY EXPANSION IN WORLD HISTORY

**QUESTION:** What has caused the present, largest-ever-in-history financial bubble and stock market buying frenzy?

**ANSWER:** *The most massive monetary expansion, the most massive injection of financial liquidity into a financial system totaling trillions of dollars in U.S. or world history.* It has been done by the Fed, the U.S. Treasury, and other monetary authorities since 1994 but especially over the past 16 months since September 1998. It has created the greatest speculative buying frenzy (in U.S. financial assets) since the ill-fated Tulip Mania and financial collapse in Holland in 1637. Only this mania is a hundred times larger.

In October/November '98, in the wake of the near-collapse of Long Term Capital Management, the Fed/U.S. Treasury and monetary authorities pumped over $200 billion in new liquidity into the U.S. financial system to prop up the faltering U.S. stock market. In the last 13 weeks of 1999, the Fed pumped in another $194 billion to keep the bubble market expanding and to insulate against a Y2K-induced financial collapse which the Fed desperately feared.

In the last 60 days of 1999, the Fed expanded the adjusted monetary base at an unprecedented annualized rate of over 48%—the highest in U.S. history! Much of that excess liquidity has flowed into the U.S. stock market. The public is now stampeding into stocks like at no time in history, with stocks that have no earnings or near term prospects for earnings (i.e., they are losing money) going up 10, 15, 20, or 25 times in 1999.

*In November '99 alone, margin debt rose $24 billion to $206 billion, a $65 billion or 46% increase in margin debt for the year.* An explosion of derivatives trading in stocks has added massive leverage to the stock market. And that does not include all the indirect borrowing that has made its way into the stock market from an increase in mortgage and other debt for the household sector as well as unprecedented stock buybacks by the corporate sector.

Underscoring the present buying panic and mania is the fact that *from October 27 to December 22 (less than 60 days) the Nasdaq grew 40%; that is an incomprehensible $1.4 trillion increase in market value or new wealth. Over the past nine weeks, over $2 trillion in stock market wealth has been created.*

Over the past 14 weeks, our already overleveraged financial sector increased its commercial paper borrowings another $123 billion to $1.1 trillion, while *the broad money supply (M3) increased $230 billion to $6.8 trillion.* We are presently seeing the greatest credit expansion in U.S. history and most of it is pouring into the stock market. Some is also beginning to pour into real estate.

### ARE WE ENTERING HYPERINFLATION?

**QUESTION:** What is happening?

**ANSWER:** *The Fed and the U.S. monetary authorities have triggered a hyperinflation which is currently manifesting itself in financial assets (primarily stock).* It is now beginning to roll into real estate where prices in certain California real estate markets are now rising 25% to 35% per year. *It is likely that at some point in the coming months, this hyperinflation in financial assets will roll into wages and prices.* Indeed, industrial commodities were up almost 40% in price in 1999.

*If the present hyperinflation in financial assets rolls into the real economy, our currency could be destroyed in a matter of days or weeks.* This phenomenon is beginning to take hold all over the world. Hyperinflations are normally followed by financial/economic collapse and the rise of a dictatorship. The hyperinflation of the German Weimar Republic was followed by economic collapse and the rise of Adolf Hitler and the Nazi Third Reich.

### WHAT IS A "CRACK-UP BOOM"?

Ludwig Von Mises, history's greatest free market (Austrian) economist, wrote in his epic work *The Theory of Money and Credit* about a concept he called the "crack-up boom." As he wrote: *"The boom can last only as long as the credit expansion progresses at an ever-accelerated pace. The boom comes to an end as soon as additional quantities of fiduciary media are no longer thrown upon the loan market. But it could not last forever even if inflation and credit expansion were to go on endlessly. It would then encounter the barriers which prevent the boundless expansion of circulation credit. It would lead to the crack-up boom and the breakdown of the whole monetary system."*

Dr. Frank Shostak, a leading Austrian economist and Chief Economist at Ord Minnett in Sydney, Australia, explained the concept of *"crack-up boom."* According to Von Mises, *"whenever people are observing ever expanding money supply they start to form expectations that the purchasing power of money will fall. Once they become convinced that the monetary pumping will never stop and consequently prices of goods and services will continue to rise, they will spend their money as fast as possible,"* i.e., their demand for money will fall.

*"Ultimately this could reach an extreme,"* i.e., no one wants to hold money and there is a flight to real goods. This Von Mises calls a crack-up boom. *"In other words, the increase in the money supply that generates expectations of a fall in money's purchasing power leads to the fall in the demand for money. Eventually, prices of real goods are rising to such high levels that people don't have enough money to buy them. Consequently it is not possible to conduct monetary transactions. The monetary system breaks down."*

When Von Mises wrote about credit excesses precipitating a flight to real goods (i.e., super or hyperinflation), he may not have envisioned today's stampede into stocks. Nevertheless, there are some strong similarities in his "crack-up boom" and in the stampede to convert money into stocks today fed and exacerbated by the Fed's promiscuous, non-stop monetary expansion. So we have the masses dumping cash to borrow more money to buy more stock. The same is beginning to happen in the real estate market and could begin to happen in commodities and other real goods including the much maligned, manipulated, and suppressed gold and silver markets.

The Fed may be losing control. *Von Mises describes an accelerating situation which finally eventuates, wherein the monetary authorities must keep injecting more and more financial credit on an accelerating basis into the bubble to keep it going. When they slow it down, to stop the monetary inflating, the bubble collapses.*

This is like a drug addict who must take ever increasing doses of drugs to maintain the same high. There is a principle of diminishing returns at work and if he levels off, slows down, or stops the drug intake, he will crash. The same thing applies in accelerating inflation, hyperinflation, or a "crack-up boom."

For the first time since the 1970s, this writer now believes that there is the potential for high and rising inflation in the U.S. possibly leading to super or hyperinflation. A financial collapse will surely follow.

### IN SUMMARY

Americans are still partying on the deck of the *Titanic* driven by raw unadulterated greed, materialism, pride, and arrogance believing that nothing can touch them, nothing can bring them down. They are very wise and indestructible in their own eyes. They just dodged the Y2K bullet (or so they believe) or was it an iceberg? But they don't see that there are other, even larger icebergs directly ahead. The Bible says that *"pride comes before the fall."* Americans are a very proud and prosperous people and this writer suspects they are headed for a major fall in the not-too-distant future.

Mr. McAlvany and I have some disagreements, most notably on the severity of the damage that will be wrought (more on this later), but—and this is what's important—on substance, particularly the manipulation of the market via expansionistic monetary policy, we are in total agreement. Without runaway monetary expansion, the extent of the overselling and overvaluation of the late 1990s stock market would not have become a reality.

But enough of the bad news. Believe it or not, notwithstanding what I've said so far, the stock market is an excellent place to make a fortune regardless of the market's condition, if. . . .

I'm going to show you how to turn the stock market into your own personal money machine, but for that to happen you must, based on strong information and reasoning, jettison any preconceived notions regarding investing and the market—because, perhaps more than anything else, they will ensure that you ultimately fail in the economy of the new millennium.

Stop doing what everyone else is doing! It worked during the run-up of the 1990s, but it won't work again. The days of investing in the market in a general sense instead of in individual stocks probably are, or soon will be, over. Even the few nonpros who have the requisite stock market education and intellect to be successful don't usually have enough money to compete fairly. Using a no-limit poker game as an analogy: Take two players with identical talent. Give one a bankroll substantially larger than the other. The better-funded player (like the market insiders) will be able to play to his or her skill potential and win the game. The other (small, individual investors), being forced to play defensively because of limited resources, will make costly self-defeating mistakes. Likewise, the average stock market investor will lose in the long run.

Over time, the big fish feed on the little fish. I'm going to say that again, because it's critical: Over time, the big fish feed on the little fish. It is irrelevant that this truth has seemed untrue the past few years. In a historical time line, a few years or even a decade means little. In the long run, the axiom remains valid.

That's why most investment guides are a waste of money. They treat you like the small fish (individual investor) you are (no offense meant)—and that means the advice you're getting will ultimately lead to disaster. This book, on the other hand, is going to show you how to be a big fish regardless of your market knowledge or financial standing.

## My Track Record

My advice is based on an extensive professional record. A few examples: On the record, I calculated the collapse of the savings and loan industry long before congressional hearings even acknowledged that there might be a problem. I also forecast the true cost to taxpayers back when the FSLIC said the cost would not exceed five billion dollars. I warned of the collapse of the Japanese banking model at the time it was being held up as the jewel of the world's banking industry. Perhaps the October crash of 1987 proves the point best, as it was predicted by very few—I was one of them. Allow me a quote from the April 1987 edition of my newsletter. "The stock market will continue (allowing for controlled swings) to be bullish. So much so that a Dow of 3,000 plus is foreseeable and probable. That is, up and until a correction occurs—the likes of which may have never been seen in recent memory. There are many factors at play here, but be warned. The market is poised for disaster. You can't afford to be aboard when it happens."

At present, the market is at 11,000+. I happen to believe my 1987 advice is equally applicable today, and it will be just as accurate. The market is poised for disaster. How much will be lost for the market? The best-case scenario would be a 20 percent loss of market valuation (the traditional standard of a "crash"). As much as a 50 percent loss is possible. A complete collapse is remotely possible but *highly* unlikely.

It is also likely that the crash will occur over a period of time, which may confuse many people who, when they think about a crash, do so in the context of a few days. This crash, to play out completely, may take months or years. Bear markets often work like this—the market retreats and then rebounds, retreats and then rebounds, for weeks or months, with each retreat becoming larger and/or each rebound gaining slightly less than the previous rebound. The market can retreat in this manner so slowly that, if you're not paying attention, you're not even aware that things have taken a turn for the worse. It's like the frog that is placed in a pot of cold water.

He's perfectly happy to swim around and doesn't even realize it when the burner under the pot is turned on. Slowly the water warms, so slowly that the frog doesn't know he's in trouble until it's too late. A slow burn in the market can do the same to unsuspecting investors.

There is another possibility too, that of a "stagnant crash," where the market heads into an extended period of time where basically nothing happens for years. In such a case, present investors will sit and watch their investments return virtually nothing while their "principal" is inflationarily reduced. The Dow would fluctuate between slim parameters, allowing reality to catch up to overvaluation. Regardless of what form it takes, an adjustment of major proportions must take place (yet it must be noted that the market could go much higher before it does). However, the longer the crash is avoided through overt or covert manipulation, the more serious the consequences. Again, depending on when you're reading this, you know, or soon will know, how right I am again.

It also must be noted that in the future the market will substantially eclipse the record highs of today.

Notwithstanding my accuracy, for most investors at any time predicting the market or listening to someone predicting the market is dangerous, very dangerous. The only way to accurately predict it is knowing what the insiders and big money are going to do before everyone else does. The amazing discovery contained here does just that. It is as safe as any investment strategy can be and requires only 10 minutes to a half hour a day to produce winning trade after winning trade—proving that the adage "Less is more" is applicable even in the complex world of stock market finance. And even though market knowledge is going to be at a premium when the market's salad days end, it doesn't matter if you know virtually nothing about the stock market, bear or bull, because you're going to base your investments on the knowledge of those that, for all intents and purposes, unduly influence the market. It can't get any better than that.

Does it sound too good to be true? It isn't. Sometimes the simplest, most productive things are the hardest to see, but once you understand them, they keep proving themselves. That's been my experience, and it will be yours, too. You're going to become a market insider by easily deciphering information from the real insiders. This is critical once the can't-miss market is exposed for what it is. Anyone could have made money in the stock market of the mid to late 1990s. That's no longer, or soon will no longer be, the case. In a true market, one not manipulated to severe overvaluation, dumb luck means nothing.

Unlike other stock market investment books, many of which are huge volumes of technically confusing, useless information, my strategy works because it gives you the information you need to be your own expert in the simplest, quickest form possible. It's based on the principle contained in the maxim: "Give a man a fish and he eats but one meal. Teach him how to fish and he eats for a lifetime." It works in a bull market; it works in a bear market. Even in times of stock market chaos, the volatility of the market often works to the plan's advantage. These are just a few of the considerations that make this book unique.

I'm making my discovery available because for years readers of my newsletter *Money Insider* begged me to show them how I was choosing my individual stock recommendations that were making them so much money. I promised that at some point I would make the information available, because I believe that everyone, especially the individual small investor, deserves the opportunity this discovery offers. This book is a promise kept.

Let me make the bottom line of my strategy by using a baseball analogy. Assume you are the manager of a major-league baseball team. What do you think your winning percentage would be if you were able to steal every sign of the opposing team—if you knew in advance that the other side was going to bunt, steal a base, hit-and-run, or pitch out? You, notwithstanding the fact that you might have lesser talent, would probably make the play-offs every year and be a World Series victor every other year. Knowing what the other team was going to do before they did it would provide an almost unbeatable edge. That's what this book gives you, an unbeatable edge. You are going to know much of what is going to happen before the fact because you are going to tap into the forces that influence the game (market).

The market goes up and the market comes down, and it does so for a reason; one of the main reasons being insiders' and big money players' influence—undue influence—makes it do so or contributes inordinately. After reading this book you'll know, long before the average investor, when a given stock is going to move long term in either direction. That's going to allow you to buy stocks on their way to the moon or sell short and watch the stock drop like a rock. You'll also know when it's time to get out of the market and when to get back in. That is why this book is special and why your investment potential is about to become unlimited.

Do you know how Wall Street got its name? The legend goes that it got its name from the wall that was erected around the original exchange building solely for the purpose of keeping the common folk from bothering the wealthy elite who owned the exchange and/or traded stocks.

They, the insiders, may have long ago torn down the physical wall, but in many very real ways the wall is still there to keep the common folk outside looking in. By the way, just because you invest in the market and own some stock doesn't mean you're not on the outside looking in, because, as explained throughout this book, you are—and if you don't do something about it and instead remain on the outside, you're not going to realize the wealth that the stock market can provide those who truly understand the nature of the beast.

The trading system and advice in this book isn't a polite attempt to get those inside the wall to play the game aboveboard. It's an in-your-face system that kicks the wall down, smashes in the front door, and says, "I understand what's going on and I'm here for my fair share—and I won't settle for a dime less."

# CHAPTER 2

# The Basics

## Winners and Losers

Investing in the stock market is an act of optimism—or at least it used to be. Now, in this era of "can't miss" hysteria, investing in the stock market is more a matter of false optimism based on sales hype instead of corporate earnings. But whichever motivates you, optimism or false optimism, the fact is that you invest in the stock market so that your financial resources grow and expand. And for that to happen you have to plan and manage your assets. While it has been easy to make money in the market over the past few years, the truth is that we live in a time of financial turmoil and extremely fast change—witness the economies of Russia and Japan—change that can occur so rapidly that most people cannot react appropriately. At best they react, as opposed to act.

World events, for example, can happen when and where no one expects. An incident in the Middle East can dramatically affect oil stocks within minutes. That can be good for your holdings or it can be bad, very bad. And now, since most of us have more and more control of our retirement investments, you can see even a well planned out stock market retirement plan/future wiped out in minutes. I am not trying to frighten you here or anywhere else in this book. I am, however, trying to get you to understand what you're investing in. The past few amazing bull years are not representative of what the stock market really is or will be. This bull run is an aberration. Sooner or later things will even out, and when they do it will be too late to start your market education. You need to know now, before the fact. The world is changing, technology is changing, and so you'd better change, too.

If you're an investor or you are considering investing in the stock market, it may look confusing. It's supposed to—that's the way the inside professionals want it to appear, so you believe you need them to survive. You don't.

You don't if you plan your personal financial future along with your investment plan and then dovetail the two. The two must go hand in hand. You may think that you have this covered, but, based on my consulting experience, I know most don't. For example, let's go back to retirement investments. With the market so strong (as I write this) too many people have forgotten that their retirement investments should not have the same risk factor (exposure to loss) as their risk capital. If, however, you have a plan for your financial future, which, of course, would include differentiation of investment funds, confusion of risk and retirement monies wouldn't happen. You'd stay the course knowing that in the end all things even out—historical trend lines eventually overtake periodic spikes (even those that last years).

Realistic investing isn't as hard as it at first might seem, especially if you're smart enough to see through the market facade. You don't need to be a market insider, a floor trader, or a broker to reap the benefits the market can produce. In fact, I would argue that the further you distance yourself from the usual market trappings the better off you'll be. There are a million self-styled market experts ready and willing to sell you their advice or their service. But here's a fact—most of them don't always act in your best interest. Shocked? Don't be. There are market players who make a very good if not extravagant living not from the stock market proper, but from "suckers" (their categorization, not mine) whom they convince through cold calls, direct mail, and so on that they can help make a fortune.

Stay away from technical insiders or you stand in real danger of becoming intellectually constipated. If you read every piece of relevant stock market information, subscribed to an insider hot sheet, listened to your broker, and so on every day in an attempt to make the wisest stock picks, you'd be a day behind every day. It doesn't even matter if the information is right on the money—it's too much. Here's one of those areas where I differ from most investment writers. They tell you to read everything, get reports, subscribe to this, that, and the other thing in order to get ahead of the curve. I suggest that this is a huge mistake. You don't have the time, and then, too, many of the experts disagree. One expert says buy stock X at the same time others are recommending selling stock X. How do you cancel one out against the other? How do you know which is right? My system, the one described later in detail, functions under the premise that you should take all the stock market info you can get your hands on and burn it. It's useless. I'll explain this later, but for right now just start thinking that this is a new day for you and your investments. And it's a good thing, too, because there is a new day dawning in the market.

That's not to say that you don't have to retain traditional financial thinking to be successful. For instance, you have to have investment goals. You have to know what your investment timetable is. You have to understand risk and reward. The latter is a critical issue as the market returns to "normal." The present risk/reward ratio has been skewed because of the record bull run we've been on, and many investors, especially new investors in the market, have never known anything but what they've seen recently. To them, a record bull run with low risk and high returns is the norm. They, especially, are in danger. Lately there has been little appreciable risk—when the risk/reward ratio balances out, the risk will have to escalate dramatically to bring the market within normal, historical trend lines.

Sanity must prevail if you are ultimately to be successful in the market. I talk to people every day who call asking what, where, how to invest. Mostly I am asked which stocks will return the highest yield. Seldom am I asked about the corresponding risk that comes with the potential reward. The past few years have done, or will do, an injustice to many investors by leading them to believe that the standard risk/reward factor—which states that the bigger the risk (potential for loss), the bigger the reward (potential for gain)—no longer exists. It does.

There are other traditional considerations, such as tax aspects, appreciation, dividends, diversification, and so on, all of which are part of any successful long-term investment plan. What I want you to realize is that what has had value recently—reward without thought or risk—will soon be valueless (if it isn't already), and what has been discarded as "old thinking," a system of trading based on historic trend lines, will again have prominence. So we have a seeming paradox. On the one hand I am suggesting that you dump the traditional trappings of the market proper (brokers, experts, etc.) while I am encouraging traditional financial thinking. Friends, that's not a paradox at all. It's simply suggesting that it is wise not to base your investing strategy on what amounts to the stock market's pet rock (hot today, gone tomorrow) and instead to replace it with something of substance. Which brings us to an important part of any winning investment plan/strategy.

### *Your Personality Traits Are Important to Your Success*

The individual personality of the investor is a critical factor in the success or failure of any investment strategy. Not all investors belong in the stock market. Further, some people have to narrow the scope of their stock market investments. For example, some people, if they require a predetermined monthly income, should never leave the solid-gold blue chips if they want to sleep at night.

Sometimes these positions change. For instance, when a couple is starting out in life, they may be able to invest only small sums in varying markets due to limited resources. As their net worth grows, they may opt to speculate with their risk capital (money they can afford to lose) while continuing to invest the remainder of their liquid capital. As they near retirement, they may decide to invest in long-term vehicles, such as bonds, that will protect their income. Later, if one spouse passes away, the survivor may wish to continue a portion of the investment portfolio while making other arrangements for additional family members (trusts, wills, gifts, etc.). The point is, there is no one right way to invest. There isn't even one right way to invest for a specific person or couple. All things do not remain constant. Needs change. The market changes. This is another reason why this book is so very valuable. You can apply its principles at every stage of your investment life, in every situation, bull or bear.

Never underestimate the role your personality plays in the investment process. You may have some traits or financial flaws that will make certain types of investing very difficult for you to profit by. You have to recognize these traits, or your plan—no matter how well conceived—will fail. Winning in the stock market is a combination of market circumstances, the vehicle chosen, and the financial complexity of the individual making the decisions. I can't make your investment decisions for you, and neither can someone else. But I can give you some insight into what characteristics make up the winners and losers in the stock market. See if you don't recognize some personality/investment traits of your own on my list in Figure 2.1.

It's not only the market, or what vehicle you choose, but also your investment personality that decides whether you win or lose. If your temperament is ill suited to an investment choice, you will ultimately lose regardless of the success of the vehicle. Certain disciplines are required in the stock market. If you don't qualify, you should invest elsewhere. Maybe your money should be in bonds or high-yield savings accounts.

| | |
|---|---|
| Resources: | Winner: Substantial capitalization. Can absorb losses. |
| | Loser: Undercapitalized. |
| Resource management: | Winner: Has long-term, sizable reserves. |
| | Loser: Seldom has reserve position. |
| Self-control: | Winner: Reacts to trading system signals. |
| | Loser: Emotional. Takes big losses, small profits. |
| Market skill: | Winner: Is the equivalent of a professional. |
| | Loser: Little market knowledge. |
| Market position: | Winner: Always diversified. No more than 20% of capital in one position. |
| | Loser: Single positions. |
| Market education: | Winner: Well-researched positions. |
| | Loser: Little knowledge. Relies on broker, newsletters, etc. |
| Strategy: | Winner: Doesn't deviate from trading system. |
| | Loser: No plan—constantly changes direction. |
| Timing: | Winner: Acts on trading system signals only. Usually ahead of the market. |
| | Loser: Acts when he/she gets a hot tip or when broker calls. |
| Objectives: | Winner: Long-term expectations. |
| | Loser: Wants to make quick killing. |
| Damage control: | Winner: Uses stops. |
| | Loser: Takes risks. Positions are frequently wiped out. |
| Market focus: | Winner: Devotes quality time to portfolio. |
| | Loser: Gives part-time attention at best. |

**FIGURE 2.1 Winners and losers.**
*Source:* John R. Mrkvicka.

I believe strongly that people can learn and make adjustments to fill their investment needs. However, I also believe that average investors, those who do not follow the market full-time or as a career, will never be as prosperous as they should be because they can't put in the time needed. If you'll be honest, the chart you just reviewed showed you one thing: You can't, on your own, consistently win because you have too many negative traits. All part-time investors do. However, don't despair. I didn't present the chart to show your strengths, but rather the inherent weaknesses of most investors. It was my way of showing that the average person will, in the long term, due to human nature and the nature of the system, lose money or make less than they should have. Market insiders have all the winning traits. The rest of us ultimately lose because we have negative traits.

You need an investment strategy that repairs any losing investment traits—and, unless you are a market authority, you may have many. My trading system, however, solves every negative trait on the chart, and you don't have to do a thing other than follow its rules. It also amplifies positive traits, which means it will enhance the semipro's results, too. More importantly, it will lead you in the direction of winning individual stock trades. The plan doesn't make a specific choice (but it shows you how); that's your responsibility. You will choose the investment vehicle and then apply the strategy's management principles. Much of the information is geared toward helping you make that important choice, but don't confuse that personal decision with basic market guiding philosophies. They are distinctly separate yet necessarily symbiotic.

### More on Winning Investment Traits

I'd like to take my winners and losers chart one step further by quoting a similar list from psychologist and noted stock market expert Jonathan Myers's *Profits without Panic,* so you can see another perspective on this issue. There are, as noted, certain characteristics that stock market winners possess. For example:

- "Clarity and acute realism—often seeing financial opportunities before others do." My system will help you be continually ahead of the noninsider crowd.

- "Forward looking—not letting past habits dominate future actions." If you follow my system your investment past becomes moot.

- "Taking responsibility for their actions—both good and bad." If you follow my strategy you and you alone control your investment future.

- "High level of commitment and motivation to succeed." If you weren't motivated you wouldn't be reading this book.

- "Not relying on luck, but a strategy consistently applied." With my system there is no luck involved. You're investing on facts and figures and inside information.

- "Faith in their own decisions." You're going to have faith in your own decisions if you decide to trade using my strategy.

- "Goal-oriented outlook." Throughout the book I will be talking about why and how to set investment goals.

- "Good self-control—keeping in check any personal tendencies or characteristics that are counterproductive to success." This is a terribly important point, which is why my system takes "personal tendencies" completely out of the picture. As you'll find as you read further, my strategy is the zenith of self-control, because everything is decided for you. All you have to do is follow the plan.

- "Not being easily influenced by other people or events." Trade my system and you'll never listen to your broker again, you'll never listen to more than a few seconds of a cold sales call, and you'll never be moved to make a trade because of a hot tip from a TV talking head.

- "Often passionate about investing." Again, you bought this book, so it is only reasonable to believe you have a degree of passion about the market. You want to learn something new about the market, which brings me to an interesting point: I believe that many of you purchased this book because the title caught your attention. Of course, that's what titles are supposed to do. It interested you because, if nowhere other than your subconscious, you know, and, as I say right at the beginning of this book, there's always been an element of secrecy in the stock market. You also know there are market insiders that have an undue influence, and you know the market is overvalued and oversold. Those are good things to know, and I applaud your perception.

Mr. Myers and I agree that there are characteristics of a winning stock investor. I wanted to include his thinking as well as mine, so you will give the issue weight when you are deciding to invest and/or whether you want to follow my advice. A good investment program is one that stands on its own without the burden of the personality of the investor. Frankly, I don't think anyone has all the winning characteristics that one needs to be successful in the market. If that's true, then we have to look for a system/strategy that does what we cannot. Even if you possess only a few losing characteristics, they are enough to overshadow the winning characteristics you have and bring into play. That's why I say that the smartest thing you can do with your money is admit your inability to beat a system designed by the pros for the pros. That's why you need to rely on a strategy/trading system that has all the winning investing attributes most of us don't. This is that plan.

## Developing a Winning Perspective

Do you know what "TNO" stands for? Those of us who have been around longer than we'd like to admit know it stands for "trust no one." That admonition is no more true anywhere than in the stock market. TNO. However, you can trust me—and it's not just because I'm a nice guy, which, of course, I am. No, you can trust me because I'm not trying to sell you anything. I've already made every penny from you I am going to make. I have no additional vested interest. Can the same be said for your broker? The brokerage house? Stock market newsletters? Market "experts"? No, everyone you'll run into in your stock market experience is trying to sell you something, and that's why they are suspect.

Let's use another example to expand the TNO axiom. Many experts tell their clients to read company year-end reports or a prospectus before buying a stock. That makes sense—or does it? I am a retired bank president, chief executive officer, and chairman of the board of a national bank. At one point in my career I was, according to the American Bankers Association, the youngest bank president in the United States. I was 31 at a time when bank presidents had to be at least 50, bald or balding, and fat. I wasn't.

The reason I mention this is because I've been around the park a few times in the fast lane. I have seen the deceit of accounting practices that can make a company that should be closed look like a great investment opportunity. As the saying goes, "Figures don't lie, but liars always figure." The point: TNO. Everyone wants to make a buck. They'll tell you what you want to hear. They'll hire accountants and public relations (PR) firms that will convince you up is down and down is up. Consequently, you can do all the research you want and still end up holding the fuzzy end of the lollipop.

That's not to say that every year-end report is a fraud, because most aren't. But they could be. I ask rhetorically, how are you going to know if what you're reading is fact or fiction? I swear, and most accountants will agree in private, that given the opportunity, they can make something out of less than nothing without coming close to breaking a law. TNO.

And realistically, why would/should you trust virtual strangers?

You, and you alone, are responsible for your financial well-being. Looking to someone else to plan for your future almost never works. It's up to you. Managing your money and investments isn't that hard, but you do need to have a winning perspective.

### Goal Setting

To get a winning perspective you'll need goals to judge your progress. I'm not talking about general meaningless goals such as "I want to be financially secure." What does that really mean? To me it means one thing; to a homeless man, it means something else; and to the Kennedy family it means something altogether different. Omnibus goals won't help you get where you want to go. In fact, they may hurt the process.

For those of you who have started to panic, thinking I'm going to talk about financial management by objectives and so on, relax. All I am trying to impart here is that goal setting, which is necessary for financial success, should be direct and to the point. For example, "I will be a millionaire by the age of 45" is a worthy, usable goal. Having set a goal that is financially specific, you can then judge your progress at any given point and make adjustments when needed. Specific goals give you a perspective by their nature. Specific goals break down easily to checkpoints along the way. For example, if at age 25 you set a goal to be a millionaire by the age of 45 and have only $100 in equities at the age of 43, your plan is in trouble. Of course, you would have known that long before the age of 43. However, if you're 43 and are just setting that goal for 45, you know by design that you are going to have to be very, very aggressive.

Regardless, with specific goals you will be able to set short-term, mid-term, and long-term goals. Using our millionaire example again, if you want to be a millionaire by 45 you will have to have equities of $100,000 by the age of 30, $300,000 by 38, and so on. Your perspective of achievement is easily explained and understood. If your goals are ambiguous, this built-in planning perspective doesn't design itself.

Let your financial goals give you your financial planning perspective. But a winning perspective requires more than that.

Making money consistently in the stock market takes belief in, and dedication to, a reliable plan. Anything less will ultimately fail.

It is impossible to overemphasize the importance of specific planning. Frankly, I don't know why anyone would even consider making an investment without having a plan. You wouldn't attempt to drive from Chicago to Seattle without a map, would you? You'll actually find more twists and turns in the road called Wall Street than you would on your way West. But people don't plan because they are trusting someone else, like their broker. I don't mean to pick on brokers—or anyone else for that matter—but the next time your expert gives you advice, ask this simple question: What will the Dow finish at tomorrow? Surely if they are as good as they say they are, they should be able to give you an answer. Sadly, if you do ask, many will attempt to tell you. But I, and any other honest market expert, will tell you, "I don't know." Yet, as I said, many will try to call tops and bottoms, closings, and so on. What nonsense! Check it out—if your expert gives you an answer I'll bet you it is wrong. And if he or she is wrong on an estimate 24 hours away, why would you listen to this expert for any long-term advice? TNO— have a realistic perspective.

On this subject, here's another analogy regarding our trip to Seattle. Would anyone undertake such a trip without a spare tire? I hope not. Yet, in effect, that's what many investors do by not having a plan or having a plan that doesn't take into account likely negative scenarios such as short- or long-term market reversals. If you're going to invest in the stock market for the next X number of years, I can assure you it's not going to be all beer and skittles, as the saying goes. There is going to be a flat tire every once in a while, and if you haven't included a contingency plan (such as having a reserve fund for emergencies) in your master plan you're going to get wiped out. Maybe not tomorrow, maybe not next month, or maybe not next year, but you will be wiped out. That's not a guess on my part; based on my consulting experience, that's a fact.

There are many roads to investing success (real estate, collectibles, etc.), and it would be foolish of me to think my stock market strategy is the only way. Of course, for me, and for the dedicated readers of my newsletter, it is, but the purpose of this chapter isn't to convince you of the wisdom of my discovery. Rather it is to explain that no matter what method you employ, you must have an investing perspective that is compatible with your philosophy of life. If they're in conflict (for example, a financial conservative should not be buying penny stocks), you're going to fail even with a good plan.

### Financial Perspective

It's mandatory to have a sense of balance in your financial life. You invest to make money. But money is only green paper until it's used for a worthwhile purpose. Investing should be part of your life, not your entire life, and that's what it is to too many investors. They wake up to check the foreign markets, ride the train to work reading the *Wall Street Journal*, spend too many hours at work trying to earn more money, watch cable TV to check the market closings, review each stock in their portfolios, and then, just before turning in, spend time planning tomorrow's strategy. That kind of time devoted to investing is as close to a priority sin as one can get. It's wrong because you're wasting time that could be put to better use—which brings us to the point: Why are you investing?

If you're investing as part of your devotion to the right things in life, such as providing for your family and your retirement, then you can be a smashing success. If you're investing to invest or beat the game, you lose no matter how much you earn, because you'll never have peace of mind in a marketplace that by itself creates chaos.

My suggestion is this: Find a balance. There's a place for investments in your life, and while I wouldn't be so presumptuous as to tell you exactly what it should be, I will tell you you'd better find it. Having done that, you'll be far better equipped to reach your financial goals. Investing doesn't have to be a zero-sum proposition whereby you give up your peace of mind in order to be rich. It is that only if you lose your perspective. If this sit-back-and-relax approach seems in conflict with the previous chapter, it's not. My investment strategy offers all the advantages and results of a 24-hours-a-day, 7-days-a-week effort, but it takes only minutes per day.

Probably the single most critical aspect that causes one to lose his or her perspective is greed.

Financial markets are fueled by greed. There's nothing terribly wrong with that, as we all want to make more money. In fact, those who don't save and invest are making a ruinous mistake. But being one of the players in a market, even a player with altruistic motivation, is not the problem. The problem arises when greed starts eclipsing your personal financial logic.

That's why the should-have-been-obvious stock market overvaluation of the 1990s fooled so many people. It appealed to their greed. But that shouldn't happen. All one has to remember is: If it sounds too good to be true, it almost always is. When the "experts" and TV talking heads started talking about how it was virtually impossible to lose money anymore in the market, it should have been a red flag that warned you something was wrong, terribly wrong.

Greed doesn't always have to culminate in an actual actionable swindle to cause difficulty. Subtle market greed can be equally devastating. Even then greed can cause you to lose perspective. It can cause those who are looking for investments to end up with speculations. In that case, you become the perpetrator and the victim in that you deceive yourself.

Defining your needs and expectations is necessary for investment success. Once that is accomplished, don't deviate from your plan. Don't let greed talk you into commodity futures when you really belong in blue chip stocks. That is a greed-generated value judgment that will produce results that are disastrous.

Of course, the greed factor also causes investors to look for exact tops and bottoms. It causes people to hold on when they should sell and sell when they should hold on. Regardless of the actual circumstances, greed in the market, any market, can compel people to make many erroneous judgments that if they could do over again they would do differently.

Certainly there are exceptions when greed and luck cause an unusual windfall for some lucky person, but long-term successful investing isn't a crapshoot. Frankly, when I hear of such cases, the parties involved, because of their avaricious natures, eventually give back (lose) their winnings, so it can be said that greed ultimately overtakes luck.

For the rest of us, it is prudent to remember that greed is a player in all financial markets. Therefore, you must recognize the ruinous nature of the force it commands.

### *Overcoming Greed*

Can greed be overcome? It sure can. I'd like to offer two simple rules that will tame greed and make it an impotent enemy:

**1. *Don't panic.*** Greed, as it pertains to an investment increasing in value, is often determined by its potential for loss (perhaps just the opposite of what you may have thought). All investments should have a short-term potential of a 50 percent profit to offset losses with other investments; that is, you can't win them all, so you have to let your winners pay for those judgments that didn't pan out.

But greed can cloud one's thinking when an investment turns against you. That's why many investors sell shortly after they make a stock purchase. The stock retreats for a day or so and they panic. They sell. Shortly thereafter the stock regains its loss and starts making gains from their original purchase point. Of course, sometimes a stock heads south right after a purchase, and the sooner you realize that the better. But stock, or any investment for that matter, seldom goes straight up or down. There is almost always a cycle involved.

As it's impossible to consistently pick an investment's top or bottom, you may have to ride out some negative positions to realize a profit. If you're following this book's plan, the investment will probably head in your direction at some point (sooner rather than later), but that won't matter if you've panicked and sold. An investment's profit potential can only be fully realized by letting it remain open until a clear pattern emerges or your stop is hit (more on this later).

**2. *Plan your profits.*** Taking profits is an art form. You can't grab them haphazardly. If you do, you end up with results that are less than they should have been.

When you buy an investment you should know two things: your target profit and your target term. When you set a target profit for an investment and stick to it, greed seldom gets in your way. When you reach the target, you sell. It's that simple.

Some may question this strategy, because you might make more if you hold on. True, but the reverse may occur, too—your profit and more may disappear.

However, understand that even though your target profit has been reached, you can "sell" without selling. By using a rolling stop-loss (this is discussed in depth in the section in Chapter 4 entitled "Win Big, Lose Small") you can lock in your present profit if you think there is more to be realized. By using a stop in this manner, in effect, you've "sold-out" your position by changing the investment's dynamics. You now control the floor. I can't possibly overstate the necessity of stop-loss orders. They protect capital, and they protect profits. Stops are something too many investors don't use, and even those that do seldom use them correctly.

There's nothing wrong in changing your target profit of 50 percent on the upside, as long as you ensure your original target price has been met and that almost all the profit gained has been banked. When stops are used, greed is effectively emasculated.

Your target term is also important. You wouldn't purchase a certificate of deposit without knowing its term. Nor would you sign a mortgage agreement without knowing its term. Then why do almost all investors invest without knowing what the investment's term is?

An investment should have a profit potential of X percent (whatever level you've set—again, I recommend at least 50 percent) prior to committing capital. Once that level has been met, you sell, in fact, or change the target, but you take action determined by facts in effect when the investment was purchased. The other ingredient is time. Time, as the saying goes, is money. That's why you have to have an anticipated target exit date when making an investment. Everything is relative. For example, a target date for a bank CD may be measured in months while a date for a real estate investment is probably measured in years. Then, too, investment objectives play a role. A family investing for a down payment on a house will have different maturity needs than one investing for retirement. The actual date mechanism isn't important. What's critical is employing one.

Either profit or term will determine when you sell an investment. Your profit will be hit (and perhaps restructed and protected) or your target date will arrive, whichever comes first. At that point, greed becomes a nonfactor. You will act in accordance with a specific plan instead of mimicking most investors, who play hunches or react because they got a call from their broker. Emotions should not infiltrate investment judgment, but they will if you don't have a plan for each individual investment that coexists with an overall portfolio philosophy.

Of course, there are other factors with regard to coping with greed. We're talking about basic investment criteria—for instance, trading with risk capital only, diversification, account management, and so on. But most investors know all that. So why aren't they rich? In many cases the answer is greed. Sadly, greed, by its very definition, is never satisfied.

Greed is a human frailty. Learn how to control its destructive nature, and you dramatically improve your odds of investment success. Allow me to state one of my favorite stock market axioms, as, on the subject of perspective, it's apropos: Bulls make money, bears make money—pigs get slaughtered.

I can't design a winning perspective for you. Each of us is different emotionally, each has different goals, each has a different timetable. I have, however, outlined a few aspects that are important to everyone. Build on them, and mold them to your specific needs. Do so before you invest a dime. Define your winning perspective, your goals, and your timetable, and my strategy will do the rest.

## Garbage In, Garbage Out

A principal factor to the failure of average investors to reach their financial goals is this: Too many transactions are confusing. They can also lead investors to the wrong conclusions. Unscrupulous brokers and market gurus depend on that fact. Then, too, when some of the so-called financial experts don't understand the nuances of a certain deal or investment, they simply pass on their confusion. For example, many brokers have little training or market experience, yet they make recommendations to clients—recommendations they are told to push by their bosses without understanding why or how the recommendations will affect their clients.

The financial world plays hardball, especially the stock market. Under certain circumstances, you could lose your entire life savings in a day. Again, you stand little chance of being successful, or as wealthy as you should be, even if you understand everything, because others in the marketplace make their money by taking yours. Realizing the unlevel playing field, just think how damaging these judgments are to your effectiveness. You didn't understand what you were doing even though you thought you did. A quiz to make the point:

First, what rate of return is required to equal a 20 percent average growth on $1,000 over 10 years?

| Year | Investing $1,000 | Yields |
|---|---|---|
| 1 | +20% | $1,200 |
| 2 | +20% | $1,440 |
| 3 | +20% | $1,728 |
| 4 | +20% | $2,074 |
| 5 | +20% | $2,489 |
| 6 | +20% | $2,987 |
| 7 | +20% | $3,584 |
| 8 | +20% | $4,301 |
| 9 | +20% | $5,161 |
| 10 | +20% | $6,193 |

That's what we are trying to achieve: a 20 percent average growth over 10 years that returns, in dollars, $6,193. Now, what if every other year you lose 10 percent?

The most common response is that you need a return of 50 percent in the profitable years to average a gain of 20 percent. That seems logical, as 50 percent minus 10 percent equals 40 percent, which, when divided by 2, equals 20 percent. Double-checking, you have five years at plus 50 percent; which equals 250 percent, and five years at minus 10 percent, which equals minus 50 percent; 250 percent minus 50 percent equals 200 percent—which is exactly what 20 percent times 10 years equals. Obviously, that must be the answer. But let's check, using the same procedural chart as before:

| Year | Investing $1,000 | Yields |
|---|---|---|
| 1 | +50% | $1,500 |
| 2 | −10% | $1,350 |
| 3 | +50% | $2,025 |

| Year | Investing $1,000 | Yields |
|------|------------------|--------|
| 4 | −10% | $1,823 |
| 5 | +50% | $2,735 |
| 6 | −10% | $2,462 |
| 7 | +50% | $3,693 |
| 8 | −10% | $3,324 |
| 9 | +50% | $4,986 |
| 10 | −10% | $4,487 |

Wait a minute. We're $1,706 short ($6,193 − $4,487). The percentages added up. How can that be?

This is a perfect example of how things can appear to be something they're not. That's why you may have come to the wrong conclusion/answer, as does almost everyone. Sadly, many don't even get this close to the right solution.

Let me give you the right answer prior to explaining why, on its face, it appears to be wrong. To return a 20 percent average growth over 10 years, the plus years have to be calculated at 60 percent:

| Year | Investing $1,000 | Yields |
|------|------------------|--------|
| 1 | +60% | $1,600 |
| 2 | −10% | $1,440 |
| 3 | +60% | $2,304 |
| 4 | −10% | $2,074 |
| 5 | +60% | $3,318 |
| 6 | −10% | $2,986 |
| 7 | +60% | $4,778 |
| 8 | −10% | $4,300 |
| 9 | +60% | $6,880 |
| 10 | −10% | $6,193 |

Have you figured out why the seemingly logical, most often given answer was wrong? It's in error because of the compounding factor;

that is, each year the account is building or losing on its principal plus previous interest growth/loss. Simply stated, you are earning, using straight savings as an example, interest on interest. In our quiz, that magnifies the good and bad years.

What I am trying to make clear is that investors have to be thorough when making financial decisions; otherwise, you may be making a determination based on a false or misunderstood premise.

One more quick example to make the point. If an investment loses 50 percent, are you aware that you must earn 100 percent on what's left of your capital just to get back to a break-even position? Unfortunately, losses compound, too. Not understanding such a crucial principle can put your portfolio in an unenviable position, as when's the last time you earned 100 percent on anything? Examples like this are why you must use stops. Most people, however, don't examine a loss beyond its immediate implications. Its impact on remaining capital is just as important. That's a consideration that must be made prior to making an investment rather than after a loss. Understanding only a portion of a transaction is death in the stock market.

But there is more to this than just not understanding a given transaction. Earlier we talked briefly about how a good accountant can make a year-end report look better than the company's bottom line would actually call for. That's bad enough—but what about those facts you're relying on that are written so that you can't understand them? To make the point, let's use a prospectus, as after all a prospectus is the very essence of a stock, its root as it were. If you can't understand such a document, you're in trouble. And remember, most experts say reading a prospectus is mandatory. Almost every book ever written about the stock market and investing includes at least one chapter on how to read a prospectus. It's critical, they all say. I say they are wrong—not because you shouldn't be informed; no, it's my argument that the information available to individual investors is, while compliant with the law, useless. It was designed and written to be useless and confusing.

### Most of What You're Supposed to Read Is a Waste of Time

Many of you may doubt my conclusion, so I am going to take a random prospectus and try to elucidate it.

I've chosen a relatively simple section containing no complicated mathematics so no one can say that I picked a difficult subject to make my point. Here goes (under the section entitled "Shares Eligible for Future Sale"). For obvious reasons I am redacting anything that might reveal a company name or indicate same by deduction.

Upon completion of the offering, we expect to have X,XXX,XXX shares of common stock outstanding, assuming no exercise of outstanding options or warrants, or X,XXX,XXX shares if the underwriter's over-allotment is exercised in full. Of these shares, the X,XXX,XXX shares of common stock, and the shares of common stock issue upon exercise of the warrants, issued as part of the units sold in the offering will be freely tradeable without restrictions or further registration under the Securities Act, except that any shares purchased by our "affiliates," as that term is defined under the Securities Act, may generally only be sold in compliance with the limitations of Rule 144 under the Securities Act. All of the remaining outstanding shares of common stock are restricted securities within the meaning of Rule 144 and may not be sold in absence of registration under the Securities Act unless an exemption from registration is available, including the exemption from registration offered by Rule 144.

Holders of more than 95% of our restricted shares of common stock, other than those beneficially owned by ABC have agreed (the "Lock-Up Agreements") not to sell or otherwise dispose of any of their shares of common stock for a period of one year after completion of the offering, without the prior written consent of ABC, Inc. and XYZ, Inc., subject to certain limited exceptions. XYZ has a six-month lock-up period. After the expiration of these lock-up periods, or earlier with the prior written consent of ABC and XYZ, X,XXX,XXX shares of the common stock may be sold in the public market pursuant to Rule 144.

In general, under Rule 144, as current in effect, beginning 90 days after the date of this prospectus, a person who has beneficially owned restricted shares for at least one year, including a person who may be deemed to be our affiliate, may sell within a three-month period a number of shares of common stock that does not exceed a maximum number of shares. The maximum is equal to the greater of 1% of the then outstanding shares of our common stock or the average weekly trading volume in the common stock during the four calendar weeks immediately preceding the sale. Sales under Rule 144 are also subject to restrictions relating to manner of sale, notice and availability of current public information about us. In addition, under Rule 144(k) of the Securities Act, a person who is not our affiliate, has not been an affiliate of ours within three months prior to the sale and has beneficially owned shares for at least two years, would be entitled to sell such shares immediately without regard to volume limitations, manner of sale provisions, notice or other requirements of Rule 144.

I stop here, halfway through the section, hoping I've made my point. Remember, this is one of the easiest-to-understand sections in the entire 83-page—that's right, 83-page—prospectus. As you can see, garbage comes in many forms.

So, did you understand everything? Did you whip out your copy of the Securities Act to double-check Rule 144? Do you understand who's doing what to whom? Some will say yes; others will say no. I say, who cares? The entire prospectus could be distilled down to a few pages and have far more meaning and relevance to a potential investor. We're playing a game here. The game is this—the company wants to ensure it is compliant with all SEC regulations in such a manner that investors are enticed to spend their money. Too often, far too often, a company entices through confusion—which sends investors back to their brokers. Making large commissions by selling the company's stock to investors, brokers do nothing to explain the prospectus adequately, which was the problem in the first place.

Let's also remember that there are thousands of stocks traded publicly. If you're going to be an educated investor by the standard extolled by the "experts" (i.e., reading everything available on a given stock or stocks), you're going to have to quit your job—you've got enough reading to do in one year to last a lifetime.

The point I am trying to make is this: Even if the information available was decipherable, which most is not, it is impossible for you to adequately avail yourself of the details contained in all of the documentation. That's exactly what the insiders had in mind in the first place. They want to be able to crow about how they are so highly regulated, while at the same time ensuring they have a captive audience of investors that have, by the confusing nature of the prospectus, year-end report, and so on, determined they need the insiders to survive. Again, the stock market is designed by the insiders/pros for the insiders/pros.

The financial marketplace can, over the long term, take as much of your money as you allow it to, so it's critical to understand every aspect of a transaction before acting. Then, check, check, and check again. Turn your answer upside down and sideways. Overlook nothing. You see, much of what traditional stock market thinking says is not wrong. What's wrong is the method the "experts" tell you is a means to that end. And that's why you need this book. I'm going to show you a different way, a better way. The beauty of my discovery is this: In a matter of minutes you will have "read" everything worth reading about every stock on the exchange. Better yet, my strategy gives you the right answers even if you don't know the right questions.

Let me give you one example of how buying into conventional wisdom can be costly. One of the biggest financial myths during my lifetime is that the middle class has done pretty well during the 1990s. Unfortunately, the truth is that the middle class has been robbed during the 1990s without even knowing it. While their financial situation may have remained constant or even improved somewhat, it did so because two wage earners were now providing what one wage earner used to be able to provide. That's not financial progress; that's running financially backward. What's next, putting our kids to work so we can continue to believe the lie of our affluence into the next century? While not pertaining to the stock market per se, this example, and what it represents, says that not being able to see through the conventional explanations is the kind of mistake that has serious financial and personal repercussions. If you're not careful, the "experts" will have you believing things you should clearly know are false.

We all know that even the best, most sophisticated computer is rendered useless if its input is garbage (i.e., incorrect). So would be your ability to profit in the stock market if you input into your strategy the garbage disseminated by publicly held corporations and then propagated by brokers and their houses, government, the SEC, TV talking heads, newsletter "experts," and others.

## To Invest Successfully You Have to Have Something to Invest

You have to invest. If you don't invest, you'll just be one of the millions of people who hope they can send their kids to college, hope the Social Security system really isn't bankrupt, hope they win the lottery, and so on. That, unfortunately, is the financial plan for too many families in the United States.

And if you have wealth at present and don't invest, your wealth will disappear, as Table 2.1 shows. Bear in mind that this chart ignores the devastating effect of personal income taxes.

Regardless of your present situation, you have to invest; you have no choice. And, since most of us aren't rich to start with, we have to start by building a fund with which we can start investing. This is critical. To invest, you have to have something to invest with. (If you already have a substantial portfolio, this subject is irrelevant, and you can skip to the next chapter.)

Understandably, to most people the subject of savings is boring at

**TABLE 2.1** What Today's $100,000 Will Be Worth

| Rate of Inflation | Today's Value | Value in 5 Years | Value in 15 Years | Value in 25 Years |
| --- | --- | --- | --- | --- |
| 2% | $100,000 | $89,108 | $62,250 | $43,986 |
| 4% | $100,000 | $81,526 | $52,117 | $31,990 |
| 6% | $100,000 | $74,726 | $41,727 | $23,300 |
| 8% | $100,000 | $68,058 | $31,524 | $14,602 |
| 10% | $100,000 | $62,092 | $23,939 | $ 9,230 |
| 12% | $100,000 | $56,743 | $18,270 | $ 5,882 |

*Source:* John R. Mrkvicka.

best. The word immediately brings to mind the picture of a savings passbook at a local financial institution. A passbook that, as of this writing, pays under 5 percent interest. A passbook that, after taxes and inflation, is a net loss. It's hard to get excited about an "investment" vehicle like that.

Will Rogers said, "Forget about a return on my money, what I want is a return of my money." As cute as that is, and it was probably quite appropriate when said, that's nonsense. If it weren't, the best place to put your money would be to bury it. That would indeed ensure the return of your money, but it is not prudent or wise. Today, while people aren't burying their money, they aren't saving any, either. They're taking fliers on every new stock and investment opportunity that comes down the pike, because everything works! No one seems to be losing any money, and they're making a bundle. Again, that's somewhat true now, but it won't be forever. Reality will once again return to the market. So what are we talking about here—should you invest in nothing, or put your money in a certificate of deposit, a savings bond, a money market, a NOW account, or what? Which is safest? Should you be concerned with Federal Deposit Insurance Corporation (FDIC) insurance? Should you shop for better rates? How about offshore banking?

### Savings: A New Definition

Forget all of this about traditional savings choices; none of it matters. I want you to consider another, more exciting definition of savings. Savings is a systematic program, based on a percentage of your salary, that is used for the purpose of acquiring wealth through the buying and selling of stock. It's not the vehicle that determines if you are saving, it's the continuum of putting aside monies on a predetermined basis that counts.

Savings cannot involve any form of speculation since that destroys the ability to reasonably foresee the end results of your efforts. For example, if you set aside X dollars per month for savings, and then speculate in commodities, how can you estimate your capital in 5, 10, 15 years? Obviously you can't. By its very nature, speculation precludes that.

If you set aside X dollars per month and invest in the stock market, are you saving or investing? It's speculation if you have no stock market investment plan. You're saving if you do, because while you must be careful in the market, the fact is that stocks, withstanding even major corrections, have an acceptable and predictable time-line track record of return that takes them out of the speculation realm. However, if you're buying this and selling that without a strategy/system/plan, you negate the market's historical semi-predictability.

As you can see, savings can take on many forms, so don't mistakenly reject the savings principle.

There are two generally accepted principles that determine whether a vehicle is a savings vehicle: (1) Savings have to be liquid (easily accessible/redeemable). Notice that I said liquid, not risk free. (2) Savings have to be relatively safe. Notice I said relatively safe, not risk free. The stock market has both of these qualifications. You can, under normal circumstances, buy and sell stocks immediately. You can, under normal circumstances, know, within certain parameters, that your investment is relatively safe and—and this is important—you are in charge of your investment's safety. You and you alone have control of your stocks if not the market itself.

In today's high-pressured financial environment, many of us have amassed little or nothing in the way of liquid assets. In other words, we have no savings plans. Saving money is not easy, especially when many of us have to spend every dollar we earn just to make ends meet. No, it's not easy, but it's mandatory for financial success.

Many years ago, everyone saved. Our parents or grandparents were products of the Depression, an event our generation cannot truly comprehend. Because of that experience, our parents believe that if you don't save, you will be at the mercy of an uncertain future.

With double-digit inflation and the arrival of the I-want-it-now generation, savings in the United States, the richest nation in the world, declined. Today we have one of the lowest savings ratios of any industrialized nation. Are we so smart or are our elders stupid?

The truth is, we're the stupid ones. Saving has been replaced with buying things we cannot afford and in most cases don't need. That principle has bankrupted our country. Learn from that mistake. As every millionaire knows, you must pay yourself before you pay others. A substantial portion of your earnings must be saved each month.

Saving requires dedication and hard work. It takes time. You can't make a million overnight, but you can make a million. Saving works primarily due to the effect of accumulating numbers. That is the key to any savings plan.

Tables 2.2 and 2.3 use a conservative 10 percent return. Even in a tough market, you should be able to average substantially better than 10 percent. In fact, as explained throughout this book, you're going to be making 50 to 200 percent or more!

Return can be accrued through either interest, appreciation, inflation, or any combination. Don't get confused and limit your consideration to just one aspect of an investment's potential. The wealthy realize and utilize all factors that contribute to the net return.

Both these tables are in keeping with my Golden Rule of Savings, which states that you must save a minimum of 5 percent of your gross

**TABLE 2.2** 5% Savings, 10% Return

| Salary | Monthly Savings | Value in 10 Years | Value in 20 Years | Value in 30 Years |
|---|---|---|---|---|
| $20,000 | $ 83.33 | $17,069.73 | $ 63,278.21 | $188,366.46 |
| $25,000 | $104.17 | $21,337.68 | $ 79,099.66 | $235,463.72 |
| $30,000 | $125.00 | $25,605.62 | $ 94,921.11 | $282,560.98 |
| $35,000 | $145.83 | $29,872.54 | $110,738.76 | $329,646.94 |
| $40,000 | $166.67 | $34,140.49 | $126,560.20 | $376,744.21 |
| $45,000 | $187.50 | $38,408.44 | $142,381.65 | $423,841.42 |
| $50,000 | $208.33 | $42,675.35 | $158,199.30 | $470,927.43 |

*Source:* John R. Mrkvicka.

salary every month. To further elaborate the principle of savings as a means to financial independence, Table 2.3 is a chart for the same salaries as in Table 2.2 but using an ideal 10 percent savings figure for the more ambitious.

These monthly savings will go into your stock account.

These tables clearly show that savings can accumulate enormously. To make the point, look at the 10 percent savings chart in the salary line

**TABLE 2.3** 10% Savings, 10% Return

| Salary | Monthly Savings | Value in 10 Years | Value in 20 Years | Value in 30 Years |
|---|---|---|---|---|
| $20,000 | $166.66 | $34,139.46 | $126,566.41 | $376,732.91 |
| $25,000 | $208.33 | $42,675.35 | $158,199.31 | $470,927.44 |
| $30,000 | $250.00 | $51,211.24 | $189,842.21 | $565,121.97 |
| $35,000 | $291.66 | $59,745.08 | $221,477.51 | $659,293.89 |
| $40,000 | $333.33 | $68,280.97 | $253,120.41 | $753,488.42 |
| $45,000 | $375.00 | $76,816.87 | $284,763.31 | $847,682.95 |
| $50,000 | $416.66 | $85,350.71 | $316,398.61 | $941,854.87 |

*Source:* John R. Mrkvicka.

of $30,000. After 10 years you have a balance of $51,211.24. During that time you deposited a total of $30,000, which means your nondeposited return is $21,211.24. At the 20-year mark, you have a balance of $189,842.21. During that time you actually paid in a total of $60,000, which means you earned a whopping $129,842.21. You have accumulated more than double what you paid in. The figures become staggering the further down the line we go.

And all we require is 5 or 10 percent of your gross income. Even if you are 45 years old when you start saving, you can amass a sizable fortune by age 65. The savings principle works regardless of age. One thing's for certain: If you don't save and subsequently invest your savings, I can assure you that you will be substantially poorer in 20 years than those who did.

There's another characteristic to this methodical approach that is often overlooked: Percentage savings is inflation proof in an indirect way. Almost everyone, especially in times of high inflation, receives a yearly raise that includes an additional cost-of-living adjustment. Since your savings plan is predicated on a percentage, your savings positioning should remain at a movable constant that reflects the status quo. In the charts I used a specific yearly amount to show how investments grow monthly. In actuality, your balance in 10 or 20 years should be far in excess of the charts. Again, the percentage factor. You may start out with a salary of $20,000 per year, but wind up at $75,000 at career end. Obviously, then, your monthly savings amount will constantly increase and, consequently, so will your ultimate balance.

Again, these are conservative estimates. My experience suggests you'll do much, much better. Percentage savings and dedication on your part will allow this book's strategy to perform at its maximum, because the more money you have the easier it is to make more money. And when you put the additional money to good use, it multiplies through appreciation and reinvestment of dividends, interest, inflationary considerations, and so on.

### "Small" Mistakes in Judgment Can Be Very Costly

Let's try another quiz. Imagine you're offered a 30-day summer job. You are offered two pay scales. You can be paid $100,000 per day or a salary that starts out at $.01 and doubles every day. On the second day you will be paid $.02, the third day $.04, the fourth day $.08, and so on. Remember, now, this job lasts only 30 days. You have five seconds to choose one or the other or lose the job. Most people, even though they are wary because of the nature of the quiz, choose the $100,000 per day. They can quickly, in their heads, even in five seconds, realize that at $100,000 per day they are going to make $3 million, and it seems unlikely that a penny starting salary can better that, especially in only 30 days.

Extrapolating the doubling salary goes like this: Day (1) $.01, (2) $.02, (3) $.04, (4) $.08, (5) $.16, (6) $.32, (7) $.64, (8) $1.28, (9) $2.56, (10) $5.12, (11) $10.24, (12) $20.48, (13) $40.96, (14) $81.92, (15) $163.84.

At the end of the first half of our 30-day job the $100,000 salary has earned $1,500,000. The doubling salary has made a total of only $327.67. It hardly seems possible that the doubling salary can catch up, must less pass the $100,000-a-day total. Let's continue.

Day (16) $327.68, (17) $655.36, (18) $1,310.72, (19) $2,621.44, (20) $5,242.88, (21) $10,485.76, (22) $20,971.52, (23) $41,943.04, (24) $83,886.08, (25) $167,772.16, (26) $335,544.32. Only four days left. The $100,000-per-day salary has made $2,600,000, while the doubling salary has earned only $671,088.63.

Day (27) $671,088.64, (28) $1,342,177.28, (29) $2,684,354.56, (30) $5,368,709.12, for a total of $10,737,418.23.

Those who understand the principle of accumulating numbers do the best. In fact, they make $7,737,418.23 more than those who take the seemingly better, at first blush, $100,000-a-day salary. But I offer this quiz for more than just the value of the quiz itself and the principle of accumulating numbers. There is more to be learned. First, once again we can see that things aren't necessarily what they appear to be, especially at first glance. We learn that financial decisions deserve considerable consideration. We learn that financial mistakes can be extremely costly. We are reminded that slow and steady often wins the race. We are reminded, too, that money, when used correctly, can make more money.

What I have tried to show here is that saving is a principle. Your return, as noted earlier, can be made through interest, dividends, appreciation, sales profit, or a combination thereof. Regardless, what makes the magic of the stock market work is a dedication to the concept of savings using that vehicle.

In my consulting, especially when dealing with younger investors, I am asked about this stock or that one. After listening to the usual market double-talk, learned no doubt from their brokers or brothers-in-law, I often ask, "And how much are you saving each month to invest in the stock market?" Usually that's met with a blank stare and dead silence. New investors have the fever, but they often don't have the bread. Oh, they'll grab their year-end bonus, an inheritance, and the like and shove it into an episodically growing portfolio, but they have no plan—they're not saving to invest; they're trying to invest to save. Friends, that's putting the cart in front of the horse, and that means that the cart won't consistently head in the right direction.

Even though you might not be able to save a lot, our charts show how a little money applied to a savings/investment plan over time will make you rich. And for those of you who truly believe you can't save, that you just don't have any extra money to put away, I ask that you participate in a month long test of your finances. Starting today, and for the next 30 days, write down, on a list you carry with you, every penny you spend and why you spend it. It doesn't matter if it's cash, check, or credit card; write down every expenditure for the next 30 days. If you spend $100 on a sweater and charge it, write it down. If you spend 50 cents on a pack of gum, write it down. If you pay a credit card bill from last month with a check, write it down. At the end of the month you should be able to account for every penny you spent and why you spent it.

Why should you go to this trouble? Because, if you're at all like most people, you're going to be stunned at how much you've spent/wasted and what you spent/wasted it on. You're going to quickly realize that you've wasted a bundle, money that would have been better spent buying stock. There isn't anyone who buys this book who cannot afford or find the money to save and invest. There isn't anyone who doesn't save and invest who will ever be wealthy (short of a rich relative dying and leaving you a fortune, or hitting the lottery). This rather pedestrian subject of saving is critical to your investing success. You can't hit a home run if you don't step up to the plate. You can't win a marathon without running. You can't win the Indy 500 without starting your car. Likewise, you can't get rich unless you pay yourself first out of your income, regardless of what you make, and then invest those savings.

Stop and think about what you're doing. Think long-term, because that's what your stock market relationship should be—quick killings are seldom made and often lost at a later date. You want a plan. And part of that plan must include saving. Don't just blurt out and act upon the first thing that runs through your mind. Remember our summer job quiz—don't make a multimillion-dollar mistake. Once again, you save to invest; you don't invest to save.

## The Ten Commandments of Stock Market Success

The average investors are likely to rely on brokers or market gurus for market recommendations, which are dangerous errors. Either that or they are entirely on their own with no plan—which is equally dangerous. The latter is often a compulsive person who, instead of going to Las Vegas, turns to the market for a gambling fix. Usually overinvested, this type of investor loves to trade on the latest hot tip, and is unhappy when nothing is happening. Making a trade is even more important than holding onto a winner.

It doesn't matter what your problem with the market is, though, you first have to admit you have one and then work to correct it. How do you know if you've even got a problem? Look at your record. Are you making big money in all market conditions? After expenses, are you showing a profit and at what rate? If you're returning, as an example, only 15 percent net on your stocks, I suggest you get out of the market, because you're risking 100 percent of your investment capital for a limited return.

Basically, there are four kinds of market players: the big winners, the small winners, the small losers, and the big losers. The big winners are the Wall Street traders. The small winners are insiders/brokers and a small portion of individual investors. The small losers are individual traders. The big losers are the compulsive individual traders. In the end, as in all games designed for a predetermined outcome, only the insiders ultimately win. If the crash hasn't happened yet, don't let the fact that you've won a few hands go to your head. You're just being set up for a fall.

However, as the adage goes, a high tide raises all boats. That's what is/was going on prior to the crash. Consequently, in a bull market all positions tend to improve. There is nothing wrong with profiting from that fact. However, as mentioned earlier, most individual traders lose all their winnings when the market turns around. Amateurs normally win only in a can't-lose situation. Professionals win all the time. The bottom line: Don't allow success in the best of times to cloud your thinking and lead you into believing that the market is a win/win situation—it's not.

Nevertheless, the stock market has certain investment advantages. It's easy to get into, and trading costs can be low if you use an online or discount broker/house. Most importantly, returns can be substantial.

Realizing that the market is unduly influenced by insiders, to be successful you need a set of rules that you can follow without question to counteract the inequity. That, of course, is something your broker and other market pros hope you'll never realize.

## The Ten Commandments

Here are my Ten Commandments of Stock Market Success:

**1. *Invest only*.** You cannot afford to speculate in vehicles with a high degree of exposure to loss.

Far too many people are speculating while believing they're investing in relatively safe vehicles. And, of course, invest with risk capital only.

I have heard more than one person say that they are investing in the commodities markets, such as corn, oil, or gold futures. I shake my head in wonderment that someone could be in commodities, a highly charged and volatile market, and not even understand that they are not investing; they are speculating. They are in a market that has no predictability to it (regardless of what some commodity pundits say) and has a risk factor that for most individuals highly eclipses its profit potential, and they think they are investing. Amazing—it is no wonder that the vast majority of losing commodity trades are made by individual nonprofessional investors.

Let's look at two aspects of the difference between investments and speculations:

First, you hold an investment. Speculation is geared toward a quick turnover. An investment is long-term. A speculation is entered into with the anticipation of a short-term devotion of funds.

But a bigger difference is this—an investment has minimal risks associated with the vehicle choice, while a speculation often assumes tremendous risks in anticipation of greater rewards. This more than anything determines the difference between an investment and a speculation.

**2. *Diversify*.** All-your-eggs-in-one-basket is not wise. Trade 5 to 10 positions.

This is done for more than the obvious reasons. What we're trying to do is protect your portfolio. This demands that you trade 5 to 10 stocks in the stock portion of your investment portfolio, so that the failure of one or two companies won't hurt your overall gains. Then, too, if you diversify, the odds are that you'll be in more than one industry genre (i.e., tech stocks, Internet stocks, etc.). Therefore, should one industry get hurt as a whole, you will suffer only a minor hit.

It has to be noted that many investors have made a fortune knowing and trading just one or two stocks or just one industry. I don't fault them, as actually that's a very productive strategy. However, it is not for the average small investor, who needs an across-the-board investment strategy that offers an element of safety through its wider parameters.

Diversification should enter your entire investment portfolio, not just your stock account—meaning that you shouldn't have 100 percent of your investments in the stock market, real estate, bonds, or cash equivalents. I won't tell you what percentages should be where, because your needs and the investment climate should make that determination. I will repeat, however, that if you're 100 percent invested in one thing, you're making a mistake.

Some people get a little confused on the issue of diversification. They think if they have 10 different stocks they are diversified. That's like a real estate investor saying he is diversified because he owns 10 single-family houses in a given community. That's not diversification. A tumble in real estate prices in that area and each house will be reduced in value.

This is somewhat true with certain mutual funds that specialize in particular stocks—there is a false sense of diversification when, in fact, there may not be any. The fund may specialize in a certain group/genre of stocks that will all be hit hard if the genre changes direction or falls out of favor.

The goal we are trying to accomplish here is safety. Most people understand the concept of diversification, but find it difficult or impossible to achieve, because they really haven't thought it through. Diversification has many tiers, not just the one people normally think of. You want diversification with your portfolio, and then you also want diversification with your stocks, and so on. Diversification might not sound like a big deal and may be somewhat of a pain to achieve, but it may save you from some tremendous losses. The Trinity Trading System (TTS) offers its users diversification by picking stocks in a most unique way, as described in Chapter 3, "Picking Winning Stocks."

**3. *Trade active stocks only.*** And review your positions on a daily basis. Buying inactive stocks is like mortality; once locked in, you won't be able to change things easily even though you may wish to.

You'll be glad to know, as with other aspects of my 10 rules, that the TTS you'll read about in the next chapter solves the active stock problem, as that's all you're going to be trading.

Let me give you a personal example of how trading anything that is not active can kill you. I had, very early on in my commodity trading experience, taken a position in eggs that was historically rock solid when I made it. It was a trade, based on past history, that had a success rate of over 90 percent. Can't beat that, right? I had additionally put the appropriate stop on my position, so I wasn't exposing myself to a loss that would not be in line with my commandment percentages (I applied them to commodities, too, even back when I was an investment accident waiting to happen—of course, I didn't know that at the time). Well, for the first time in years the trade was a loser. Not to worry, I said to myself, that's what stops are for. That's right, except for one thing. Someone has to buy you out of your position whether you are in commodities or the stock market, thereby exercising your stop. No one ever did until I had lost thousands of dollars. The missing ingredient was this—no one was trading eggs, no one. I had to sit there and watch what should have been, at worst, a small loss turn into a large loss. Why? Because I made a fatal error. I traded a commodity that had had no transactions for days. I learned a valuable lesson the hard way. Don't let this happen to you, because the same thing can happen in the stock market, although it is far less likely than in commodities. But if you trade active stocks, this is moot. Check on volume and activity—your broker can help.

**4. *Become a professional.*** Your personal finances are important and deserve your attention.

The best way to achieve the equivalent of professional status is devotion to the strategy contained in this book.

Some of you may be thinking, Boy, this guy is beating this "professional" thing to death—what's the big deal? Maybe I can explain the "big deal" better by asking you a few questions. Would you use a bank if you realized that every employee was untrained and had just started last week? Would you hire a financial planner who wasn't certified? Would you entertain using your brother-in-law who has no discernible skills to do your personal and corporate taxes? The obvious answer to all is a resounding no. So why would you treat your investments, your retirement future, with any less concern? If you are not a "professional" with regard to your investments you could be settling for a lot less than you could have had.

Do you see the interesting paradox? You're not a professional and you can't trust those that are. Fortunately, my strategy solves the problem.

**5. *Never lose hands-on control.*** This is probably the most important rule of investing. Once you turn over your portfolio to another, in actuality or in principle, you stand very little chance of winning the game. I have never met any truly wealthy people (excluding those who inherited wealth) who didn't have complete control of their finances.

It's your money, and it must be taken hold of. One of the questions I like to ask people who have come to me for advice is this: "How well do you know your broker?" The answer usually goes something like this, "Well, uh, he's a nice guy, I guess. Why do you ask?" I ask because those people who rely solely on their brokers have entrusted a great deal of money to someone they don't know. They don't know where, or even if, the brokers went to school, how much experience they have, or whether they have ever been brought up on charges in the financial industry. They, in many cases, wouldn't even know their brokers if they passed them on the street. Think about this: They have given people they don't know, virtual strangers, access to their money. They use their advice to make investment decisions. It's no big deal, some would say, because they are really relying on the records of their brokerage houses. Regardless, no rational person gives that much access to one's financial future to a person, even one who may work for a reputable stock house, but last week may have been a used car salesman. You must have hands-on control. This is not an option; it's mandatory. The TTS forces you to follow this advice.

Let me give you a few specific reasons why you should empower yourself in such a way:

• Only you know why you're investing, which is a key component to a successful trading system. Sure, you can discuss goals with brokers, but, ultimately, they have little reason to be responsible to you. Before you know it they'll be calling about this stock flier and that stock flier when all you want to do is make sure you have a comfortable retirement.

The trading system outlined in the next chapter will pick a broad-based list of stocks daily for you to choose from. Portfolio value, the dollar value of your investments, will help you narrow the list down to the stocks that are right for you. Knowing why you're investing will narrow that list even further, as if you have only five years before your kid(s) start college and haven't saved a dime, you might be looking for a different stock than if you have 30 years until retirement. And if by chance you don't know why you're investing, or it's a thrill thing, watch out—you're headed for trouble. Any good investment plan starts with an answer to the question of why.

• Only you can determine your investment timetable. Obviously, the longer the time you have to reach your goal the more likely that it will be reached. The shorter the time factor the greater the element of risk (exposure to potential loss) you may have to absorb to get where you want to go. Regardless, this, too, must be determined before you plunge headlong into the stock market. Someone else (a broker, adviser, etc.), even though you may explain in great detail your timetable, will, eventually, make their timetable your timetable—and guess who loses when that happens.

• Only you can determine what risk you are willing to accept. Fortunately, as you are about to find out, the system described in this book will help you eliminate much of the normal risk associated with any stock pick. But the issue of risk is still germain, since if you personally aren't trading my system, no one you hire is going to trade it for you.

• Only you can stay focused on what you want from your investments. If you listen to others, in short order you're going to be heading in about 20 different directions at once. This broker says this, that TV expert says that; the newspaper says they're both wrong, and this afternoon's cold sales call said offshore banking is where the money is to be made. I can tell you as a fact that a shotgun approach to investing doesn't work. The more focused you are, the better your chances of being pleased with the results.

Lastly on this subject I would like to relate a study I did years ago for my newsletter. I then wrote an article entitled "The Keys to Wealth." Every wealthy person I interviewed said at one point that he or she doesn't trust anyone with their money (remember TNO?). That's not as crass as it might sound, and it coincided with my experience within the banking community. Many wealthy people think everyone is a crook. I can remember one older gentleman I met early on in my banking career. We got onto the subject of wealth (which he had a ton of), and he said, "Let me tell you something: No one is ever going to make you rich. If you want to be rich, you're going to have to do it yourself." He then asked me an interesting question to make the point. "Ed, why would anyone, except maybe your dad, want to make you rich? Why would they take the time? Why would they make the effort?" I had no answer. He had made his point. The only one who had enough at stake in my welfare to make me wealthy was me—no one else had any serious vested interest.

For those of you who may be thinking that a broker or trusted financial adviser has a vested interest in you, because "if you make money he or she makes money," you're wrong. As I said earlier, your broker wins every time you make a trade, period; you don't. Here's the bottom line—no one, except your family, has as much to lose or gain as you do every time you make a decision regarding your finances.

**6. *Never trade more than 20 percent of your investment capital on one trade.*** This will stop you from overtrading and/or overexposing your portfolio to excessive risk.

Here again I am trying to force you into prudence. You would have to make five consecutive bad/complete wipeout trades to zero yourself out. With my system that is more than highly unlikely, so you have an almost guaranteed lifetime ticket to the game (notwithstanding any small stumbles).

**7. *Use stop-loss orders.*** Always protect your capital, profits, and individual trades. You should know going in what you expect from the trade and what you are willing to accept as a loss.

Never lose more than 10 percent of your total capital on one trade. With this addendum/further clarification to Rule 6, you would now have to have 10 total wipeout trades in a row to lose your portfolio. Depending on how many trades you execute at 20 percent of your portfolio, this number could go even higher. What we're doing is, without fanfare, packing on layer after layer of safety.

Lock in profits whenever possible.

I go into this in detail later on due to its importance.

**8. *When in doubt, don't.*** Whether it's the market in general or a specific stock, if you've got any doubt, pass. You don't have to trade all the time. In fact, there are times when you should be out of the market. An uncertain trade is almost always a loser.

I don't believe in hunches, but I'd encourage you to listen to that little voice in the back of your head that has doubts about a trade. As unobjective as this may be, this is a strong signal that shouldn't be ignored. I wish I had a dollar for every time I heard a market player say, "I knew I shouldn't have done that—I should have listened to myself!"

**9.** *You have to win in bull and bear markets.* As mentioned earlier, anyone can win in a bull market. The real test comes when the bear arrives. Winners make money because they understand and can profit from both markets. If all you know is how to buy and/or you can win only when everyone does, you've got problems.

Most individual small investors don't fare well in a bear market. My system/strategy changes all that. The principle, and what makes my system work, holds true when the market is going up or down. You'll be amazed at how easy it is. A bear market is nothing to fear; it's just a different set of circumstances. In fact, many huge fortunes have been made when the stock market heads south.

**10.** *Retain (set aside) a 10 percent liquid capital savings account.* Add to it with every winning trade. As corny as it may sound, a rainy-day account may mean the difference between having to accept being wiped out and being able to hang in there and trade later when conditions improve. Think of it as your market/investment insurance policy. You'll be glad you planned ahead.

You also need to know that your investments should be judged on a portfolio basis. Individual trades are important, but may mean little at the end of the year (the number of winners and losers doesn't necessarily matter). The only thing that counts then is, how much money did you make? A loss is a loss. By itself it means nothing. If your ego can't stand the strain of short-term defeat(s), get out of the market before you lose it all.

As mentioned earlier, look for a potential profit of 50 percent on each investment choice. Refuse to invest in any vehicle that does not have a reasonable short-term potential of at least that amount, the reason being that the winners you'll have must offset the losers and then some. Don't forget, when looking for a 50 percent return, you have to appraise an investment's entire potential: growth, dividends, appreciation, and so on. There are many investors who have made a fortune by understanding that buying and selling aren't all there is. For instance, some stocks that have appreciated little over the past 10 years have made their owners rich in dividends.

If you've made initially wise decisions, you will be able to stay the course, which is an important consideration, because the potential for future profit may be there even though your original investment positioning may have been slightly flawed or unusual events made your plan temporarily worthless. If you believe in your investment choices, don't let short-term reversals sway your thinking. It may just take a little longer for you to be proven right. It's equally important to recognize an obvious error and curtail its effect immediately.

If you're going to be in the market you must understand the rules, and not those outlined by the brokers and self-appointed experts who make money not by being right, but by being good salespeople. Truth is, no one in the market proper or who sells monthly advice is going to make you rich in the stock market. Again, if you succeed, you'll do so on your own.

It should be noted that you'll be far more successful in the market if you don't get too fancy. For example, don't hedge (see Glossary). There are times when hedging is appropriate (for example, for farmers trying to protect their crop profits), but not for the average investor. Then, too, it's best if you don't pyramid (see Glossary). Using margins is emotionally draining and increases the risk factor. The point is, there are very complicated trading addenda that you'll hear about and want to consider making a part of your investment strategy—don't do it. You're not equipped to do so. And if you rely on another for these additions, you'll be violating Rule 5. Follow the KISS method—keep it simple, stupid. That's one of the smartest things you'll ever do in the market.

Notice, I have yet to mention picking stocks. Nor will there be a listing, as is done in so many financial publications, where you'll hear about the top-ten Hottest Stock Picks. That kind of fuzzy-headed thinking is what gets investors in trouble. It's like reading a new car guide for consumers after you've bought a new car. Learn the rules first, then look at stocks.

Please read this book over and over until everything contained in it is committed to memory. Each piece of information is designed to take you out of the amateur ranks and into the big leagues as quickly and simply as possible.

But is that all there is to this, picking winning stocks? No, my system does more for you than just picking winning stocks, although surely that would be enough to make most people happy.

### Additional Important Benefits

Throughout this book I will refer to this consideration or that and then follow with the fact that my strategy solves what is a problem for others who are not following my system. Actually, I find that aspect of the TTS the most interesting; that is, not only does it pick winning stocks, it cures a number of expensive and costly errors that too many investors make.

For example, it cures falling for the dreaded cold sales call that we all get all too often. You know, the one from that guy or gal—and a house you never heard of—who is willing to give you the greatest hot tip of all time, the one that is going to make you rich and handsome at the same time. These salespeople are good, really good, but, if you're devoted to my trading system, you will not allow yourself to buy into the hype; until you get a buy signal from the system, you're not going to do anything, much less listen to a total stranger for investment advice.

My trading system will also stop you from trading or acting upon tonight's newscast or "market wrap-up" show, because, once again, the system will tell you what to do, and until the time is right, you're not going to overreact based on what you heard on TV.

In fact, my trading system will allow you, perhaps for the first time since you entered the market, to sleep at night. You can watch television if you want, but you won't be inclined to insomnia. That's one of the advantages my system offers the user—peace of mind and isolation from all those investment/speculation schemes. "Just say no!" That's my motto. Remember the old saying, "Even a fish wouldn't get into trouble if it kept its big mouth shut." Say no and hang up when solicited over the phone. People don't get rich dealing with cold call salespeople; only the salespeople do. This may not seem like much of a side benefit, but, believe me, it is. If I had but an infinitesimal percentage of the monies lost by innocent investors to cold stock calls, my fortune would make Bill Gates look like a poor man.

My system also stops you from going craze crazy. Let me give you a most relevant example—Internet stocks. Of course, this could also apply to biotechnology stocks, computer stocks, and anything else deemed high tech. If salespeople can somehow use the words "cutting edge" when discussing a genre of stocks, they always seem to be able to find buyers who can't wait to plunk down their money. Sadly, that's more true today than ever.

Earlier I mentioned Alan Greenspan's opinion of investing in Internet stocks, but here I'd like to go further. In the mid-1990s Internet stocks were snapped up. Initial public offerings (IPOs) were gone quickly as well. Prices skyrocketed. Stocks were selling for hundreds of times earnings, and in some cases the companies had no earnings and wouldn't have for the foreseeable future. Yet they sold and doubled and tripled in price. It was hard to keep up with the stampede. Oversold, overbought, overvalued hysteria. Sure, lots of people made money in Internet stocks, but lots of people lost money because they got in at the wrong time, a time when reality set in and the price of many hot Internet stocks went in the tank. But there were those, like myself, who knew that things couldn't continue. You see, Internet stocks became a perfect representative of what has happened to the market in general. What happened to Internet stocks in months is the same thing that has been happening to the market for most of the past decade.

Following my strategy, however, you would not have purchased Internet stocks at their inception, because any stock with less than a 52-week track record is ignored. Although you may be thinking, "I could have made a bundle and this system would have kept me out," remember that many people did make money in Internet stocks, but that many more now wish they had stayed away. You see, with many new issues, Internet stocks being one class, you are, in effect, playing the stock market's equivalent of Old Maid. Eventually the hype is eclipsed by reality, the stocks plummet, and someone is stuck holding the Old Maid. If that's your idea of investing, take your retirement money and go to Las Vegas, because you're gambling.

There is an element of excitement in the stock market. Couple that with the fact that most of us, and this includes me, are at some point in our lives gullible—and headed for trouble. Maybe greed enters the picture as well. We get tempted and start looking for the once-in-a-lifetime killing. We take chances. I could go on with this, but why? The point is this—do you want to gamble, speculate, or invest? If the answer is the latter, you bought the right book because, as you'll find out in the next chapter, I have unlocked the stock market's dirtiest secret and in the process given you keys that will allow you to unlock the daily secret code to picking winning stocks. And in the process, if you'll stick to the system and apply the account/portfolio management techniques discussed here and later, you will, without even knowing it, make yourself into a lean, mean trading machine that will not get sidetracked by the trappings that usually destroy other individual investors. The market goes up, the market eventually goes down; but this we know, too: Someone, regardless of market condition, bull or bear, is always making money in the stock market. Do you think the winners are the mom-and-pop investors or the big money boys and the market insiders? You know the answer to that question, and that—what the big money boys and market insiders know—is what you're going to tap into, and that's why you're going to win the game.

Gambling in California, as in most states, is illegal—yet there are legal poker clubs where they play for real, sometimes for big money. To most people this would seem like an inconsistency, but it's not, because the State of California recognizes that straight poker isn't gambling! It's a skill. Putting $10 on red is gambling. Putting a dollar in a slot machine is gambling. Playing blackjack is gambling because the house has better odds. But straight poker is a skill, because it's how you play the cards, not necessarily the cards you're dealt, that matters, and it is therefore allowed. The odds are even for everyone. Can you see a parallel with the stock market? The market, just like a house in Vegas, has odds that say eventually you'll lose or earn less than you should or could have. There is no skill in that. But, if you, in effect, level the odds by knowing what the house knows, that's skill. Once you know what they know, you'll win, because the house always wins.

Let me give you another gambling analogy. Question: Why is a hot tip from your broker unlike a hot tip on a horse running in the third race? Answer: It's not. You see how you can get sucked in if you're not trading a system. That hot tip from your broker may not have any more information behind it than a hot tip on a horse from a total stranger. It is just as likely that the broker never heard of the stock, or certainly never researched it, prior to a boss trying to push it. Having said that, that hot horse tip suddenly doesn't sound too bad in comparison.

People have been brutally murdered for a few bucks, so it is not too hard to believe that some people, some market insiders, would lie or bend the rules to make millions. There are thousands of investment schemes out there. Believe it or not, there are still variations on the decades-old Ponzi scheme still being practiced today, and people still fall for it. You need to protect yourself.

My Ten Commandments of Stock Market Success, as practiced with the system described in the following chapter, will do just that.

# CHAPTER 3

# Picking Winning Stocks

## Part I

Here's the key to your future financial success in the stock market. This is the chapter that explains the market's "secret code" and how I broke it.

The basis of picking winning stocks in this manner is an admission that, on your own, and in a normal market, the task is next to impossible. We've already discussed some of the reasons why.

If picking winning stocks is that difficult, why continue to agonize over the process? Wouldn't it be better to use the data insiders are using to make mega-profits? Of course, but where can that information be found? Strangely enough, it's available. It's printed every day in an end-result form in the *Wall Street Journal*. Before I tell you exactly where, let me explain why you can rely on the information.

We all know the stock market axiom "Buy low, sell high." Ideally, that scenario would make the best stock choice. Unfortunately, while millions of individual investors are searching daily for that Holy Grail of the market, the pros are laughing at their efforts and profiting from their misdirection.

Professional traders know that the only way to win and make money consistently is not to waste time looking for stocks that can be bought at their bottoms and sold at their tops. Those animals, from an individual investor's perspective, are mythical. No, the real money is made by riding stocks that are already winners, not wasting time, money, and effort looking for those that might become winners.

To the end of locating winning stocks that others have yet to recognize as such, a critical feature of my strategy that all good commodity traders are familiar with is the concept of market resistance. It's a point (price) that big-money market insiders have determined a commodity's value does not exceed. Conversely, on the short side, they have determined (by using their money to influence the market) that the price should not fall below a price of $X. What you have over a period of time is a trading range of price fluctuation with a top and bottom called resistance barriers.

For example, January corn contracts may have a range of $2.50 to $3.27 per bushel. Month after month the price will go up, then down, then up, then sideways, and so on, but almost always within the high and low range the market has set. Seasoned commodity traders know that the biggest market moves are triggered when a contract breaks through an established resistance barrier. This holds true with stocks, too.

Charting the movement of stocks in the same manner commodity speculators do gives us some amazing results and principles. For example, stock prices move up or down—that's it, right? Wrong. Prices also move sideways, and that's important. That's what gives us a range from which the price will break out and give us direction, as once a stock breaks through its barriers it has a tendency, a very strong tendency, to continue in that direction for an extended period of time. The momentum of the forces that caused the stock to break out are almost always that strong.

It is important to remind you that price ranges are set, in effect, by insiders, the experts, the big accounts. They're the only ones with enough purchasing power and influence on others in the stock market to have their decisions reflected in a stock price moving as a result of their actions. Individual traders add to the mix, but they can't move/manipulate a stock by themselves.

### Insider Influence

This would be a good place to "prove" the issue of insider influence, as it is critical to my strategy. From the book *Midas Investing* (1996), by Jonathan Steinberg, editor in chief of *Individual Investor* magazine:

> Knowing about insider buying can boost your returns in two ways: 1. It helps align you with some of the savviest investors on Wall Street. 2. It allows you to discover hidden gems early.
>
> By tracking insider transactions, you have a wonderful source for new ideas about little-known companies. You can zero in on great profit-making opportunities before most investors discover them. . . .
>
> From time to time, insider buying sweeps through an industry. This is extremely bullish.
>
> It means that competing companies think the prospects for the sector are improving. Finding such a consensus improves your odds. Would you rather buy into a sector that is emerging from a trough or one that is about to fall off a cliff? . . .
>
> Some investors find the method too straightforward for their tastes. This is especially true of people who are determined to use investing as a forum to prove how smart they are. Piggy-backing on someone else's transactions, they feel, isn't a sufficiently brilliant technique. It's too easy.

Of course, as you probably know, you can subscribe to one of the very expensive insider transactions services that chart insider trades. I wouldn't suggest it because the information they offer isn't going to help you much and contains an element of risk (because they don't show end results, only transactions). That is not acceptable. Steinberg, however, does acknowledge the importance of insider transactions. Although his trading system is different from mine, the principle is much the same; that is, it's important to know what the big-money insiders are doing. And by the way, there can be no other conclusion from his discourse than that there is insider influence in the stock market, although we would probably disagree on the magnitude of the influence. I reiterate that for those who doubted much of what I have said up to this point.

But I don't want to stop there. Marshall Loeb, managing editor of *Fortune* magazine, in his 1989 *Money Guide* has an entire section entitled "Watch the Insiders," where he, too, remarks about the importance of legal market insider transactions, once again proving that insiders have influence and can create trends and often know things the rest of us, the outsiders, don't. More importantly, he states in the section entitled "Buying What the Big Winners Buy":

> Have you ever heard of a 13D filing? No, it is not something that you would find in a dentist's office or on a clerk's desk. It is one of those obscure government reports that might give you a clue to making some money in the stock market.
>
> For that clue, recall that Damon Runyon used to say, "If you rub up against money long enough, some of it might rub up against you." Some of it might rub off on you—if you follow the purchases of the handful of multimillionaire investors who make audacious bids in the stock market to take over whole companies.

(Any investor who buys more than 5 percent of a listed company's stock must file a 13D with the Securities and Exchange Commission within 10 days.)

Here again, the point Mr. Loeb is making in his book is slightly different from my point, but the principle is exactly the same: Big-monied investors can and do influence the market for a given stock. Book after book written by the big names in the market say the same thing. It is a recurring theme because it's true. Money, big money, buys influence—in this case influence in the stock market. I am belaboring this point because you must understand that this important point is not the meanderings of just myself—it is acknowledged by virtually everyone whom most perceive as a market expert. However, these writers devote just small sections in their books to this truth for whatever points they might be making and/or to sell subscriptions to the many newsletters that track insider and big-money stock transactions. My purpose is more direct. You need to know that the stock market is not the pure exchange of capitalism it is portrayed to be. Once realizing that, you must understand there is a way to profit from that unfair truth.

That leaves us with another important truth: The best way to beat the market is to admit defeat and acknowledge that if you can't beat 'em you might as well join 'em. This important revelation dawned on me while I was discussing the simplistic brilliance of the Serenity Prayer. It says, "God, grant me the serenity to accept the things I cannot change, courage to change the things I can, and wisdom to know the difference." The market is influenced, sometimes unduly influenced, by big money and insiders. I can't change that. There is no reason to continue to pick a fight with a foe I can't beat. However, I can change the standard method of picking stocks that most individual investors use (broker recommendations, analyzing annual reports, or systems) by tapping directly into the insider knowledge of those who have some control. That, my friends, is wisdom.

### Resistance Barriers: Where to Find Them, How to Use Them

Where can you find resistance barrier breakthroughs in the stock market? In the highs and lows of a stock. They are listed every day in the *Wall Street Journal* in the "Money & Investing" section under the heading "NYSE Highs/Lows" (see Figure 3.1). This listing reflects new high or low prices a stock reaches within a 12-month period on the New York Stock Exchange. Therefore, it has a solid history base from which to make judgments.

I've been tracking this principle of resistance and what happens to stocks that break barriers for over a decade. Its record of consistency

# NYSE HIGHS/LOWS

Wednesday, January 5, 2000, 4:00 p.m. Eastern time

NEW 52-WK. HIGHS — 27

| | | | |
|---|---|---|---|
| Alcan | ConsNatGas | Inco | RightChoice A |
| Alcoa s | CorusGp s | Lubrizol | SuncorEngy |
| AveryDensn | Dynegy | Olin s | TaiwanFd |
| BOC Gp | Entrade n | Pechiney | TaiwanEqty |
| BrokenHill | GRC Int | PohangIron | Trnsmdia pfA n |
| ChicagoB&I | ISPAT Int A | ROC TwnFd | Wellman |
| CompnhiaSidr | Illinova | ReynMetl | |

NEW 52-WK. LOWS — 113

| | | | |
|---|---|---|---|
| ACE Ltd | ClmbsSo A | Hershey | RayJamFnl |
| AgreeRlty | Comerica | HoraceMn | Rouse QUIPS |
| AmAnnuTOPrS | ComrcBcpNJ | ITT EduclSvc | SLM Hldg |
| AmGreetgs | CommCap pfT | JSB Fnl | S&P PrtEquty n |
| AmReCp quip | ComrclFed | JeffPilot ACES | SafetyKleen |
| AmWtrWks pfA | CornellCorr | Kellogg | Smucker B |
| AmSoBcp s | DsgnrFin TOPR | LoewsCp | SnapOn |
| AnnTaylor | DevDivRlty | LA Cap QUIPS | SoCarEG pf |
| AssocFst A | DuPont pfA | MEPC pfA | SoCplll QUIPS |
| BCH Cap pfB | ElPasoPtnr pf | Meritage | SowestGas |
| BSCH Fin prG | Enel ADS n | MinrlTch | SowestGas pfA |
| BancWest s | EnhncFnlSvc | MT Pwr QUIPS | SvrnStrg pfB n |
| BankAm | ExcelsrInco | Morgan JP pfH | StdRegstr |
| BkMontreal | FannieMae pfA | Morgan JP pf | StrwdFnl |
| BkOne | FannieMae pfB | MorganKeg | StdPrCrTS B n |
| BkUtd PIES n | Finova | MSDW MIT | SummitBcp |
| BarnesNoble | FstAmCap pfT | MuniyldInsFd | SunAm pfV |
| BearStearn pfE | FleetBosFnl | NationsRent | TlsmnEgy pfB n |
| BerkHathwy A | FredMac | NoForkBcp | UnPlantr |
| Blkbstr A n | GTE FL pfA | NoStPwr pfG | UtdAssetMgt |
| BurlNthSF | GTE FL pfB | NuvMA Prm | UtdCapFd pfA |
| BurnhmPacif | GlblVacGp | OH Pwr pfA | Utilicp PEPS n |
| CampblSoup | GldnState | PLC Cp TOPrS | VestaurSec |
| Caribnrlnt | Gdrch QUIPS | PP&L pfA | ViadCp pf |
| CrlPwr QUC | GtLksREIT pfA n | PciCpQDSB | Wachovia |
| CascadeCp | GrnptFnl | PetsecEngy | WashMut |
| ChevyCh pfA | Hasbro s | PharmUpjhn | WstnRs QUIPB |
| CstlCplnc n | Heinz | PSEG pfC | ZweigFd |
| ColonlBcgp | | | |

s–Split or stock dividend of 25 percent or more in the past 52 weeks. High-low range is adjusted from old stock. n-New issue in past 52 weeks and does not cover the entire 52 week period.

**FIGURE 3.1** NYSE Highs/Lows.

*Source:* Reprinted from the *Wall Street Journal*, July 5, 2000.

is truly remarkable, but not unexpected. I've known for years that the stock market was not a true reflection of free market forces—meaning a stock's price has little or nothing to do with the accounting worth of the company. Nor does it have the relationship to corporate earnings it once had. Again, it's largely and most often determined by insiders, large traders, rumor, and, most importantly, overselling. Armed with that understanding, I started looking for a way to tap into the information the insiders were using to make huge profits. That was a difficult task, because it's not just a matter of knowing what the big money players and insiders are doing, which is why I believe subscribing to newsletters that relate such transactions is a waste of money. What is important is knowing at what point their transactions impact the price of a given stock. Eventually I was led to look for keys that would let me profit from the actions of insiders even if I wasn't privy to the process or information they used to make a market decision. Logically, that led to the commodity principle of resistance and what happens when resistance barriers are broken. And that led to stocks that were setting the new highs and new lows. That's where the rubber meets the road—when brokerage houses, brokers, big money, and insider transactions produce results (stock price movement).

It should be obvious then that, in theory, you should buy when a stock breaks through to a new high and short the stock when it reaches a new low—just the opposite of what most investors do. I want to repeat that—my trading system recommends, based on historical statistics that are repeated, that you do just the opposite of what almost every other investor is doing. Of course, there were missing parts to the puzzle. First, how many such breakthrough signals offered the surest sign of potential profit while still offering adequate safety? Secondly, during what time span must the unknown number of breakthroughs take place to magnify the breakthrough's signal? In short, I was looking for the key to the paradox of locating stocks that offered the equivalent of FDIC bank certificate of deposit safety coupled with the often staggering return potential of commodity futures.

In analyzing the records (past trading statistics) I found that a stock's third breakthrough was the key, which is why I named my discovery the Trinity Trading System (TTS). Why three breakthroughs and not one, two, four, five, or more? I have no idea, nor do I, as a financial pragmatist, care. I look for answers that give results; I am not often concerned with the "why" of the answer. I've charted breakthroughs until I was sick of looking at the figures, and three is the number that consistently produces the best results. Quick trend reversals after three breakthroughs were almost nonexistent. Huge profits were almost always the rule—provided the breakthroughs occurred within a relatively short period of time. Analyzing the records further, I found that 24 calendar days is the longest time span for the three breakthroughs to occur. Why 24 days? Here again, I don't know exactly; it just works out that way. If they don't happen within 24 days, the signals are too weak to act on, and you have to start over. Obviously, the quicker the breakthroughs happen, the better the indication of trend strength. For example, if a stock has three new breakthroughs within a week, it's a better bet than a stock that has its three breakthroughs just under the 24-day limit. However, they are both worthy of consideration.

It is worth noting the obvious fact that 24 calendar days can offer a varying number of trading days, as, depending on when you start the count for a particular stock, there may be a holiday, an extra weekend, or an extra weekend day involved. That was of concern at first, as, logically, the exact number of days is extremely important, just as is the number of breakthroughs within that time period. So why not use trading days? Because 24 calendar days gives the best average response. Again, I charted stocks until I was blue in the face, went back and looked at past history, and found that a period of 24 calendar days or less is what works. Playing amateur psychiatrist, my guess is that there is a market dynamic here that says it is not the number of trading days, but the number of calendar days because the psyche of investors, as it pertains to a particular stock, works over a set period of time (all things being equal and no special market event occurring, such as possible war, an oil crisis, etc.). It is almost like investors have, as a group, a 24 calendar days biorhythm that focuses on a stock as it is starting to make new highs or lows. After 24 days, interest wanes and momentum evaporates. This cycle and the force behind three new highs or lows through a previous resistance barrier are what make a stock worthy of your consideration.

It takes only a few minutes a day to find winning stocks. Take a sheet of paper for each letter of the alphabet (see Figure 3.2). Every day, on the appropriate alphabetical page, list all the stocks in your price range that make the *WSJ*'s "NYSE Highs/Lows." Next to the name of the stock write the date it first shows up on the listing and when it broke its high or low barrier (indicate low breakthroughs with a minus sign). Then write the date the next time it shows up on the list heading in the same direction and so on. The moment it

**A**
**(Stock Price Range under $10)**

Buy Signal
Aeroflex: 7/8, 7/9, 7/17, 9/8

Start over — Buy Signal
Allwaste: 7/9, 7/11, 8/6, 8/7, 8/12, 8/14

Start over
Am West Air: 7/8, 7/11, 8/13, 8/14

Argosy Gaming: 7/17

Start over — Short Signal
Atlas Cp: –7/9, –7/11, –8/7, –8/9, –8/12, –8/19

Aviall: 7/8, 7/12, 8/13

(Minus sign indicates a new low)
(This page is for example purposes only)

**FIGURE 3.2** **Sample page of stocks.**
*Source:* John R. Mrkvicka.

makes an arrival the third time within 24 days, buy or sell it. I don't recommend short selling stock (trading in anticipation of a stock going down in price) to start out with—although it's not that difficult, it confuses some people. Wait until you're comfortable with the market. If it doesn't make our target of three breakthroughs within 24 days, forget it and start over. The hypothetical chart in Figure 3.2 is an example of a page representing those stocks one might chart that start with the letter *A*.

Profits tend to be magnified if you're buying a stock in a bear market and shorting in a bull market. This important contrarian addendum is why market direction is so important (a subject discussed later). This anomaly only makes sense. Think of the pressure that is being exerted to push a stock to three new highs when the market is heading in the opposite direction. Conversely, as a rising tide lifts all boats, imagine the pressure pushing a stock to three new lows during a bull run.

Profits can be magnified even further if a group of stocks are uniquely affected. For example, pharmaceutical stocks that were setting new lows after the industry came under attack from the Clinton administration (even though the market was in a strong bull position) made excellent profits for those who shorted the market.

Another interesting finding: Although stocks seldom go straight up or straight down, trend lines that solidify get stronger. And in those cases you'll see your stock pick establish new high after new high, month after month—the result being that a top resistance barrier, once broken, often becomes the bottom resistance barrier once a new range is established. The reverse can happen with a stock establishing a new low; that is, the bottom resistance barrier, once broken, can become the top resistance barrier when the new range solidifies. If you see either scenario develop, you are in the position of realizing exceptional profits if you choose to build on your position (buy or sell additional shares of the same stock). You will also, to a large degree, be able to see a stock's future trading range before it becomes obvious to most investors. That's the kind of information that can lead to mega-profits.

### *Finding the Right Stocks for Your Portfolio*

However, the key to the process of picking winning stocks isn't simply a matter of buying every stock that makes three new highs and shorting every one that sets three new lows. Your portfolio determines which of the stocks you will choose. As we don't want to have any more than 20 percent of our investment capital in one stock (from our previously discussed commandments), which stocks you can consider is determined for you. For example, if you have a $20,000 portfolio, you wouldn't invest more than $4,000 in one stock, and you would use a stop to ensure you didn't lose any more than 10 percent of your capital on the trade (again from our commandments). Under these circumstances a stock that has broken through its top barrier at $65 wouldn't make much sense even though it might skyrocket. Why? Because you could purchase only 61 shares, and that will likely limit your dollar return (more on this later), as rapidity of growth is often influenced by present costs; that is, it is more likely to see a stock at $5 a share double in X number of weeks than a stock at $70 a share double in the same time span. This is an amazing result of the psychological mind-set of investors and has nothing to do with actualities of the market or individual stocks. A more likely price range of stocks appropriate for this portfolio would be those valued at $10 per share or below.

There is also a hidden benefit of using my discovery. Look again at the sample NYSE Highs/Lows chart. Read the note at the bottom— the one that says "n—New issue in past 52 weeks and does not cover the entire 52 week period." You should ignore all stocks that have an "n" designation. They don't have a track record that allows this system to work. I have known for years that investing in initial public offerings (IPOs) is a huge investing mistake even though I didn't have, until recently, the facts or statistics to back up that claim. What I knew would eventually be proven; namely, IPOs are a bad bet. "Wait a minute!" many of you may be screaming. "That eliminates IPOs. Are you crazy? I've been looking for another Microsoft or Amazon.com."

I've argued about this with many people who should have known better, but I think even they have had their eyes glazed over by the very rare success of a few offerings. The Microsofts notwithstanding, I believed IPOs were an investing mistake.

Recently two professors, Tim Loughran and Jay Ritter, documented the paths of all the IPOs since 1970. The results proved the point: The average return on IPO stocks has been 5 percent a year, while other stocks have averaged 12 percent. Remember, that paltry 5 percent average for IPOs includes the blockbuster rarities like Amazon and Microsoft. Imagine the average return for IPOs as a group without including the profits of these monster winners. But you might say, "That's what I'm looking for, another Microsoft." If that's your plan—to find another Microsoft on the ground floor—all I can say is, good luck. Better that you go to Vegas with your financial future; your odds might be better. I am not saying that there will never be another Microsoft or something similar. What I am saying is this—looking for the next Microsoft is not an investment strategy that will make you rich. The odds say, based on the number of IPOs available every year, that you'll go broke before you do. I said earlier—and it bears repeating here—investing should not be a crapshoot. Stay away from IPOs. Stay away from stocks annotated with an "n."

### Simple, Complicated—Who Cares? It Works

My trading strategy is so simple that it may offend your investment intelligence. After all, something this simple surely can't work. Don't make the mistake of believing that. This is not a simple plan—it's just simple to use. You see, although you have to do very little, the research work and/or manipulation pressure by the Wall Street insiders that led them to push a stock through purchases or hype to three new highs or three new lows within 24 days didn't come easy. Perhaps thousands of man-hours went into the buying or selling decision(s) that caused a stock to come to your attention via the new "NYSE Highs/Lows." Don't be put off because you didn't come to some brilliant conclusion on your own; rather, rejoice in the fact that you've broken the code and discovered how to profit from the work of the insiders.

I want to requote Jonathan Steinberg in *Midas Investing*. "Some investors find the method too straightforward for their tastes. This is especially true of people who are determined to use investing as a forum to prove how smart they are. Piggy-backing on someone else's transactions, they feel, isn't a sufficiently brilliant technique. It's too easy." While he was talking about a technique only slightly similar to mine in principle, and I believe substantially less accurate and potentially far less rewarding, I know many will meet my system with the same skepticism. Why? Because it's just too easy, that's why. Things have to be complicated to work, right? You need newsletters, TV talking-head opinions, year-end reports, and so on, and that's just to get started. Then you need a formula or secret system and on and on and on. I'll tell you what, use my strategy, make a fortune, and then tell everyone you use your own personally designed trading system that you and you alone thought up. If that makes you feel better, great, do it. Just don't pass up what I've discovered because you've got an ego that's more important to you than the bottom line. Remember, the bottom line is the bottom line. You can't buy anything with ego.

There is another response to my strategy that I want to warn you about. Practically every broker and market "expert" in the business will tell you it won't work because—say it with me now—"It's too simple." The market is too complicated. They will take this approach because if you realize the TTS potential, they're out of business, as least as far as you're concerned. I said earlier and I'll say again that once you learn this system you don't need anyone's help to make a fortune in the market, and that includes me. I am, for all intents and purposes, gladly putting myself out of business, too. Opinions of those still having a vested interest should be suspect and ultimately discarded by any serious, or soon to be serious, investor.

Of course, it's important to again note that system is not simple.

In fact, in terms of what went into the results, it may be the most complicated strategy ever. You shouldn't let the fact that it takes you only minutes to use the results of the system be off-putting. I liken my discovery to a computer program that virtually no one can understand, but that gives immediate answers to math problems heretofore unsolvable. It might, if one looked at what went into the answer, take perhaps a thousand pages of programming computations to allow the computer to come to an immediate answer. In such a case, would it be wise for anyone to look at the answer and reject it because it appears too simple in response time for complicated math problems? No, of course not. That would be ignoring the behind-the-scenes work that was done to arrive at the "simple" answer. That's true with my strategy. You're getting perhaps a thousand pages of calculations and thousands of man-hours distilled down to one simple answer.

Remember this: When a stock breaks through an established resistance barrier three times within a matter of weeks, it's trying to tell you something of major importance—be smart enough to listen.

## Part II

The myth of stock market wizards who can predict the future of the market or a given stock is ingrained in the psyche of most individual investors. So deep is that belief that I know many readers will be thinking I am dead wrong on this subject. But let me quote from *The Warren Buffett Way: Investment Strategies of the World's Greatest Investor*, by Robert G. Hagstrom, Jr. (1994):

> Graham said, "The farther away one gets from Wall Street, the more skepticism one will find as to the pretensions of stock-market forecasting or timing." Since Omaha is a good distance from New York, it is not surprising that Buffett gives zero credence to market predictions. Buffett cannot predict short-term market movements and does not believe that anyone

else can. He has long felt that the only value of stock forecasters is to make fortune tellers look good.

Are you subscribing to a newsletter or service that predicts short-term market or stock movements? Does your broker call with prediction tips? Warren Buffett, the man many believe is the world's greatest investor (and with a record to back him up) says not even he can predict what many others are claiming. Think about that as a general principle. Statistically, market experts are wrong more than they are right. This means that almost all available services that attempt to foretell virtually anything in the market are a waste of money.

The people who do win in the market, especially winning individual investors, hitch their wagons to a rising or falling star and ride it for all it's worth. Remember, you want to invest in proven/known winners, not in stocks that might, at some later date, do well. To cement the belief, Figures 3.3 through 3.60 are examples of stock picks from my newsletter *Money Insider*. There are a considerable number to review, but they've been included for a reason. I could show you a few selected winners, but what would that prove? Nothing. But a substantial representation inspires the trust you need to pursue this strategy without reservation. Review each example carefully. I haven't included them just to take up space. I did so because "a picture is worth a thousand words," and the charts will add immeasurably to your understanding of what this system can actually produce. It's one thing to talk about monster profits; it's another seeing them. I have, at random, chosen from our "Stocks to Watch" column a few stocks each month for three years. On the charts I've noted the buy entry point(s) with an arrow. Exit points are not noted, as that is up to each investor based on one's target profit. Of course, as the stock picks continued to rise, they were continually recommended as long as they met the criteria of the TTS. However, the charts note only the original recommendation from that time period.

For those who may be thinking stock X or Y could have made more money if it had been bought earlier (before the third breakthrough criterion), I must remind you that trying to pick tops and bottoms is a guaranteed losing strategy. The big money is made by picking winning stock after winning stock and then maximizing their return through portfolio management and the employment of options when appropriate (more on options later).

Then, too, as the examples are from the years 1991–1993, it's possible that the stock was recommended numerous times previously and/or subsequently. The important thing for your reference is what the stock did after my recommendation, not trying to figure out why it wasn't recommended earlier or again later. As noted, it may or may not have been.

No short sales or options are shown because they are not included in *Money Insider*. However, as the key to both is the consistent, successful picking of stocks, and that is verified in these examples, you can easily see how that information can be applied to those possibilities.

You'll remember from earlier chapters that I said a stock must have a realizable return potential of at least 50 percent. That may have startled you. Not to worry. My system picks stocks that most often return that and more. This is another positive feature of my discovery. It picks the best stocks with the biggest potential. Check the annualized returns in the examples! 70, 80, 90, 100, 200 percent and, in many cases, much, much more. Are you doing that well on your own? Is your broker? No, these returns are in a class by themselves, often because a buy signal was reached only to be subsequently followed by an extremely profitable stock split that was, at the time, unknown to the general public. Such is the powerful nature of three barrier breakthroughs. It's important to restate that the discovery in my strategy reveals the results of hundreds or thousands of hours of professional research, including, in many cases, inside information, in a matter of seconds.

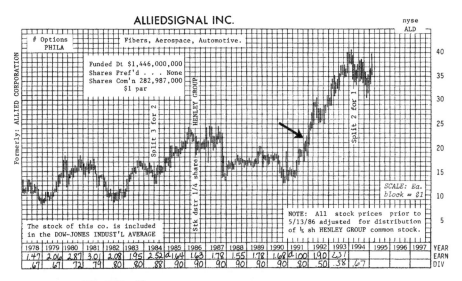

**FIGURE 3.3** AlliedSignal Inc.

*Source:* Used by permission of M. C. Horsey & Company, Inc.

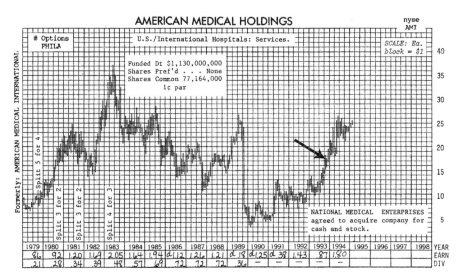

**FIGURE 3.4** American Medical Holdings.

*Source:* Used by permission of M. C. Horsey & Company, Inc.

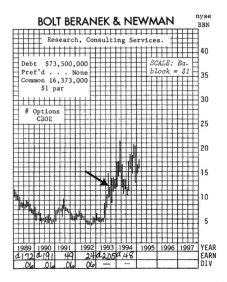

FIGURE 3.5 Bolt Beranek & Newman.

*Source:* Used by permission of M. C. Horsey & Company, Inc.

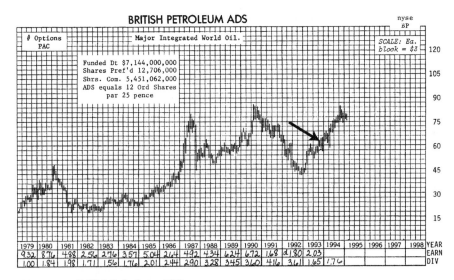

FIGURE 3.6 British Petroleum ADS.

*Source:* Used by permission of M. C. Horsey & Company, Inc.

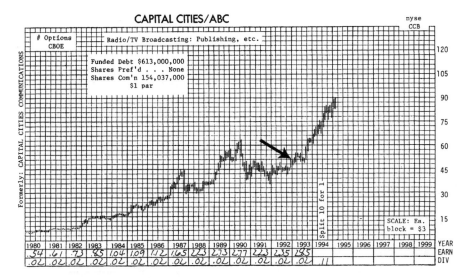

**FIGURE 3.7** Capital Cities/ABC.

*Source:* Used by permission of M. C. Horsey & Company, Inc.

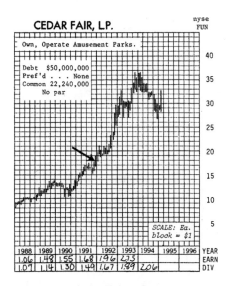

**FIGURE 3.8** Cedar Fair, L.P.

*Source:* Used by permission of M. C. Horsey & Company, Inc.

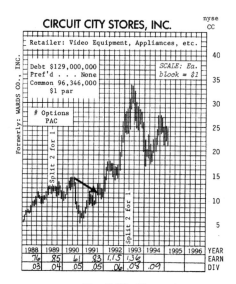

**FIGURE 3.9** Circuit City Stores, Inc.

*Source:* Used by permission of M. C. Horsey & Company, Inc.

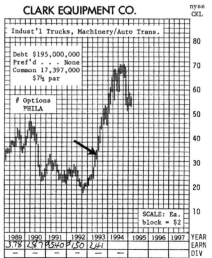

**FIGURE 3.10** Clark Equipment Co.

*Source:* Used by permission of M. C. Horsey & Company, Inc.

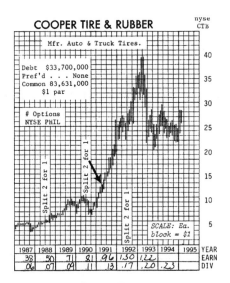

**FIGURE 3.11** Cooper Tire & Rubber.

*Source:* Used by permission of M. C. Horsey & Company, Inc.

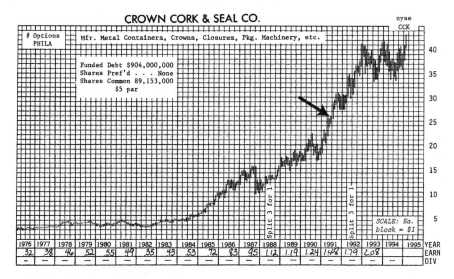

**FIGURE 3.12** Crown Cork & Seal Co.

*Source:* Used by permission of M. C. Horsey & Company, Inc.

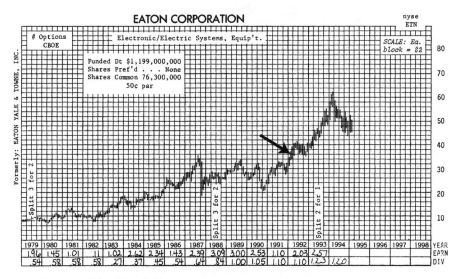

**FIGURE 3.13** Eaton Corporation.

*Source:* Used by permission of M. C. Horsey & Company, Inc.

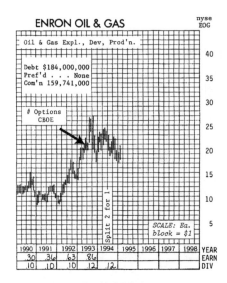

FIGURE 3.14 Enron Oil & Gas.
*Source:* Used by permission of M. C. Horsey & Company, Inc.

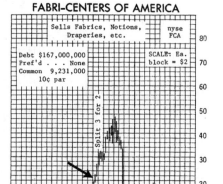

FIGURE 3.15 Fabri-Centers of America.
*Source:* Used by permission of M. C. Horsey & Company, Inc.

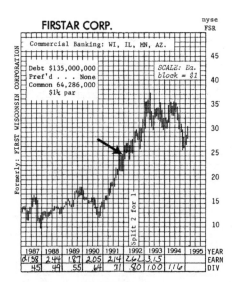

FIGURE 3.16 Firstar Corp.
*Source:* Used by permission of M. C. Horsey & Company, Inc.

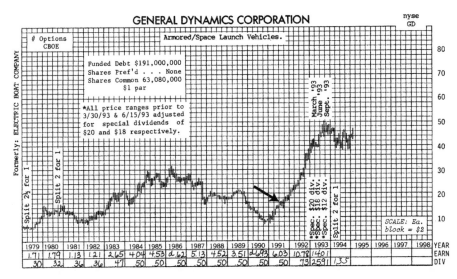

**FIGURE 3.17** General Dynamics Corporation.

*Source:* Used by permission of M. C. Horsey & Company, Inc.

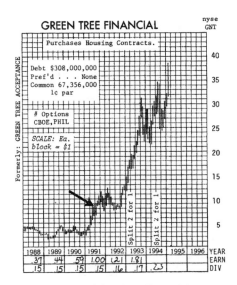

**FIGURE 3.18** Green Tree Financial.

*Source:* Used by permission of M. C. Horsey & Company, Inc.

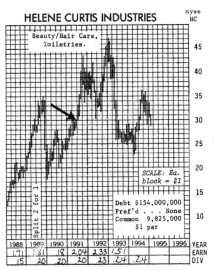

**FIGURE 3.19** Helene Curtis Industries.

*Source:* Used by permission of M. C. Horsey & Company, Inc.

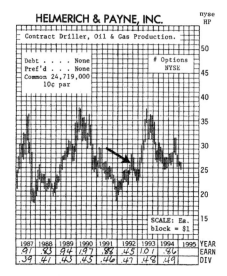

**FIGURE 3.20** Helmerich & Payne, Inc.

*Source:* Used by permission of M. C. Horsey & Company, Inc.

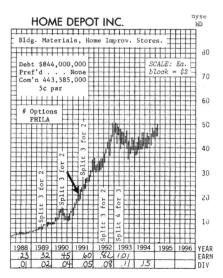

**FIGURE 3.21** Home Depot Inc.

*Source:* Used by permission of M. C. Horsey & Company, Inc.

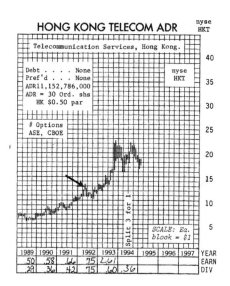

**FIGURE 3.22** Hong Kong Telecom ADR.

*Source:* Used by permission of M. C. Horsey & Company, Inc.

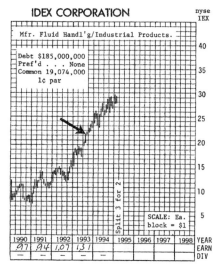

**FIGURE 3.23** IDEX Corporation.

*Source:* Used by permission of M. C. Horsey & Company, Inc.

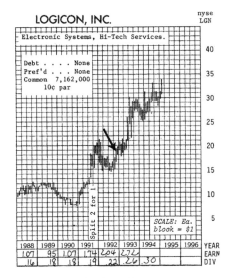

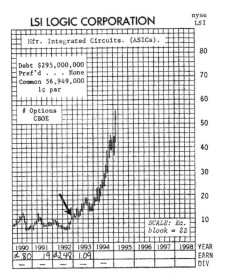

**FIGURE 3.24** Logicon, Inc.
*Source:* Used by permission of M. C. Horsey & Company, Inc.

**FIGURE 3.25** LSI Logic Corporation.
*Source:* Used by permission of M. C. Horsey & Company, Inc.

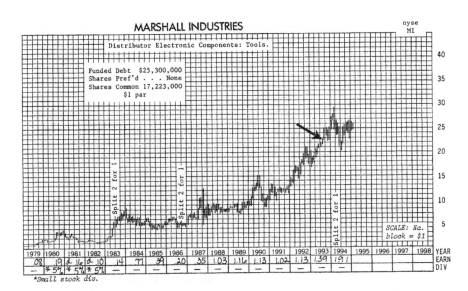

**FIGURE 3.26** Marshall Industries.
*Source:* Used by permission of M. C. Horsey & Company, Inc.

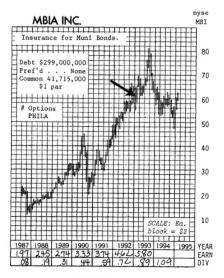

**FIGURE 3.27 MBIA Inc.**

*Source:* Used by permission of M. C. Horsey & Company, Inc.

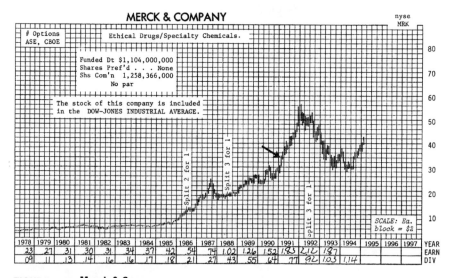

**FIGURE 3.28 Merck & Company.**

*Source:* Used by permission of M. C. Horsey & Company, Inc.

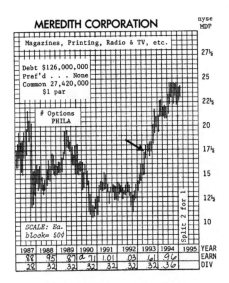

FIGURE 3.29 Meredith Corporation.

*Source:* Used by permission of M. C. Horsey & Company, Inc.

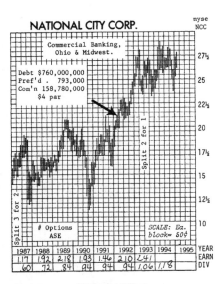

FIGURE 3.30 National City Corp.

*Source:* Used by permission of M. C. Horsey & Company, Inc.

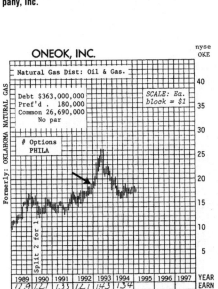

FIGURE 3.31 Oneok, Inc.

*Source:* Used by permission of M. C. Horsey & Company, Inc.

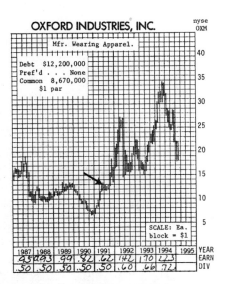

FIGURE 3.32 Oxford Industries, Inc.

*Source:* Used by permission of M. C. Horsey & Company, Inc.

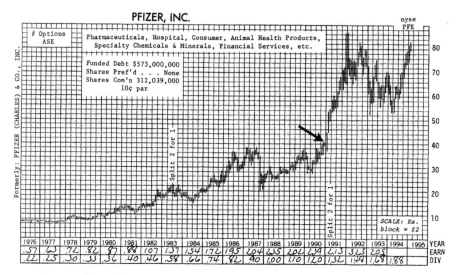

**FIGURE 3.33** Pfizer, Inc.

*Source:* Used by permission of M. C. Horsey & Company, Inc.

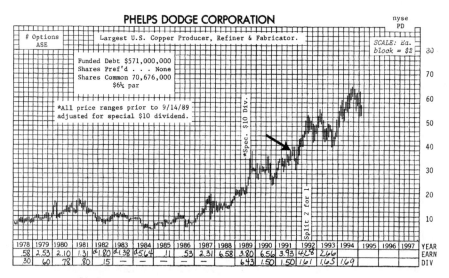

**FIGURE 3.34** Phelps Dodge Corporation.

*Source:* Used by permission of M. C. Horsey & Company, Inc.

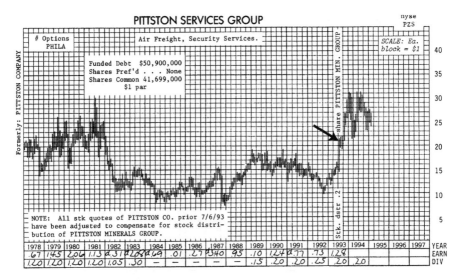

**FIGURE 3.35** Pittston Services Group.

*Source:* Used by permission of M. C. Horsey & Company, Inc.

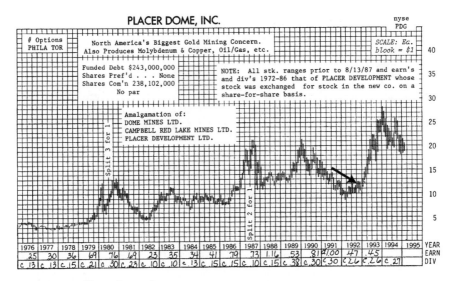

**FIGURE 3.36** Placer Dome, Inc.

*Source:* Used by permission of M. C. Horsey & Company, Inc.

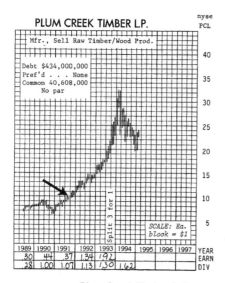

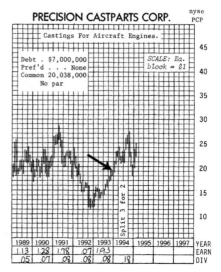

**FIGURE 3.37** Plum Creek Timber L.P.

*Source:* Used by permission of M. C. Horsey & Company, Inc.

**FIGURE 3.38** Precision Castparts Corp.

*Source:* Used by permission of M. C. Horsey & Company, Inc.

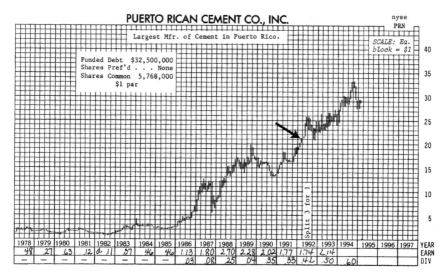

**FIGURE 3.39** Puerto Rican Cement Co., Inc.

*Source:* Used by permission of M. C. Horsey & Company, Inc.

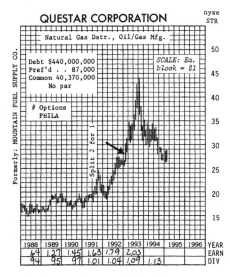

### QUESTAR CORPORATION
nyse STR

Natural Gas Dstr., Oil/Gas Mfg.

Debt $440,000,000
Pref'd . . 87,000
Common 40,370,000
No par

SCALE: Ea. block = $1

# Options PHILA

Split 2 for 1

Formerly: MOUNTAIN FUEL SUPPLY CO.

| YEAR | 1988 | 1989 | 1990 | 1991 | 1992 | 1993 | 1994 | 1995 | 1996 |
|------|------|------|------|------|------|------|------|------|------|
| EARN | .64 | 1.27 | 1.45 | 1.63 | 1.79 | 2.03 | | | |
| DIV | .94 | .95 | .97 | 1.01 | 1.04 | 1.09 | 1.13 | | |

**FIGURE 3.40** Questar Corporation.

*Source:* Used by permission of M. C. Horsey & Company, Inc.

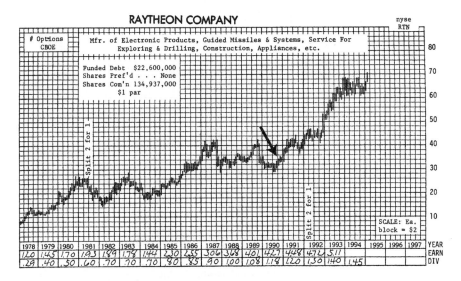

### RAYTHEON COMPANY
nyse RTN

# Options CBOE

Mfr. of Electronic Products, Guided Missiles & Systems, Service For Exploring & Drilling, Construction, Appliances, etc.

Funded Debt  $22,600,000
Shares Pref'd . . . None
Shares Com'n 134,937,000
$1 par

Split 2 for 1

Split 2 for 1

SCALE: Ea. block = $2

| YEAR | 1978 | 1979 | 1980 | 1981 | 1982 | 1983 | 1984 | 1985 | 1986 | 1987 | 1988 | 1989 | 1990 | 1991 | 1992 | 1993 | 1994 | 1995 | 1996 | 1997 |
|------|------|------|------|------|------|------|------|------|------|------|------|------|------|------|------|------|------|------|------|------|
| EARN | 1.20 | 1.45 | 1.70 | 1.93 | 1.89 | 1.78 | 1.44 | 2.30 | 2.55 | 3.06 | 3.68 | 4.01 | 4.27 | 4.48 | 4.72 | 5.11 | | | | |
| DIV | .29 | .40 | .50 | .60 | .70 | .70 | .70 | .80 | .85 | .90 | 1.00 | 1.08 | 1.18 | 1.20 | 1.30 | 1.40 | 1.45 | | | |

**FIGURE 3.41** Raytheon Company.

*Source:* Used by permission of M. C. Horsey & Company, Inc.

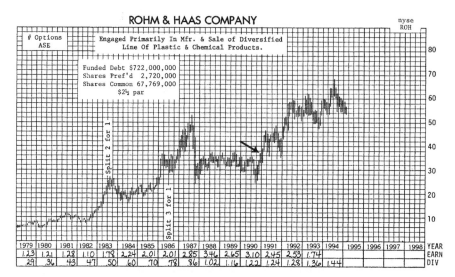

**FIGURE 3.42** Rohm & Haas Company.

*Source:* Used by permission of M. C. Horsey & Company, Inc.

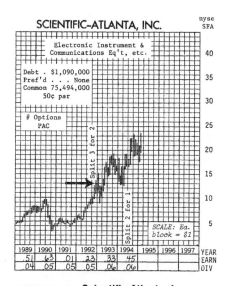

**FIGURE 3.43** Scientific-Atlanta, Inc.

*Source:* Used by permission of M. C. Horsey & Company, Inc.

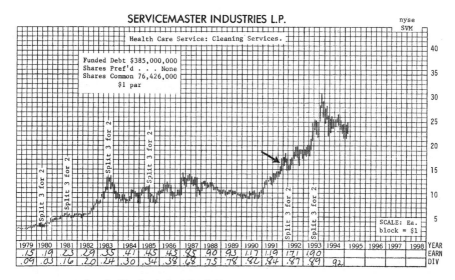

SERVICEMASTER INDUSTRIES L.P.

nyse
SVM

Health Care Service: Cleaning Services.

Funded Debt $385,000,000
Shares Pref'd . . . None
Shares Common 76,426,000
$1 par

SCALE: Ea.
block = $1

| YEAR | 1979 | 1980 | 1981 | 1982 | 1983 | 1984 | 1985 | 1986 | 1987 | 1988 | 1989 | 1990 | 1991 | 1992 | 1993 | 1994 | 1995 | 1996 | 1997 | 1998 |
|---|---|---|---|---|---|---|---|---|---|---|---|---|---|---|---|---|---|---|---|---|
| EARN | .15 | .19 | .23 | .29 | .35 | .41 | .45 | .45 | .85 | .90 | .93 | 1.17 | 1.19 | 1.71 | 1.90 | | | | | |
| DIV | .09 | .03 | .16 | .20 | .24 | .30 | .34 | .38 | .68 | .75 | .78 | .82 | .84 | .87 | .89 | .92 | | | | |

**FIGURE 3.44** ServiceMaster Industries L.P.
*Source:* Used by permission of M. C. Horsey & Company, Inc.

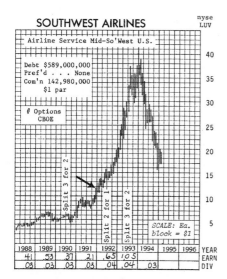

SOUTHWEST AIRLINES

nyse
LUV

Airline Service Mid-So'West U.S.

Debt $589,000,000
Pref'd . . . None
Com'n 142,980,000
$1 par

# Options
CBOE

SCALE: Ea.
block = $1

| YEAR | 1988 | 1989 | 1990 | 1991 | 1992 | 1993 | 1994 | 1995 | 1996 |
|---|---|---|---|---|---|---|---|---|---|
| EARN | .41 | .53 | .37 | .21 | .65 | 1.05 | | | |
| DIV | .03 | .03 | .03 | .03 | .04 | .04 | .03 | | |

**FIGURE 3.45** Southwest Airlines.
*Source:* Used by permission of M. C. Horsey & Company, Inc.

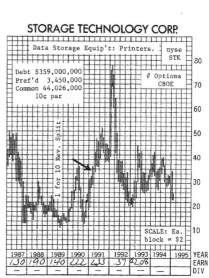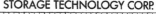

STORAGE TECHNOLOGY CORP.

nyse
STK

Data Storage Equip't: Printers.

Debt $359,000,000
Pref'd 3,450,000
Common 44,026,000
10¢ par

# Options
CBOE

SCALE: Ea.
block = $2

| YEAR | 1987 | 1988 | 1989 | 1990 | 1991 | 1992 | 1993 | 1994 | 1995 |
|---|---|---|---|---|---|---|---|---|---|
| EARN | 1.30 | 1.90 | 1.40 | 2.22 | 2.33 | .37 | d2.08 | | |
| DIV | — | — | — | — | — | — | — | — | |

**FIGURE 3.46** Storage Technology Corp.
*Source:* Used by permission of M. C. Horsey & Company, Inc.

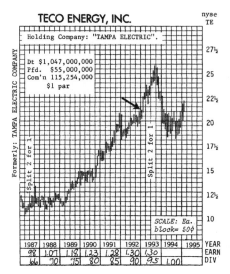

**FIGURE 3.47 TECO Energy, Inc.**

*Source:* Used by permission of M. C. Horsey & Company, Inc.

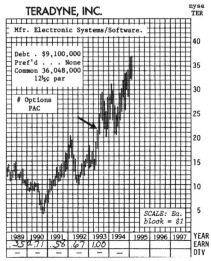

**FIGURE 3.48 Teradyne, Inc.**

*Source:* Used by permission of M. C. Horsey & Company, Inc.

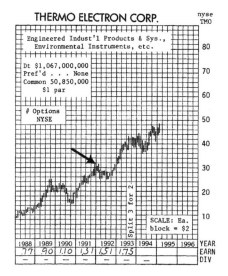

**FIGURE 3.49 Thermo Electron Corp.**

*Source:* Used by permission of M. C. Horsey & Company, Inc.

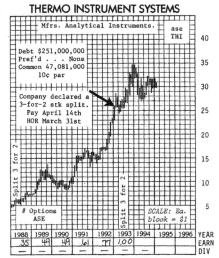

**FIGURE 3.50 Thermo Instrument Systems.**

*Source:* Used by permission of M. C. Horsey & Company, Inc.

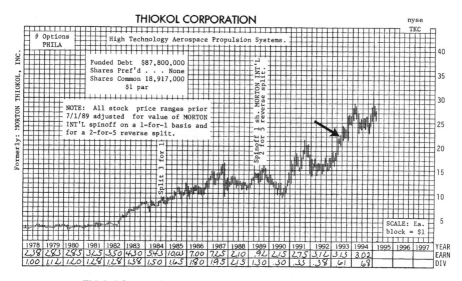

## THIOKOL CORPORATION

FIGURE 3.51  Thiokol Corporation.

*Source:* Used by permission of M. C. Horsey & Company, Inc.

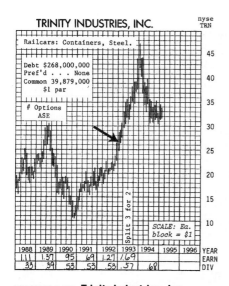

FIGURE 3.52  Trinity Industries, Inc.

*Source:* Used by permission of M. C. Horsey & Company, Inc.

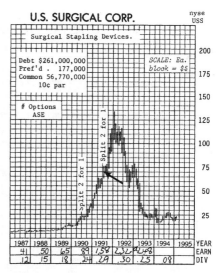

FIGURE 3.53  U.S. Surgical Corp.

*Source:* Used by permission of M. C. Horsey & Company, Inc.

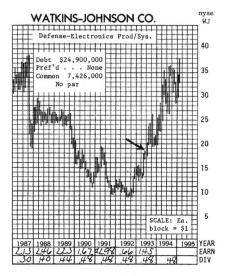

**FIGURE 3.54** Watkins-Johnson Co.

*Source:* Used by permission of M. C. Horsey & Company, Inc.

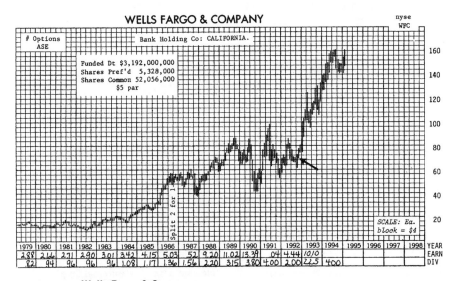

**FIGURE 3.55** Wells Fargo & Company.

*Source:* Used by permission of M. C. Horsey & Company, Inc.

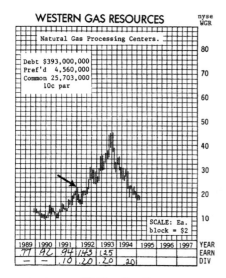

**FIGURE 3.56** Western Gas Resources.

*Source:* Used by permission of M. C. Horsey & Company, Inc.

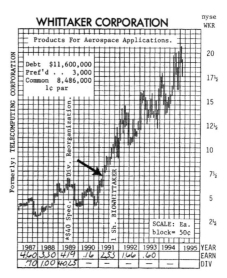

**FIGURE 3.57** Whittaker Corporation.

*Source:* Used by permission of M. C. Horsey & Company, Inc.

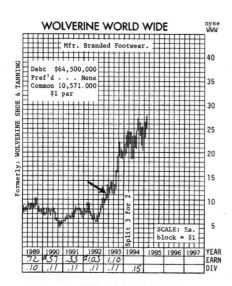

**FIGURE 3.58** Wolverine World Wide.

*Source:* Used by permission of M. C. Horsey & Company, Inc.

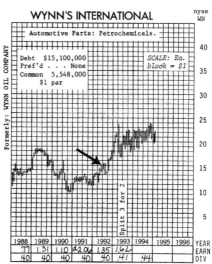

**FIGURE 3.59** Wynn's International.

*Source:* Used by permission of M. C. Horsey & Company, Inc.

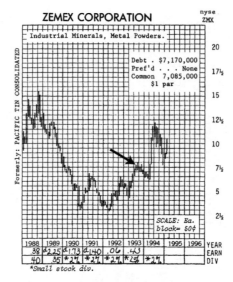

**FIGURE 3.60** Zemex Corporation.
*Source:* Used by permission of M. C. Horsey & Company, Inc.

## Let's Look at the Record

Let's review a few of the stocks I recommended, but before we do I want to remind you that the entry point indicated by an arrow was *an* entry point, not necessarily the *only* entry point. I may have recommended the stock many times prior to the entry shown here and I may have recommended it month after month for a number of months. Nothing is reflected here except one buy signal. You must understand this for the charts to make sense.

- Cedar Fair, L.P., was recommended just prior to the start of 1992 at $19. Two years later it was selling for $36. A return of 90 percent annualized at 45 percent.

- Circuit City Stores, Inc., was recommended in late 1991 at $11. By the end of 1992 it was at $26. By mid-1993 it was at almost $34, where it split two shares for one.

- Cooper Tire was recommended in early 1991 at $13. By mid-1992 it was selling at $26. It then split two for one and by early 1993 it was at almost $40.

- Enron Oil and Gas was recommended in mid-1993 at $22. A little over three months later it was at $27. That's an annualized return of over 90 percent.

- Fabri-Centers of America was selling at $22 in early 1991. After I recommended it, it split three shares for two after the first quarter and went to over $46 by the end of 1991.

- General Dynamics was recommended mid-1991 at $16. By the end of 1992 it was at $38. In 1993 it declared three special dividends—$20 in March, $18 in June, and $12 in September. At the end of 1993 it was at $50.

- Green Tree Financial was selling at a little more than $8 when I made my buy recommendation. This was in mid-1991. First quarter 1993 it split two for one. In mid-1994 it split two for one again. By the first quarter of 1995 it was at a high of over $38. If you had bought as little as 100 shares for $800 in mid-1991, by early 1995 you would have owned 400 shares valued at over $15,000. That's an annualized return of over 400 percent.

- Home Depot was an interesting pick. My recommendation was at the end of the first quarter of 1991 when the stock was at $20. At the end of the next quarter the stock split three for two. Mid-1992 the stock split again three for two. First quarter 1993 the stock once again split, this time four for three. At the end of the first quarter 1993 the stock was selling for $50 a share.

- Logicon, Inc., was a quick return. I recommended it at $19 in the last quarter of 1992. By mid-1993 it was selling at $30.

- LSI Logic went from a little over $10 at the start of 1993 to almost $56 by mid-first quarter 1995. Annualized return, 230 percent.

- National City Corp. was unusual. Although I don't, in general, like bank stocks, I recommended it at the end of the first quarter of 1992 at $21. Notwithstandng my personal feelings, the trading system said buy. It went to $28 by the same time the next year, when it split two for one and then climbed to $29 per share by the end of the first quarter of 1994.

- Oxford Industries, Inc., was a recommendation at $13 in mid-1991. A year later it was at $27.

- Pfizer was an excellent recommendation at $40 right before the start of 1991, because at the end of the first quarter it split two for one. From there it went to $83 by the end of 1991.

- Placer Dome, Inc., went from $12 to $28 in about 15 months.

- Plum Creek Timber L.P. was a real winner. Recommended at $10 the third quarter of 1991, it started a steady rise. It was at $20 when it split three for one. It rose to over $32 by the first quarter of 1994. That's a return of 860 percent in 30 months.

- Questar Corporation was a quick hitter. In mid-first quarter 1993 I recommended it at $28. By the end of the third quarter that year it was selling at almost $43.

- Southwest Airlines was discovered by my system at the very end of 1991 at almost $12. In mid-1992 it split two shares for one. In mid-1993 it split again, this time three shares for two. By the end of 1993 it was selling at almost $39. A $1,200 investment that purchased 100 shares would have returned in just over two years 300 shares valued at $11,700.

- Storage Technology Corp. is interesting. I recommended it at $35 near the end of the first quarter of 1991. Almost exactly a year later it was selling at $78.

- Trinity Industries, Inc., was a buy at almost $27 early in the first quarter of 1993. At mid-year it split three for two. It rose to $47 a year later.

- Wells Fargo, another banking stock, was recommended in the late fourth quarter of 1992 at slightly below $75. By mid-1994 it was at $160.

- Zemex shows that there were a few reversals during this time span. This was a bummer. I recommended it at slightly below $8 and it retreated to $6 nine months later. However, it did rebound to over $12 by mid-1994 for a return (annualized) of 50 percent.

That's not to say that the system didn't recommend any losers, because, as nothing is perfect, it did. They were few and far between, but there were a few. But, by using the stop-loss method and portfolio management techniques discussed throughout this book, losses were kept to an absolute minimum.

Many of the examples I've included are not as spectacular as some of the ones just mentioned. I included those, too, to show the balance of my strategy. But even those that didn't do so well did better than most picks made by others during this same time span. And it is very important to note that I made these recommendations without ever reading a prospectus, a year-end report, a press release, or anything else for that matter. In some cases I had no idea what the company made, produced, serviced, or whatever. But it didn't matter, because I was basing my pick on the efforts of those who did read every report, did know what the company made or serviced, did know the quality of the management, and so on. And once their influence became apparent by pushing the stock to three new yearly highs within 24 days, I was ready to get on the profit bandwagon. Again, study these charts. See how many times a stock split shortly after I recommended it. I had no idea that the stock was going to split, but, again, those who pushed the stock to my attention through new highs did. Honestly, this discovery is unbelievable. It distills so much reliable information down to one criterion—new highs through a 12-month resistance barrier.

Think of my discovery like this: If Alan Greenspan, the president of the United States, the chairman of the SEC, and Warren Buffett all came to you and said, "Buy Disney right now," would you hesitate until they explained in detail why they were making such a recommendation, or would you call your broker the next minute? You'd call immediately, because you'd realize that when you have inside information and recommendations from those who can influence the market, all you really need to know is what stock(s) to buy and when to buy—you don't need to know why. That's what my system gives you. It tells you what and when. The why is a waste of time.

*Note:* The examples are not "outdated." This time span was chosen specifically due to the fact that recent years have been too easy; that is, because of the market's strength and record highs, anyone could have been somewhat successful. The period 1991–1993 presents a much better, more difficult test of my discovery. In coming years, when things get tough again after the crash, you'll be glad you're not relying on a strategy that was profitable only during the boom years.

If you've been an investor for the past 10 years, go back to your records during the years I'm referring to and see what your portfolio returned. I think most, if not close to all, will have to admit you would have gladly exchanged your picks and those of your broker for mine—and that, folks, is the real bottom line.

# CHAPTER 4

# Wringing Every Penny of Profit Out of Every Opportunity

## Market Direction

Again, the stock market has little or nothing to do with normal financial reality. If the market was simply a reflection of true corporate worth, the crash of 1987 would not have occurred. Actual book value (corporate assets divided by the number of shares outstanding) of stock didn't change from one day to the next. Neither did corporate earnings. What changed was the rejection of overvaluation, thereby proving the market has no accounting-based worth. After book value is eclipsed by sale price, it's all perception. So, based on history, the concept of a crash caused by overvaluation and overselling is moved from the theory to the fact category. I mention this for those who don't believe an overvaluation/overselling crash is possible—the fact is it has happened before, and it can happen again. The float—the difference between true corporate stock value and market fantasy (sale price)—allows manipulation of the market for the aggrandizement of insiders.

Now, before you say that the pros lost in the 1987 crash, too, I remind you that they experienced the result of their own hyperselling excesses. They weren't market victims; they were the cause of the crash (we discussed this briefly in Chapter 1). They produced the overvaluation. They profited many times over by the overvaluation, and they did so for many years. They profited on commissions and trades. Any losses they experienced were minimal compared to their previous gains. Additionally, many of the results of Black Monday were triggered by the systematic, computer-generated trading methods many pros still employ. Then, too, most got out long before their individual clients were afforded the luxury. Events continue to make clear the undeniable fact that the stock market is quite often a major deception. Those who refuse to believe that are (one of my favorite investment sayings) "an investment accident looking for a place to happen."

To explain further, let's look at an example. If the stock market were a true reflection of corporate America you would have to admit that stock value in a stable, profitable corporation should not have been adversely affected by the crash of 1987, yet all stocks were. Why? Again, it's perception. Much of the stock available on the market is, at the time of this writing, so severely overvalued and manipulated that stocks having a book value of as little as 50 cents are selling for as much as $25 or substantially more. This proves the hypothesis that stock market sale price usually has little connection to hard-value accounting analysis. The selling price of an individual stock is all too often the result of broker salesmanship as opposed to actual book value or even corporate earnings.

This brings us to the fact that regardless of the stock, it is, to some extent, a pawn of the insider-influenced market. When you invest in stock you are, to a degree, making a system bet—that is, an investment in the direction of the market and not necessarily just a given stock. Granted, the choice of stocks is important and their impact on your net results cannot be ignored. But equally important in the total equation is market direction and what it means for that stock.

## Indicators: The Big Four

Four specific indicators that will help you quickly determine where the market is headed include:

**1. *Employment trends.*** Movement in the number of jobs created each month gives an indication as to whether the economy is strong or retreating.

Sustained growth is perhaps the best indication of an economy showing bullish trends, while the opposite indicates a possible market retreat. Employment figures affect many variables that influence markets in general. For instance, a decline in jobs means more unemployment claims, less tax income, and reduced consumer spending.

**2. *Consumer spending.*** Obviously, this is to be coupled with employment trends to see the full impact of current events.

Here we have a measure of consumer confidence, although there are times—around Christmas, for instance—when the figures' importance must be tempered. However, consumer spending influences all aspects of business and as such helps management make decisions regarding the future, both short and long term.

**3. *Personal income.*** It should be obvious that if personal income is rising, the economy is getting stronger. The reverse is also true.

I caution, however, that personal income statistics, to have investment direction value, have to be used in conjunction with known information regarding inflation. You need to see a net effect; that is, we know inflation can drive personal income higher, but at the same time personal spending power may have decreased.

**4. *The consumer price index.*** Interest rates are affected by inflation. The consumer price index (CPI) can help give you an indication of the direction interest rates will be driven—and the direction of interest rates can often tell you the direction of the stock market.

It also gives an indication of what business borrowing will be, which affects manufacturing, which affects the market, and so on.

The overall economy is affected by many circumstances, some controlled, like the money supply, and some uncontrolled, like events in the Middle East. The market trades on rumor and changes direction suddenly on traumatic world events. This means that regardless of one's accuracy in seeing the direction of the market, there is an implied element of risk even with blue chip stock picks. Yet, if you understand the overall market concept, as opposed to just individual stock choices, your win/loss ratio will improve dramatically. Again, from Jonathan Steinberg's *Midas Investing*—"On Wall Street, they say, 'the trend is your friend,' a reference to the fact that, more often than not, a rising market continues to rise and a declining market finds new ways to sag. A trend can be your ally in a different way as well. If you understand a broad economic cycle or an enormously important industry development, you have an edge over other investors." I couldn't agree more, especially with the part about understanding a broad economic cycle. I've been preaching that for decades—in a very broad sense, the market moves stocks; stocks don't move the market.

You must review these market indicators every month to be on top of this; it only takes a few minutes. Newspapers, cable financial programs, and most Internet trading sites (see "Trading Online" in Chapter 5) are good sources. While positive news/indicators are what we are normally looking for, negative indications are just as good once you learn how to short the market.

Please also be aware of this important fact: Overheating of indicators can look positive and be, in fact, quite negative. For example, while we normally would see a rise in consumer spending and personal incomes in a favorable light, if it is rising too fast—faster than normal—that's usually a bad sign. Let me give you a banking analogy. When I was still with the industry I used to tell people that certain banks would shortly be in trouble. My fellow bankers would all laugh—right up until the bank got in trouble or was closed. How did I know? I admit I knew nothing of the bank(s) per se. What I did know, however, was this—they were growing at too slow or fast a rate. That can mean only one thing. They were, for some unknown yet important reasons, eclipsing their ability to service.

In some cases it also meant that they were drug banks—places where money was laundered, which generates huge income for a bank. You'd see a bank open up and in a few months it would have the dollar deposits of a bank that had been in the same area for decades. It didn't take a genius to conclude that something was wrong. That's the same kind of obvious thinking that led me to believe back in 1987 that there would be a major stock market reversal. I didn't know anything others didn't choose to ignore. Things were out of whack. They are really out of whack now. So understand, if you thought from some of what I've said so far that I am throwing rocks at those who try to predict the market while at the same time making predictions of my own, you're wrong. You're comparing apples and oranges. I'm really not predicting anything. I am applying common sense to the adage that history repeats itself. Of course, I try, within my limitations, to update the circumstances and adjust accordingly. That's why I don't say that when the big reversal hits this time that all that will be left will be about 11 percent of what was, as was the case in 1929. That would be stupid. History repeats itself in principle, but circumstances change. No, I don't predict anything in the market; I, like I did with banks, simply give voice to what the facts say will happen.

An economy that overheats can be as damaging as an economy that is stagnant. Which brings us to another example of that principle.

There are thousands of intelligent, successful commodity traders who trade based on a strategy that says there is a perfect order to all markets—commodities, stocks, whatever. Simply put, this complicated strategy is somewhat based on the axiom that history repeats itself. There are nuances of the strategy. For instance, some, believe it or not, trade on the cycles of the moon. There are other variations that are not worth mentioning here. Notwithstanding the "craziness" and complication of some of these bizarre, sometimes mathematical methods, the fact is that many of the traders are extremely success-ful and wealthy. Why? Because, regardless of what substrategy they subscribe to, the bottom line is that history does repeat itself, and that's a fact. It has been since the first of recorded history and it will continue to be.

So how does this apply to the stock market of the new millennium? In August of 1929 the stock market had just finished an amazing run of months whereby the market had doubled in valuation. This was an unusual and historic event. Of course, that run-up was the precursor to the Crash where the market went from 381.17 to 198.69. And the Crash was the precursor to the Great Depression where the market continued its slide until it hit a low of 41.22 just two and a half years later. In virtually the same monthly time span the current market went from 5,500 to over 11,000. Does that alone mean the market will crash? No, not necessarily. But it does mean that doubling of the mar-ket in a short time span is not common, and, as I said earlier, history does repeat itself. Stock market history is no exception. It is interest-ing to note that the combination of overvaluation and overselling was the same motivating factor of market insiders in 1929 as it is now. Truth is, everything is in place. We will see if the outcome is similar.

My expectation, as noted in Chapter 1, is that this crash will be very different from the Crash of 1929. It won't look the same—but the damage will be substantial, especially as this market holds so many retirement funds that the 1929 market did not. This means that, while the short-term effects will likely be less, perhaps far less, the long-term effects may actually be worse.

That's why you have to understand that in a most consequential way the market moves individual investments; individual investments don't move the market; that is, the rising tide lifts all boats, just as a low tide lowers all boats. Picking the right stock(s) produces profits. Picking the right stock(s) at the right time produces mega-profits.

Most investors don't understand this principle, which is one reason they are disappointed in their results.

In addition, there are trends within the stock market that need to be addressed when assessing where it is headed, because, unlike some markets, the stock market is not a zero-sum game. With each trade there isn't necessarily a winner and loser—there are, however, two traders with different opinions.

Take Company X—let's say it's selling for $14 a share. I want to buy 100 shares. Someone sells me 100 shares. What does this mean at its base level? It means that I think Company X's stock will increase in price. The seller thinks, for whatever reason, that I am wrong. Of course there are other considerations that might be in play, but when you strip away the varnish that's what this trade is all about, a difference of opinion. That difference holds true in almost all trades and, in fact, makes the market work. If everyone was in agreement on the direction of the market and particular stocks there wouldn't be any trades, because everyone would be holding on to their stock or selling at the same time. This is an important point. The market works because we all disagree most of the time.

### The Anomaly That Generates Big Profits

This is one of the underlying reasons that the buy and sell signals of my strategy are so valid. When you see a consensus of opinion driven by those in the know—and in the money—who are making things happen, you have an event you can't ignore; that is, something unusual is happening—people are coming to the same conclusion in a market that survives and thrives on opinion difference. When that opinion brings three breakthroughs of a stock's highs or lows within 24 calendar days, you have something very unusual happening. The norm, the disagreement about a stock's worth, is overshadowed by forces that are willing to buck the trend of the market in general. But you also have to take into consideration that total agreement is dangerous. Total agreement in a market that depends on disagreements gives you an oversold, overbought, overvalued market. When that happens, the only thing left is a reversal. It's a "what goes up must come down" kind of thing.

So it's important, along with the other considerations mentioned earlier, to watch the trend of the overall market to determine how strong your buy or sell signal is.

There is one other strong consideration—the economic cycle. Now, I realize that the economic cycle has been off its mark the past few years. but that doesn't mean you should ignore it. To do so would be a mistake, because it's called a cycle for a reason. While it may get stretched out or shortened, it will have its way.

The stock market moves, in part, according to the economic cycle of the country, because, at its theoretical base, the market's stock prices are a reflection of corporate earnings (or at least they should be), and the economy does affect corporate earnings.

For example, when the Fed increases or decreases the money supply, the economy/stock market begins a new cycle. When the supply is increased the stock market is usually affected in a positive, bull manner, as the new cash enters the investment market as a whole corporate expansion fuels the optimism of investors and you see the market go up. This tweaking of the economy is, in no small part, the partial cause of the present bull market we have been experiencing. On the other hand, a decrease in the money supply takes money from the stock market, which affects the number of investors and their willingness to have their money, especially retirement money, at "risk." Less money in circulation also means that people will be buying less, which will affect corporate earnings, which will, or should, affect stock prices.

### The Importance of Financial Cycles

I am trying to make an important point quickly. Because our economy is cyclical, the stock market must be cyclical also. No other course of events can take place for any extraordinary amount of time without everything breaking loose at some point. These cycles are a pressure relief valve for the buildup of excesses of the economy itself. Don't forget all the pressures that can be brought to bear on the market.

The government alone, through mismanagement, can bring down the market. The world economy can bring down the market. A few major fund frauds can bring down the market. Normal economic cycles can bring down the market. A whole host of things can bring down the market. The point? Normal cycles are the grease that helps stop the stock market from seizing up and falling prey to the outside forces the market has no control over. Which, if you think ahead, means that much of the bull run everyone is so thrilled with has destroyed, if only temporarily, the firewall the normal economic cycle offers. Tamper with the cycle, as we have done by manipulating the market (this is one of those things Mr. Greenspan and I disagree about), and you may do very well in the short run, but long-term you've set the table for disaster.

What does this have to do with market direction? Everything, as market direction and the ability to spot it are important to your ability to pick the right stocks at the right time. You need to know which economic cycle we are in and/or are headed for. The four indicators mentioned earlier will help you do that, but then you have to factor in whether the cycle we're in is manufactured or a reflection of true conditions, and the only way to do that in today's market is to place your common sense above what amounts to market nonsense masquerading as fact.

I have to say at this point that there are times when a cycle is exceptional, such as the market at the millennium. There are times when the cycle got off track in a historical context. That happens. But you'll also note when looking at a unique cycle or bull or bear run that they always cycle back in the opposite direction. If that weren't the case we wouldn't use the word "cycle." A bull run to infinity is not a cycle. Of course, as indicated, there are no absolutely repeating cycles in terms of raw numbers and dates when X or Y will occur, but there are patterns that you want to get a feel for as soon as possible.

Our economy is like a big oil tanker. I understand that to turn one of those ships you have to start turning many miles before the fact, because the weight and mass of the ship takes that long to respond and change direction. Our economy too has weight and mass and, barring the most unusual (a war, for instance), it takes time to change direction—sometimes as long as six months, sometimes longer. That truism is one of the reasons we often give much too much credit to the president when the economy is right and too much blame when it's wrong. The Clinton recovery the first year of his administration was actually George Bush's recovery—no political statement here, I am just trying to make a point. Think ahead in your commonsense reasoning regarding the economy and its effect on the stock market. If you've started to perceive cracks in the economy (such as layoffs, heavy inventories, reduced housing starts, etc.) when you read this, the effects will show up in the market about six months from now. Positive news tends to respond quicker, especially if it's of the flashy variety. Long-term positive news normally responds long-term.

Market direction is not just an intellectual pursuit; it is important to your ability to be ahead, way ahead of the curve. And it's not that hard to do. Check the indicators I've recommended. Pay attention. Think ahead. Understand economic cycles and the need for same. Apply common sense to what you discern. Once you start dovetailing this knowledge with your new ability to pick winning stocks, your picks will become more valuable than ever. You'll get a better feel for how strong your picks really are and how they will be able to exist within current market conditions.

You'll also get a feel for when something is inherently wrong with the economy and the market, and that may be the most important market direction signal you ever get. You know, not everyone lost their shirt when the market crashed in 1929. Some people got out prior to the Crash and then bought up assets, valuable assets, for pennies on the dollar after the dust settled. This is an important fact. While there were many fortunes lost during the Crash, many fortunes were made right afterward in the middle of the Depression. And who had the ability to buy up assets for pennies on the dollar? Those who traded in their stocks for cash prior to the Crash. People who applied many of the same criteria to their financial thinking that I am advocating to you now.

## Win Big, Lose Small

Knowing the odds are, long-term and in general, stacked against you, you should realize that your losing trades, regardless of their number or frequency, must be monetarily limited. On the other hand, your winners should be allowed to accrue their maximum profit potential. Even if you're a good trader, if you're not using the TTS, you may have more losers than winners; but they should have a dollar total substantially less than what the perhaps fewer winners produce. That ratio is what results in your market profit (or loss). Of course, armed with the discovery of this book, your odds of a positive winning-to-losing-trades ratio is far better than most; however, even you should look to win big and lose small.

Why then, if that ratio theory is argued by no one, do most individual investors do just the opposite—lose big, win small? The problem is human nature. People don't want to admit that they made a mistake. And then, too, "You never know when things could turn around." Some who allow their losses to run have an ego problem. They cannot deal with the realities of the market.

Even those who do have a market strategy sometimes allow their emotions to overrule their common sense. They get into a contest of wills with the market. The market almost always wins.

And for every investor who tries to buck the market, there's one who's scared of it. This is equally foolish and can be just as costly.

Knowing that an investment showing profit should run its course and then allowing it to do so are two different things, especially if you've ridden a few too many losers recently. Many investors have a tendency to offset their losses, or a portion thereof, by taking any immediate profit they can get. Ego can get in the way here, too. Many traders like to talk about their winners. They made money here, they made money there. They never bother to add it up, which, more often than not, will show at best a wash; at worst a substantial loss.

Losing big and winning small is often caused by the financially un-educated position of the investor. Some people simply don't understand the entire market picture as it pertains to their portfolios. They either listen to their brokers exclusively or they become overly concerned with individual trades rather than overall results. In contrast, the smart investor realizes what matters is the net profit or loss at year-end.

The rule is: Limit your losses, and let your winners ride. You do that by using stop-loss orders on all trades. The security principle as represented by stops is accurately expressed as, "Don't trust the market; trust your stops."

I admit that there are times when following this market axiom will cost you money. In fact, I can guarantee that at some time your stop-loss order will be hit and then the stock will turn around. But the safety a stop-loss order gives is worth the occasional loss.

With regard to a specific trade, the most important element is establishing the maximum you are willing to lose. That's what determines your stop-loss order. Being conservative here will not hurt. However, being overly conservative will, as you must be able to withstand small market swings. A stop-loss built too close to your investment entry price could result in too quick a sale. My 10 percent of capital outlay recommendation offers protection and an adequate market swing cushion.

What about the profit side? Here, too, many go wrong, because they never establish the stock's potential for gain. As mentioned earlier, there has to be a better than average potential for gain before the smart investor risks capital. Investing in the stock market just to be investing is a mistake.

A rolling stop-loss order that constantly is changed as circumstances change is the best vehicle for protecting profits, thereby allowing your winners to ride. For example, if you bought 1,000 shares of stock at $10 per share expecting it to go to $15, and are willing to lose $1,000 on the trade, you'd establish an order to sell at $9. A wise investor, when the stock moves to $11, would move the stop. While some would move it to $10, I'd move it to $9.50, which would reduce the loss potential 50 percent while giving more maneuvering room if the stock experiences a short-term turnaround. With each incremental movement your stop-loss should be moved so you never experience a loss of more than you were originally willing to risk even though you're now playing with profit.

I am often asked what is the best time to sell out a stock—is there a sign, a system? Earlier I purposely avoided this question in the discussion regarding stock picks, as ultimately every investor's portfolio will influence his or her buy/sell decisions and there is no corresponding sell system to my buy system. We've talked about that already. However, here is my general portfolio management strategy: Let the stock sell itself. You do that by using rolling stops. As the stock starts to run out of steam in its movement up or down, move the stop closer and closer to the present price. Eventually, the stock, by hitting the stop, sells itself. This allows for the greatest gain at the least cost, thereby ensuring the best net.

Another important key is to abide by the results of your determinations. Don't let pride or the results of past trades dictate your position. Just because you get out, or sell, doesn't mean you should necessarily abandon the investment choice entirely. Maybe you were right all along, but that doesn't mean you should ride out a purchase to make the point. Get out when required and then back in when the Trinity Trading System (TTS) indicates another buy. The pros realize that much can be gained this way, and they are not the least bit shy about buying a stock, selling it on reversal, and buying again whenever the signals say to do so.

What is a better than average profit potential? Your expectations will determine what you consider average, but generally speaking a return most would be satisfied with is not adequate to offset the long-term, overall portfolio's potential for loss. In fact, as previously mentioned, you should believe that your investment holds the foreseeable expectation of a return of 50 percent or better. You need that potential unless you're infallible, which you're not.

Refusing to enter any position without that potential will stop you from being rushed into stocks or any other vehicle by anyone, your broker included. My strategy takes care of this problem for you, as once the stock breaks through its resistance barrier three times, it has, based on the historical data I compiled, the potential of a 50 percent return and more. Using my strategy also eliminates most offerings (you don't pick the stock, the system does), making your ultimate choice easier. Also, if you enter a position secure in the knowledge that your market potential is not overstated, you will not be tempted to get out with limited results; that is, if you're expecting a 50 percent return, chances are you won't settle for something as small as 10 or 15 percent. That perspective helps many of us.

If limiting your losses and letting your winners run were all there was to winning in terms of year-end profit, almost all investors would be winners. A market law of averages would indicate any combination of investments would accomplish these results; but, of course, no such law exists. If you pick 20 stocks, 10 will not necessarily be losers and 10 winners. That presents an interesting problem. Not only do you have to pick the right stocks, as you will do consistently utilizing my strategy, you also have to manage your portfolio to maximize their potential.

Many investors who consider themselves to be financially savvy confine themselves to, or only understand, picking stocks. The fact is, portfolio management is just as important, if not more so. I want to repeat that: Portfolio management is just as important as picking stocks, if not more so. Why? Because of the cumulative effect of market decisions.

If you had a portfolio that had a 50 percent success ratio in terms of picking winning stocks, but your winners returned an average of only 5 percent while your losers returned a loss of 20 percent, you can see the end result. However, if your market homework and instinct were right only 15 percent of the time and your winners returned 50 percent while the losers averaged 5 percent, you can see that end result, too. The key, after stock choice, is portfolio management. Those who don't control their portfolios will see their portfolios collapse and disappear.

Your market reality has to coincide with a workable market strategy. If you know you should limit your losses and let your winners ride, why are you doing just the opposite?

### Portfolio Management Keys

Fortunately, there are seven ways to bring your portfolio back into a profitable mode—and my strategy will automatically do these critical items for you. Specifically:

**1.** Start looking at your investments on a portfolio basis. Individual trades are not unimportant per se, but they may mean little when all the dust settles. Too many traders would rather have X+ winners and X losers without giving thought to the dollar amounts both numbers represent. Frankly, it doesn't matter how many winners you had last year; what matters is how much money they made. The same holds true for losing trades. The bottom line is the bottom line. In the world of finance, nothing else matters.

**2.** Refuse to invest in any vehicle that does not have a return potential of at least 50 percent. We have talked about this numerous times. As the stock charts proved conclusively, when this strategy picks a stock for you it has this potential of return and, more often than not, more. Anything less than 50 percent isn't worth risking principal on.

**3.** Appraise market potential in its entirety. What I mean here is that dividends count. Look again at the chart of General Dynamics

(Figure 3.17 in Chapter 3). After I recommended it at about $16 in mid-1991, it paid three special dividends in 1993 of $20, $18, and $12 before it split two for one at almost $50 in early 1994. Substantial appreciation, yes, but that is of lesser immediate importance than the special dividends that by themselves were worth $50 on a $16 investment.

This is an extreme case, but it makes the point. When you judge an investment, count every dollar from every source before you determine its worth. For example, everyone in the business knows people who make investments almost solely on the dividend return—and most of them do quite well, thank you.

**4.** Remember, you're not on a level playing field (are you tired of hearing this yet?), and as such, you have to make adjustments to balance your position. Make your winners count. Here, too, I am talking about all the other guys. My discovery levels the field. You must, whether you use my system or another (although I am not aware of another that levels the field as mine does), find a way to be the equal of those who have influence in the market and/or an individual stock or group of stocks. The stock market is not a crooked card game, but there is an appropriate analogy in the comparison. No one in their right mind would sit down for a card game they knew was fixed and gamble away their fortune. Likewise, no one in their right mind should enter the stock market with all its obvious flaws and warts without trying to have the same chance of winning as an insider or an investor who has multimillions or billions of his or her influential money (or the money of others) to invest.

**5.** A loss is a loss. By itself it means nothing. If your ego cannot stand the strain of admitting defeat, get out of the market before you lose it all. Maybe you've received ads in the mail that promise a system that has a winning percentage of 99 percent or some other such nonsense. The market doesn't work that way. As mentioned earlier, even investments that were right on the money when made can turn sour due to outside circumstances that happen after the fact. That alone should tell you promises like 99 percent winning trades are not to be believed.

My system is unique because it offers winning trades, yes, but considerably more important to my mind is the fact that it offers winning trades with extraordinary potential for gain. That's one of the reasons I included the charts for review, so you can see proof of my claims. Frankly, I hoped to impress you with this important feature of my discovery. Yes, I was thrilled that I had discovered how to tap into inside information that most others weren't seeing, but what really got the juices flowing was realizing that the stocks the system was picking were absolute dynamite. Special dividends, unusual growth, unknown stock splits—these are the things that make millionaires.

**6.** The potential for future profit may be there even though your original investment buy or sell position may turn against short-term profit. Realizing that may help those with market egos. It may also help to maximize profits for those who invest and then sit forever with the same position.

My strategy will keep making recommendations if a stock that you may have sold out keeps making new highs at a later date. If you're sticking with the plan, you won't let the fact that you may have experienced a slight loss previously dissuade you from another buy signal. Too many investors take a loss on a stock personally and won't go near that stock again. That's a mistake. Stock names should be basically meaningless to you. The system, stick with the system.

**7.** The only thing that counts is year-end results. Adding up the number of your winners and losers doesn't mean anything. This is similar to the first item, but it's worth noting the difference. Yes, the condition of your portfolio matters, but year-end results are the overriding consideration. It's like a bank (excuse another bank analogy, but I was a banker for a long, long time) that has done well for the past 10 years. Suddenly it has a bad year. But it could still be said that its average condition overall is excellent—even though a recent accounting may show that the bank is now in deep trouble and likely to be closed unless corrections are made.

A year-end accounting of your profit and loss results must be accomplished in addition to looking at your portfolio. You may have made a million dollars the past five years and then lost half of it back last year. So, you could say to others that you're doing just fine; but are you? No. Last year's year-end accounting says there is something seriously wrong, and if you don't fix it you may end up losing the rest of your portfolio.

The bottom line here is: If you utilize my rolling stop-loss plan faithfully, it will solve many of the problems you may encounter with the market, because it takes investing ego out of the equation, and we've already discussed how important that is. It reduces your losses, and increases your gains. On your own you might end up doing just the opposite.

## "Overnight" Profits Up to 200 Percent or More

The risk/reward relationship of investments is well defined by Theodore Miller in *Invest Your Way to Wealth*: "The bigger the promised reward, the bigger the risk. Conversely, the bigger the risk of the investment you undertake, the bigger the potential reward should be." But what if you could turn the risk/reward relationship upside down and reduce your potential risk while at the same time increasing your potential reward? Welcome to stock options.

The normal buying and selling of stocks doesn't have the mega-profit potential of speculation. Yet the thought of speculating—in commodity futures, for example—rightfully terrifies most investors. They don't have the expertise to enter those highly dangerous markets. After all, who knows what corn, gold, or oil will cost tomorrow, the day after, next month? No one. While there are variables in the stock market, there are too many variables in the commodity markets for the average investor and his or her limited resources. Is there a middle ground to the investment spectrum? Yes—stock options.

A stock option gives the right, for a price, to buy or sell a listed stock at an agreed-upon price sometime before the date when the option expires.

Options are contracts covering 100 shares of a particular stock. The strikes (prices stated in the contracts) are fixed near the current selling price of the stock in 5-, 10-, or 20-dollar increments. When a stock's price changes substantially, the exchange issues another option or options based on the new market value. Consequently, it's possible for a stock to have many options working at the same time. Of course, that gives the aggressive trader additional possibilities for trading the same stock with differing expiration dates and strike prices.

Listed stock options can be traded through your broker.

### The Types of Options

Options fall into two categories, puts and calls, which are subdivided into buying (long) or selling (short):

**BUY (LONG)**

- Call: Purchasing the right to buy a stock at a fixed price until the expiration date.
- Put: Purchasing the right to sell a stock at a fixed price until the expiration date.

**SELL (SHORT)**

- Call: Selling the right to buy a stock from you until the expiration date.
- Put: Selling the right to sell a stock to you until the expiration date.

Of course, when you buy an option, your cost is the cost of the option only. If the option is exercised you'll have to pay the agreed-upon price for the contracted shares. For most this is a moot point as, just like commodity speculators, those who purchase stock options usually do so with the thought of the profit coming from the option itself, not from its exercise. Remember that when you safely trade options you don't normally let your position get to the point where shares actually trade hands. You want out of your position prior to the contract's expiration date.

One major word of warning: If you sell an option on a stock that you don't own at present, called "naked writing," you could be looking at a huge loss, because if the option is exercised you must sell. As you don't actually own the stock in question, this means that you must then buy stock to sell to the option holder at the agreed-upon price, thereby meeting your obligation. And you'll have to buy no matter the cost. That, in my opinion, is a tragic misuse of the tremendous potential of stock options. That's why I strongly—I repeat, *strongly*—recommend avoiding the naked option.

If you do invest—speculate—by buying an option on a stock you feel will rise in price, you can lose only the cost of the option, nothing more; so you have a known, acceptable loss exposure (or you wouldn't have purchased the option) with an unlimited potential on the upside—a good deal if you believe in a stock.

The same holds true of an option you sell because you believe stock you own ("you own" being the key) will go down in price. Equally important, with an option you can't be forced or stopped out of the position before the option date, which may be many months away. This allows many losing positions eventually to become winners. Also, there are no margin calls.

Why would someone buy an option instead of the stock itself? Leverage. It makes a little money do a lot of work. Listed stock options offer the investor/speculator (which is what I call those who buy options—it's the logical middle between investing extremes) short-term profits of up to 200 percent or more, due in large part to the leverage aspect of the equation.

Depending on when you buy an option, the leverage can be 10, 50, 100 to 1. There is no negative leverage working associated with options. There is, however, the negative of time, which isn't necessarily present with a straight stock purchase. When you buy or sell an option you're betting that X will happen within a given limited time period; this negative is one of the reasons that your option has such tremendous leverage. The following example will better explain options potential.

Let's say Company X's stock is selling for $40 a share. You, because TTS says it's a buy candidate, purchase 100 shares at a cost of $4,000. In a month the stock goes to $45. You sell for a profit of $500, or a return of 12.5 percent in 30 days. Not bad, right? Right and perhaps wrong. You see, if you thought the stock had a short-term potential of $45 a share, you could have purchased a Company X option at, let's say, two and a half, meaning for $250 you would have the right to buy Company X stock (100 shares) at a predetermined date for $40. Remembering it went to $45, you would have a contract likely worth $500, or a 30-day return of 100 percent. So, in this case, your choice was to invest $4,000 to earn $500 or $250 to earn $250 in the same time span, same transaction. That's what leverage does.

For the $4,000 worth of stock you bought you could have purchased 16 options that would have controlled 1,600 shares instead of 100. Your return in that case would be $4,000. Comparing apples to apples leaves us with this: You could have purchased 100 shares of stock at $4,000 and earned $500 or purchased 16 options at the same cost, controlling 1,600 shares of stock, and earned $4,000—thereby doubling your money. Again, such is the leverage of options. So is that what I am advising—not buying stock and buying options instead with the same amount of money invested? No, absolutely not.

Unlike stock, where your investment always has some value (theoretically) and you would have lost only a little money before your stop was hit had the stock gone in the wrong direction, you can lose it all with an option. Remember our 10 percent loss on any one trade rule and you'll understand that that's why I would, in this example, risk only two contracts (which is slightly more than the rule, but necessary as the contracts have a specific cost). In this example, as in most stock versus options examples I might use, for a fraction of the cost of buying the stock you can control the same amount of stock, and, as return is based on profit divided by the amount of dollars invested, the option return is much larger—substantially larger than the return on the same amount of shares. This also does another thing for the aggressive investor. As long as you don't forget our basic rules and percentages, it frees up money to pursue more positions with a wider diversity of stocks. Again, such is the leverage power of options.

### Fear and Greed

While we've talked about fear and greed in traditional stock transactions previously, they need to be addressed again regarding options.

When you purchase a stock option you could lose 100 percent of your investment. That's not normally true of most stock purchases, a fact that causes many investors/speculators to get nervous quickly if things don't go their way immediately. Too many sell their options too early, thereby sustaining only a small loss and avoiding losing it all. Smart? Not really, because options involve knowing, and accepting, the potential for complete loss. But that comes with the territory and is an acceptable risk. So when investors/speculators bail out without seeing the option through, they are cheating themselves out of the huge potential the option could provide within the next few days.

It is unreasonable to expect to buy an option and have it go straight to the moon. A more likely scenario is having to ride up and down before reaching your objective, which should be, at a minimum, 100 percent on your investment. For example, if your option cost was $500, you should look for a profit of $500. Wait a minute! Didn't I tell you earlier that your profit goal in the stock market should be, at a minimum, 50 percent? Yes, I did, but options are different. Gains must exceed the norms of stock investing because with options you're not just investing, you're investing/speculating.

Greed can be eliminated by establishing a target profit and sticking to it. If you get greedy and constantly up the ante, your substantial paper gain can disappear quickly.

Trading stock options, which are a market unto themselves (i.e., options can be bought and sold with no stock changing hands), can dramatically enhance your market profit potential. That's why some of the rules regarding buying stocks have to be fine-tuned, and why you must bring a new perspective to the table if this is the route you go. Remember, an option's potential may substantially outstrip the potential of the stock itself. Let's use an example to make that point, while at the same time showing how increased potential of profit can easily absorb additional losses and still show a substantial return.

You have three option positions. Each has a day-one value of $2,000, for a total of $6,000. The first two positions lose 50 percent, for a total loss of $2,000. The third returns a not uncommon 200 percent, for a total profit of $4,000. Your three positions have a net return of $2,000 profit for a percentage gain of over 33 percent. You took a major loss on two-thirds of your option investment/speculation and still made big money. Amazingly, in the option market this can happen in just a few weeks. Again, leverage is the key. The same stock purchases would not have returned anywhere near this example because your investment would have purchased substantially less profit potential (less stock) than your investment/speculation controlled. That's the beauty of stock options.

Of course, the key to successful stock option trading is picking the right stocks, and that's what the TTS has revealed to you.

### Ideal Conditions

For the stock to return the most in option form you need two things to happen:

1. The stock must move in the right direction. No, not straight up or down, because that seldom happens. A fluctuating trend line heading in your direction (up if you went long, down if you went short) is more likely, although those that just take off will return more money than you can possibly comprehend.

2. The move is quicker and larger than expected.

Remember, if you've followed my advice, your potential for loss is known and accepted. Then, too, if you do experience a loss, it doesn't have to be 100 percent of your option cost. Options are bought and sold. You can choose to turn over a position for a percentage loss. Regardless, it's important to keep in mind that, if done correctly, you'll always know your potential for loss with a stock option. Understanding that makes an option's land-office profit potential even more intriguing. Up to 200 percent or more—when's the last time you had that kind of short-term return?

Stocks that are in the process of a rally over a short time span are excellent candidates for option success. Stocks showing a strong, but somewhat less spectacular upswing will also show profit, but to realize this profit will take more patience.

Obviously, if you could pick a stock just prior to a rally you would earn the most, but that's not possible on a consistent basis—and consistency is necessary. As mentioned before, picking tops and bottoms, or trying to, is the bane of the average individual investor. Again, better to ride those stocks that are already winners. The TTS is the component in picking stocks and options. Of course, by meeting strategy criteria, you are confident of the stock's potential, which allows you to pick the lower-priced, further out-of-the-money option. And that, strangely enough, offers more than normal option safety; that is, by the time an option comes to your attention, the stock will have set three new highs (lows) within 24 calendar days. Because of that trend you won't be taking any fliers on options. Consequently, there is no reason to rush to judgment while waiting for the third breakthrough.

As options are strongly affected by not only the obvious—that is, a stock's price and direction (up or down)—it's important to consider the market as a whole entity, as was discussed with regard to market direction. Is it a bear or bull market? This must be established prior to picking stocks, because the best time to buy an option is at the beginning of a bull market, and to sell one at the beginning of a bear market. This will improve your option potential while at the same time keeping your option costs down; remember, an option usually costs about 10 percent of the price of the stock it represents. This is what you'll normally pay at the beginning of a bull market. Deep into the bull run, the option, regardless of the stock, will cost more due to the "rising tide raises all boats" theory. The point is that to maximize the already huge profit potential, you must understand and then utilize the correlation of market and stock direction.

In summary, options are sold in and out of the money, so ascertain the market direction, choose the right stock, and then find the option that fits your expectations of what the market and the stock will do.

Options, however, are not for everybody. But if you have the emotional stamina and an understanding of the concept, they offer the relative safety of traditional stock market investing and the potentially larger returns of commodity speculation.

Look in the "Money & Investing" section of the *Wall Street Journal* under the heading "Listed Options Quotations." (See Figure 4.1.)

Pick your stocks using the TTS, compare their option prices and strike prices, check their expirations, and start paper trading (trading on paper without actually making a purchase) until you feel completely comfortable. Talk with a broker; he or she can explain any details of the trading process that you're unsure of (it's okay to use brokers for general information). Again, stock options are not for everyone, because they tend to confuse most part-time investors. You've got to take the time necessary to get beyond that. But it is also foolish for those in the stock market not to at least consider trading stock options.

# LISTED OPTIONS QUOTATIONS

Wednesday, January 5, 2000

For actively traded equity and LEAPS, or long-term options, with results for the Volume figures are unofficial. Open interest is total outstanding for all exchanges Close when possible is shown for the underlying stock on primary market. CB-Chicago rican Stock Exchange. PB-Philadelphia Stock Exchange. PC-Pacific Stock Exchange. -Composite. p-Put.

## MOST ACTIVE CONTRACTS

| Last | Net Chg | a-Close | Open Int | Option/Strike | | | | Vol | Exch | Last | Net Chg | a-Close | Open Int |
|---|---|---|---|---|---|---|---|---|---|---|---|---|---|
| 3 1/2 | − 1 | 74 3/8 | 236,916 | Intel | Jan | 90 | | 6,313 | XC | 1 3/4 | + 1/8 | 83 5/8 | 161,296 |
| 1 1/4 | − 11/16, | 5 1/4 | 154,251 | Cisco | Jan | 100 | | 6,248 | XC | 5 1/2 | − 1/8 | 102 3/8 | 75,008 |
| 1 3/16 | + 5/16 | 5 1/4 | 124,215 | BellAtl | Jan | 30 | | 6,016 | XC | 30 | − 5 7/8 | 59 15/16 | 2,386 |
| 17 1/4 | − 3 5/8 | 66 3/8 | 14,236 | Micsft | Jan | 120 | | 5,911 | XC | 2 | + 3/8 | 113 13/16 | 143,668 |
| 12 1/4 | + 5/8 | 66 3/8 | 20,640 | BellAtl | Jan | 40 | | 5,716 | XC | 20 | + 1/2 | 59 15/16 | 8,016 |
| 7 1/2 | + 1 1/4 | 45 1/16 | 4,160 | Micsft | Jan | 115 | | 5,674 | XC | 3 3/4 | + 3/8 | 113 13/16 | 54,444 |
| 5 1/2 | + 1 | 45 1/16 | 59,200 | I B M | Jan | 115 | | 5,657 | XC | 7 1/4 | + 3 3/8 | 116 | 74,752 |
| 4 | + 1 1/8 | 32 5/8 | 32,862 | SunMicro | Jan | 16 1/4 | | 5,601 | XC | 56 1/4 | − 2 1/2 | 71 7/8 | 45,620 |
| 1 1/4 | + 1/8 | 27 15/16 | 266,584 | Sap AG | Jan | 55 | p | 5,500 | XC | 10 1/8 | + 1 1/8 | 45 1/16 | 24,688 |
| 10 3/4 | + 1 | 32 5/8 | 22,160 | Sap AG | Feb | 55 | p | 5,500 | XC | 11 7/8 | + 4 3/4 | 45 1/16 | 600 |
| 6 3/4 | + 1 1/8 | 83 5/8 | 150,900 | Disney | Jan | 27 1/2 | | 5,494 | XC | 5 1/2 | + 1 3/8 | 32 5/8 | 60,656 |
| 6 5/8 | + 1 | 113 13/16 | 151,572 | Cisco | Feb | 100 | | 5,370 | XC | 8 3/8 | + 1/8 | 102 3/8 | 3,642 |
| 2 1/4 | + 1 1/4 | 49 15/16 | 191,636 | AT&T | Feb | 55 | | 5,189 | XC | 1 7/16 | − 1/16 | 50 15/16 | 7,668 |
| 1 1/16 | + 5/16 | 113 13/16 | 67,432 | AmOnline | Jan | 85 | | 5,149 | XC | 2 3/8 | − 1/2 | 74 3/8 | 187,016 |
| 3 1/8 | + 1 1/8 | 32 5/8 | 104,644 | TycoLb | Feb | 35 | | 5,083 | XC | 3 7/8 | − 5/8 | 35 1/2 | 5,360 |
| 1 1/4 | − 3 1/4 | 69 3/4 | 47,780 | Intel | Jan | 85 | p | 4,774 | XC | 4 5/8 | − 3/8 | 83 5/8 | 57,608 |
| 3 3/4 | + 1/2 | 83 5/8 | 140,028 | SBC Com | Jan 01 | 40 | | 4,725 | XC | 9 7/8 | + 3/4 | 44 15/16 | ·17,520 |
| 1 1/2 | − 7/16 | 74 3/8 | 209,472 | Ph Mor | Jan | 25 | | 4,673 | XC | 1/2 | − 1/8 | 23 1/2 | 71,948 |
| 1 5/8 | − 3/8 | 17 9/16 | 460 | DellCptr | Jan | 45 | | 4,643 | XC | 5 1/2 | + 2 1/8 | 49 15/16 | 165,952 |
| 5 3/4 | − 1 1/8 | 74 3/8 | 179,216 | In Pap | Jan | 45 | | 4,550 | XC | 10 1/2 | + 1 1/4 | 56 | 25,248 |

Option listings and data are available in The Wall Street Journal at **http://wsj.com** on the Internet's World Wide Web.

| Last | Option/Strike | | Exp. | Call Vol. | Call Last | Put Vol. | Put Last |
|---|---|---|---|---|---|---|---|
| 1 1/4 | 74 3/8 | 60 | Jan | 764 | 15 5/8 | 3415 | 1 |
| 2 7/8 | 74 3/8 | 60 | Feb | 290 | 18 3/4 | 418 | 2 5/8 |
| ... | 74 3/8 | 62 1/2 | Jan | 726 | 13 1/4 | 1317 | 1 1/4 |
| ... | 74 3/8 | 65 | Jan | 886 | 11 3/4 | 1681 | 1 3/4 |
| 2 5/8 | 74 3/8 | 65 | Feb | 134 | 15 5/8 | 709 | 4 1/8 |
| 1/4 | 74 3/8 | 65 | Apr | 252 | 17 5/8 | 480 | 7 1/4 |
| 1 1/4 | 74 3/8 | 67 1/2 | Jan | 205 | 9 3/4 | 485 | 2 1/2 |
| 4 1/4 | 74 3/8 | 67 1/2 | Apr | 526 | 16 1/2 | 113 | 8 5/8 |
| ... | 74 3/8 | 70 | Jan | 3105 | 8 1/2 | 2566 | 3 1/4 |
| 1 7/8 | 74 3/8 | 70 | Feb | 391 | 11 3/8 | 616 | 5 3/4 |
| 3 3/8 | 74 3/8 | 70 | Apr | 405 | 15 1/2 | 279 | 9 1/8 |
| 2 3/4 | 74 3/8 | 72 1/2 | Jan | 460 | 6 1/4 | 1475 | 4 3/8 |
| 1/4 | 74 3/8 | 75 | Jan | 6324 | 5 3/4 | 4010 | 5 5/8 |
| 3/4 | 74 3/8 | 75 | Feb | 2598 | 8 3/4 | 382 | 8 1/2 |
| 3 1/4 | 74 3/8 | 75 | Apr | 1833 | 13 1/8 | 320 | 11 5/8 |
| 1 13/16 | 74 3/8 | 77 1/2 | Jan | 3621 | 4 5/8 | 469 | 7 1/4 |
| 3 | 74 3/8 | 80 | Jan | 22611 | 3 1/2 | 1973 | 8 1/8 |
| 7 | 74 3/8 | 80 | Feb | 4267 | 6 3/4 | 202 | 11 1/8 |
| ... | 74 3/8 | 80 | Apr | 3084 | 11 1/8 | 256 | 14 3/4 |
| 5 | 74 3/8 | 80 | Jul | 493 | 14 | 41 | 16 3/4 |
| 13/16 | 74 3/8 | 82 1/2 | Jan | 1814 | 3 | 98 | 9 1/4 |
| 3 7/8 | 74 3/8 | 85 | Jan | 5149 | 2 3/8 | 505 | 12 3/8 |
| 2 7/8 | 74 3/8 | 85 | Feb | 1352 | 5 | 80 | 14 1/4 |
| ... | 74 3/8 | 87 1/2 | Jan | 1033 | 1 15/16 | 49 | 14 1/4 |
| ... | 74 3/8 | 90 | Jan | 6787 | 1 1/2 | 180 | 16 1/4 |
| 4 | 74 3/8 | 90 | Feb | 1052 | 4 | 8 | 18 1/2 |
| 3/4 | 74 3/8 | 90 | Apr | 620 | 8 1/8 | 24 | 20 1/2 |
| 5 7/8 | 74 3/8 | 92 1/2 | Jan | 696 | 1 9/16 | ... | ... |
| 2 3/4 | 74 3/8 | 95 | Jan | 1758 | 1 | 10 | 21 3/4 |
| 4 3/8 | 74 3/8 | 95 | Feb | 532 | 3 | 10 | 23 |
| 5 1/2 | 74 3/8 | 100 | Jan | 4277 | 11/16 | 112 | 25 1/2 |
| 7 1/8 | 74 3/8 | 100 | Feb | 1035 | 2 1/2 | 2 | 25 5/8 |
| 11 1/2 | 74 3/8 | 100 | Apr | 1186 | 5 5/8 | 31 | 29 1/2 |
| 9 3/8 | 74 3/8 | 110 | Jan | 2041 | 1/2 | ... | ... |
| 14 3/4 | 74 3/8 | 110 | Feb | 814 | 1 1/2 | 1 | 36 1/2 |
| 19 | 74 3/8 | 120 | Feb | 465 | 7/8 | ... | ... |
| 13 | 74 3/8 | 120 | Apr | 1052 | 3 | ... | ... |
| 18 1/4 | AEagleOt | 45 | Jan | 46 | 1 15/16 | 700 | 4 1/8 |
| 22 | AmExpr | 170 | Jan | 671 | 1/2 | ... | ... |
| 24 | 147 1/4 | 175 | Jan | 721 | 1/4 | 2 | 24 |
| ... | Am Hom | 40 | Jan | 1117 | 3 | 413 | 7/8 |
| 31 1/8 | 41 5/8 | 45 | Jan | 198 | 15/16 | 432 | 3 5/8 |
| 31 | 41 5/8 | 45 | Feb | 644 | 1 15/16 | 26 | 4 3/8 |
| 35 7/8 | AmIntGp | 95 | Feb | 28 | 7 3/8 | 601 | 3 1/4 |
| ... | 98 19/128 | 100 | Feb | ... | ... | 758 | 5 |
| 38 | 98 19/128 | 105 | Jan | 1006 | 1 | 50 | 6 1/4 |
| ... | Amrtch | 145 | Jan | 3420 | 14 5/8 | ... | ... |
| ... | Amgen | 42 1/2 | Jan | 1442 | 18 3/8 | ... | ... |
| 1/16 | 60 5/8 | 42 1/2 | Apr | 460 | 19 | 41 | 1 1/8 |
| 1/4 | 60 5/8 | 52 1/2 | Jan | 169 | 7 7/8 | 618 | 1 |
| 4 5/8 | 60 5/8 | 55 | Jan | 1408 | 7 | 699 | 1 7/16 |

| Option/Strike | | Exp. | Call Vol. | Call Last | Put Vol. | Put Last |
|---|---|---|---|---|---|---|
| 60 5/8 | 65 | Jan | 1489 | 1 5/8 | ... | ... |
| AmSouth | 17 1/2 | Feb | 750 | 1 3/8 | 10 | 1 |
| Analog | 80 | Jan | 1004 | 9 3/4 | 15 | 2 1/4 |
| 86 7/8 | 85 | Feb | 1037 | 10 1/4 | ... | ... |
| Antec | 40 | Feb | ... | ... | 575 | 10 1/8 |
| AppleC | 90 | Jan | 398 | 18 3/4 | 499 | 2 13/16 |
| 104 | 100 | Jan | 769 | 10 3/4 | 109 | 6 |
| 104 | 105 | Jan | 1408 | 7 7/8 | 189 | 7 7/8 |
| AplMat | 105 | Jan | 1979 | 12 5/8 | 1042 | 1 7/8 |
| 115 3/4 | 110 | Jan | 386 | 10 1/8 | 474 | 2 15/16 |
| 115 3/4 | 115 | Jan | 1367 | 6 3/8 | 772 | 4 5/8 |
| 115 3/4 | 120 | Jan | 1531 | 3 3/4 | 577 | 7 5/8 |
| 115 3/4 | 125 | Jan | 554 | 2 9/16 | 65 | 11 1/8 |
| Ariba | 180 | Jan | 546 | 17 1/8 | 44 | 20 1/2 |
| Airtsoft | 20 | Feb | 945 | 1 3/4 | ... | ... |
| AspectCm | 40 | Jan | 626 | 1 1/4 | ... | ... |
| AtHome | 40 | Jan | 403 | 3 1/2 | 331 | 3 |
| 39 15/16 | 45 | Jan | 661 | 1 13/16 | 104 | 6 5/8 |
| 39 15/16 | 50 | Jan | 981 | 1 | 36 | 10 5/8 |
| 39 15/16 | 50 | Feb | 510 | 2 5/8 | 5 | 11 7/8 |
| Atl R | 70 | Jan | 1450 | 10 5/8 | 132 | 11/16 |
| 79 15/16 | 75 | Jan | 26 | 6 5/8 | 3623 | 1 5/8 |
| 79 15/16 | 80 | Jan | 321 | 3 5/8 | 3063 | 3 3/4 |
| 79 15/16 | 85 | Feb | 2506 | 3 3/4 | ... | ... |
| 79 15/16 | 90 | Feb | 785 | 2 9/16 | ... | ... |
| 79 15/16 | 100 | Feb | 700 | 5/8 | ... | ... |
| Atmel | 25 | Feb | 762 | 4 | 65 | 2 5/8 |
| 26 9/16 | 30 | Feb | 741 | 2 1/8 | ... | ... |
| AutoNatn | 10 | Jan | 100 | 1/8 | 1020 | 1 9/16 |
| 8 5/8 | 12 1/2 | Jan | ... | ... | 1500 | 3 7/8 |
| BMC Sft | 45 | Jan | 1168 | 6 3/8 | 2677 | 1 9/16 |
| 49 9/16 | 45 | Feb | 506 | 8 3/8 | 608 | 3 1/2 |
| 49 9/16 | 50 | Jan | 3641 | 3 1/2 | 1448 | 3 5/8 |
| 49 9/16 | 50 | Feb | 999 | 5 7/8 | 522 | 6 |
| 49 9/16 | 50 | May | 858 | 9 1/2 | 457 | 9 |
| 49 9/16 | 55 | Jan | 2467 | 1 11/16 | 226 | 6 3/4 |
| 49 9/16 | 55 | Feb | 1186 | 4 | 223 | 8 5/8 |
| 49 9/16 | 60 | Jan | 1267 | 7/8 | 1669 | 10 1/4 |
| 49 9/16 | 60 | Feb | 548 | 2 9/16 | 63 | 12 1/4 |
| 49 9/16 | 65 | Jan | 429 | 7/16 | 1715 | 15 5/8 |
| 49 9/16 | 75 | Jan | 161 | 1/8 | 478 | 25 |
| BP Amoco | 57 1/2 | Jan | 2198 | 3 3/8 | ... | ... |
| 60 1/2 | 60 | Jan | 2110 | 1 1/8 | 30 | 1 5/8 |
| 60 1/2 | 60 | Feb | 1877 | 3 1/8 | 307 | 3 1/4 |
| BancOne | 30 | Jan | 193 | 1 1/4 | 714 | 1 1/16 |
| Bk of Am | 45 | Jan | 279 | 2 5/8 | 503 | 1 1/2 |
| 46 1/16 | 45 | May | 783 | 5 7/8 | 364 | 4 |
| 46 1/16 | 47 1/2 | Jan | 884 | 1 3/8 | 108 | 2 5/8 |
| 46 1/16 | 50 | Jan | 1367 | 3/4 | 52 | 4 5/8 |
| 46 1/16 | 55 | May | 1092 | 2 1/16 | 57 | 10 1/4 |
| 46 1/16 | 55 | Aug | ... | ... | 1015 | 11 1/8 |

| Option/Strike | | Exp. | Call Vol. | Call Last | Put Vol. | Put Last |
|---|---|---|---|---|---|---|
| BankNY | 35 | Feb | 502 | 2 13/16 | 18 | 1 15/16 |
| BanynSys | 17 1/2 | Jan | 408 | 1 15/16 | 15 | 1 1/2 |
| BarNbl | 20 | Feb | 1884 | 1 3/4 | 15 | 2 |
| BearSt | 40 | Feb | 1092 | 1 3/4 | 60 | 3 5/8 |
| BellAtl | 30 | Jan | 6016 | 30 | ... | ... |
| 59 15/16 | 35 | Jan | 500 | 25 | ... | ... |
| 59 15/16 | 40 | Jan | 5716 | 20 | ... | ... |
| 59 15/16 | 45 | Jan | 800 | 15 | ... | ... |
| 59 15/16 | 65 | Jan | 44 | 3/8 | 1300 | 5 1/2 |
| BestBuy | 40 | Jan | 1046 | 15 7/8 | 13 | 1/8 |
| 56 | 50 | Jan | 599 | 7 5/8 | 375 | 1 5/8 |
| 56 | 55 | Jan | 908 | 4 1/2 | 96 | 3 |
| 56 | 60 | Jan | 1955 | 2 3/16 | 71 | 5 1/2 |
| 56 | 65 | Jan | 425 | 15/16 | ... | ... |
| Beth S | 10 | Jul | 447 | 1 1/16 | 10 | 2 |
| Biovail | 65 | Jan | 411 | 22 5/8 | ... | ... |
| 88 3/8 | 75 | Apr | 471 | 16 1/8 | 204 | 2 3/8 |
| Blk Dk | 45 | Aug | ... | ... | 1000 | 3 3/8 |
| Boeing | 40 | Jan | 2152 | 3 1/2 | 195 | 7/16 |
| 42 5/8 | 45 | Jan | 2255 | 9/16 | 92 | 2 13/16 |
| 42 5/8 | 45 | Feb | 1065 | 1 1/4 | 448 | 3 1/4 |
| 42 5/8 | 45 | May | 481 | 2 3/4 | 3 | 4 1/2 |
| 42 5/8 | 50 | May | 414 | 1 1/4 | 4 | 7 5/8 |
| BostSc | 25 | Jan | 519 | 1 5/16 | 205 | 1 3/16 |
| 25 1/16 | 25 | Feb | 371 | 2 1/16 | 1545 | 2 |
| 25 1/16 | 30 | Jan | 30 | 1/8 | 1010 | 5 3/8 |
| BrMSq | 55 | Jan | 3 | 5 5/8 | 735 | 15/16 |
| 58 15/16 | 70 | Jan | 114 | 3/16 | 1076 | 10 3/4 |
| 58 15/16 | 80 | Mar | 596 | 3/8 | 1 | 21 |
| BroadVis | 150 | Jan | 832 | 23 1/8 | 102 | 14 |
| 159 7/8 | 160 | Jan | 613 | 20 1/4 | 85 | 19 1/8 |
| 159 7/8 | 170 | Jan | 1108 | 15 5/8 | 47 | 24 1/4 |
| 159 7/8 | 180 | Jan | 433 | 12 1/2 | 18 | 38 3/4 |
| BrcdeCo | 150 | Jan | 906 | 24 | 35 | 6 1/4 |
| CBS Cp | 45 | Jan | 639 | 9 1/8 | ... | ... |
| 54 1/8 | 50 | Jan | 438 | 4 1/2 | 260 | 3/8 |
| 54 1/8 | 50 | Jul | 510 | 9 1/8 | ... | ... |
| 54 1/8 | 55 | Jan | 470 | 1 1/2 | 42 | 2 3/16 |
| 54 1/8 | 55 | Feb | 1696 | 2 1/2 | 1502 | 3 1/2 |
| CMGI Inc | 120 | Mar | 1135 | 71 1/8 | ... | ... |
| 283 | 200 | Jan | 859 | 91 1/8 | 408 | 3 |
| 283 | 240 | Jan | 1203 | 60 7/8 | 459 | 11 |
| 283 | 250 | Jan | 1773 | 48 3/8 | 994 | 15 |
| 283 | 250 | Jun | 460 | 84 | 20 | 42 5/8 |
| 283 | 260 | Jan | 1149 | 44 1/2 | 389 | 18 |
| 283 | 300 | Jan | 2388 | 23 1/8 | 110 | 38 1/4 |
| 283 | 300 | Feb | 441 | 37 | 7 | 55 |
| 283 | 310 | Jan | 995 | 23 7/8 | 94 | 57 1/4 |
| 283 | 320 | Jan | 2355 | 19 | 186 | 54 5/8 |
| 283 | 340 | Jan | 1302 | 13 7/8 | 4 | 64 5/8 |
| Cabltrn | 20 | Jan | 404 | 4 7/8 | 12 | 7/16 |
| 24 5/16 | 25 | Jan | 493 | 1 9/16 | 39 | 2 7/16 |
| 24 5/16 | 35 | Jan | 1750 | 1/4 | ... | ... |
| 24 5/16 | 45 | Jan | 1000 | 1/16 | ... | ... |
| Caterp | 40 | May | 2 | 9 5/8 | 400 | 1 3/8 |
| 49 1/8 | 45 | Feb | 7 | 6 | 675 | 1 1/8 |
| 49 1/8 | 50 | Jan | 450 | 1 5/8 | 199 | 2 |
| 49 1/8 | 50 | Aug | 4050 | 5 3/4 | 3 | 6 1/4 |
| 49 1/8 | 60 | May | 403 | 1 5/8 | 1 | 11 1/4 |
| Cendant | 25 | Feb | 3327 | 1 1/8 | 3 | 3 |
| Chase n | 70 | Jan | 393 | 3 | 40 | 2 7/16 |
| 70 7/16 | 70 | Jun | 69 | 8 5/8 | 1517 | 6 1/2 |
| 70 7/16 | 75 | Feb | 2039 | 2 3/4 | 23 | 6 1/2 |
| ChkPntSf | 210 | Jan | 472 | 9 3/8 | ... | ... |
| CienaCp | 50 | Jan | 2310 | 4 1/8 | 968 | 4 1/8 |
| 49 3/4 | 50 | Feb | 889 | 6 1/8 | 72 | 6 |
| 49 3/4 | 60 | Jan | 578 | 1 3/16 | 49 | 11 |
| 49 3/4 | 60 | Feb | 898 | 2 15/16 | ... | ... |
| 49 3/4 | 65 | Jan | 1708 | 11/16 | ... | ... |
| Cisco | 60 | Jan | 2744 | 43 3/4 | 10 | 1/8 |
| 102 3/8 | 72 1/2 | Jan | 3355 | 31 | 17 | 1/8 |
| 102 3/8 | 80 | Jan | 1375 | 22 3/8 | 218 | 3/8 |
| 102 3/8 | 90 | Jan | 1806 | 13 1/8 | 2148 | 1 1/8 |
| 102 3/8 | 95 | Jan | 2272 | 8 3/4 | 1739 | 1 7/8 |
| 102 3/8 | 100 | Jan | 6248 | 5 1/2 | 4031 | 3 5/8 |
| 102 3/8 | 100 | Feb | 5370 | 8 3/8 | 346 | 6 1/8 |
| 102 3/8 | 100 | Apr | 922 | 12 1/4 | 258 | 8 1/2 |
| 102 3/8 | 105 | Jan | 3904 | 3 | 1282 | 6 |
| 102 3/8 | 105 | Feb | 526 | 6 | 94 | 8 3/8 |
| 102 3/8 | 105 | Apr | 711 | 9 1/4 | 10 | 12 |
| 102 3/8 | 110 | Jan | 3261 | 1 11/16 | 323 | 8 1/8 |
| 102 3/8 | 110 | Apr | 406 | 7 3/8 | 5 | 14 5/8 |
| Citigroup o | 40 | Jan | 1315 | 11 1/8 | 2 | 1/16 |
| Citigrp | 40 | Jun | 1816 | 13 | 203 | 1 5/16 |
| 50 13/16 | 45 | Jan | 49 | 6 1/2 | 594 | 3/8 |
| 50 13/16 | 50 | Jan | 3327 | 2 7/16 | 641 | 1 7/16 |
| 50 13/16 | 50 | Feb | 1195 | 3 1/2 | 103 | 2 9/16 |
| Citigroup o | 53 3/8 | Jan | 637 | 1 1/16 | 10 | 3 |
| Citigrp | 55 | Jan | 1313 | 1/2 | 344 | 4 1/4 |
| 50 13/16 | 55 | Feb | 419 | 1 3/8 | 51 | 5 3/8 |
| Coastl | 35 | Feb | 500 | 1 3/4 | ... | ... |

| Option/Strike | | Exp. | Call Vol. | Call Last | |
|---|---|---|---|---|---|
| Coke | 55 | Jan | 147 | 3 1/8 | |
| 56 15/16 | 60 | Jan | 473 | 3/4 | |
| 56 15/16 | 75 | Jan | ... | ... | 1 |
| 56 15/16 | 80 | Jan | 1 | 1/16 | 1 |
| ColumEn | 60 | Feb | 625 | 6 1/4 | |
| 64 1/4 | 65 | Feb | 666 | 2 3/4 | |
| Comdisc | 35 | Feb | 845 | 3 3/4 | |
| Comeric | 45 | Feb | 505 | 2 1/2 | |
| ComOne | 210 | Jan | 416 | 25 1/2 | |
| Compaq | 22 1/2 | Jan | 635 | 6 1/2 | |
| 27 15/16 | 25 | Jan | 1532 | 4 1/4 | 1 |
| 27 15/16 | 25 | Apr | 911 | 5 7/8 | |
| 27 15/16 | 27 1/2 | Jan | 1103 | 2 7/16 | 1 |
| 27 15/16 | 27 1/2 | Feb | 908 | 3 3/8 | |
| 27 15/16 | 30 | Jan | 11306 | 1 1/4 | |
| 27 15/16 | 30 | Feb | 3378 | 2 5/16 | |
| 27 15/16 | 30 | Apr | 1411 | 3 5/8 | |
| 27 15/16 | 32 1/2 | Jan | 1175 | 5/8 | |
| 27 15/16 | 32 1/2 | Feb | 1413 | 1 7/16 | |
| 27 15/16 | 32 1/2 | Apr | 604 | 2 9/16 | |
| 27 15/16 | 35 | Jan | 635 | 3/8 | |
| 27 15/16 | 35 | Feb | 900 | 7/8 | |
| 27 15/16 | 35 | Apr | 678 | 1 15/16 | |
| 27 15/16 | 37 1/2 | Feb | 437 | 1/2 | |
| 27 15/16 | 40 | Jan | 483 | 1/8 | |
| CompAssoc | 55 | Jan | 125 | 9 1/4 | |
| 63 | 60 | Jan | 647 | 5 | 2 |
| 63 | 65 | Jan | 739 | 2 5/8 | |
| 63 | 65 | Feb | 99 | 4 3/8 | |
| 63 | 70 | Jan | 971 | 1 | |
| 63 | 75 | Jan | 687 | 1/4 | |
| Cmpuwr | 30 | Jan | 314 | 3 1/2 | |
| 32 1/16 | 32 1/2 | Jan | 508 | 2 1/8 | |
| 32 1/16 | 35 | Jan | 792 | 1 1/4 | |
| Comvers | 120 | Apr | 5 | 25 3/8 | |
| 136 | 120 | Jul | 500 | 33 5/8 | |
| 136 | 125 | Jul | ... | ... | |
| 136 | 140 | Jan | 1072 | 5 | |
| Conexnt | 50 | Jan | 1530 | 12 5/8 | |
| 62 3/8 | 65 | Jan | 1259 | 4 | |
| CopMntn | 50 | Jan | 440 | 6 5/8 | |
| 54 1/8 | 57 1/2 | Jan | 500 | 3 7/8 | |
| Corning | 110 | Jan | 903 | 5 1/2 | |
| 107 1/2 | 110 | Feb | 414 | 9 | |
| 107 1/2 | 120 | Jan | 462 | 1 1/2 | |
| Daisytk | 20 | Jan | 1111 | 1 3/4 | |
| 20 7/16 | 22 1/2 | Jan | 509 | 5/8 | |
| DellCptr | 10 | Jan | 401 | 39 | |
| 49 15/16 | 11 1/4 | Jan | 416 | 37 1/4 | |
| 49 15/16 | 17 1/2 | Jan | 490 | 31 | |
| 49 15/16 | 40 | Jan | 563 | 10 1/8 | |
| 49 15/16 | 40 | Feb | 140 | 10 7/8 | |
| 49 15/16 | 42 1/2 | Jan | 387 | 7 3/4 | |
| 49 15/16 | 45 | Jan | 4643 | 5 1/2 | |
| 49 15/16 | 45 | Feb | 1129 | 7 | |
| 49 15/16 | 47 1/2 | Jan | 1633 | 3 1/2 | |
| 49 15/16 | 47 1/2 | Feb | 957 | 5 3/8 | |
| 49 15/16 | 50 | Jan | 7763 | 2 1/4 | |
| 49 15/16 | 50 | Feb | 2380 | 4 1/8 | |
| 49 15/16 | 50 | May | 2143 | 6 1/2 | |
| 49 15/16 | 52 1/2 | Jan | 2405 | 1 1/4 | |
| 49 15/16 | 55 | Jan | 2563 | 11/16 | |
| 49 15/16 | 55 | Feb | 1736 | 2 3/16 | |
| 49 15/16 | 55 | May | 620 | 4 7/8 | |
| 49 15/16 | 60 | Feb | 505 | 1 1/8 | |
| 49 15/16 | 70 | Jan | 501 | 1/16 | |
| DellPneLd | 17 1/2 | Jan | 600 | 1 1/8 | |
| Digisid | 100 | Jan | 514 | 15 1/4 | |
| Disney | 25 | Jan | 3225 | 8 | |
| 32 5/8 | 25 | Jul | 1436 | 9 3/4 | |
| 32 5/8 | 27 1/2 | Jan | 5494 | 5 1/2 | |
| 32 5/8 | 27 1/2 | Apr | 2287 | 7 | |
| 32 5/8 | 30 | Jan | 7591 | 3 1/8 | |
| 32 5/8 | 30 | Feb | 12273 | 4 | |
| 32 5/8 | 30 | Apr | 710 | 4 7/8 | |
| 32 5/8 | 32 1/2 | Jan | 1864 | 1 1/2 | |
| 32 5/8 | 33 3/8 | Jan | 1572 | 1 1/2 | |
| 32 5/8 | 35 | Jan | 822 | 9/16 | |
| 32 5/8 | 35 | Feb | 1148 | 1 1/4 | |
| 32 5/8 | 35 | Apr | 723 | 2 7/16 | |
| DbleClck | 100 | Apr | ... | ... | |
| 224 | 200 | Jan | 514 | 38 | |
| 224 | 220 | Jan | 490 | 32 1/2 | |
| DuPont | 70 | Apr | 485 | 4 1/2 | |
| ETradeGr | 20 | Jan | 688 | 6 3/8 | |
| 26 1/8 | 25 | Jan | 854 | 3 1/8 | |
| 26 1/8 | 30 | Jan | 976 | 1 1/2 | |
| 26 1/8 | 30 | Feb | 697 | 2 11/16 | |
| eBay | 120 | Jan | 320 | 22 | |
| 136 9/16 | 125 | Jan | 101 | 19 | |
| 136 9/16 | 145 | Jan | 273 | 8 | |

**FIGURE 4.1** Listed Options Quotations.

*Source:* Reprinted from the *Wall Street Journal*, January 6, 2000.

This book offers consistency in stock picks and tremendous investment profit potential, the like of which you probably would never achieve on your own. This is your chance at real wealth—don't pass it up. If you want to take the next logical step, stock options can supercharge the equation.

Trade the TTS until you're comfortable. Paper trade options until you're totally comfortable. If, at some point, the two seem to mesh with your trading temperament, and you are absolutely sure you understand what you're getting into, go for it. If they don't coincide, or if you have the slightest doubt, ignore this discussion of options, as it is my guesstimate that perhaps only a small portion of the readers of this book should ever be in options. In fact, I have such strong reservations about the subject as applied to the average investor that I almost left it out of the book. But to do so would not have been fair to those who will read this and make a small fortune because of it.

Understanding the synergy between stocks and options and how that can be exploited for substantial profit may be, for some, the best, most profitable strategy of all.

### The Ten Commandments of Options Success

If you do trade options, here are a few extra measures you can take to ensure your success. We've already discussed my "Ten Commandments of Stock Market Success"; here are my "Ten Commandments of Options Success."

**1.** Just as with the outright purchase of stocks, it pays to have a diverse portfolio. So, while options allow you to control more stock for the same price it would cost to actually purchase far less stock, don't get carried away. Just because you can afford 10 options of stock X doesn't mean that you should buy 10 options. Remember our exposure to loss rules and percentages. Yes, your acceptable loss may allow you to control more stock through options, but it pays to have a variety of option positions with different stocks. Don't forget that, although your total loss potential is known when you purchase the option, under most circumstances you will never allow a 100 percent loss because you would have sold out your position before that happened, assuming that's possible.

And while we are on the subject of diversification, if you trade in options, don't do so entirely. Your portfolio should have stocks, perhaps some bonds, a few options, and so on. Anyone who is not a full-time professional in the options market needs this diversity—it's critical; it's mandatory.

**2.** Don't day trade options. I know that many people who do so have made millions, as the possibility of huge profits is tremendous. But, as with penny stocks, the potential for loss is staggering. The average investor shouldn't day trade stocks or options. You are playing financial Russian roulette when you do.

**3.** Just because a stock comes to your attention via my strategy doesn't mean that you should run out and buy an option on the stock. Some option situations are not a good buy; that is, they are too costly based on stock strength, time, and so forth. This is a key area, and the only way you're going to get a feel for options and their relative pricing is to paper trade for an extended period of time. Don't worry; you've got the time, as your stock portfolio will be doing quite well on its own. When you start showing consistent profits paper trading, you're ready to trade for real.

**4.** There are certain parts of the day when you absolutely must not trade options, because you're going to get whipsawed if you do.

Market orders are not a good idea first thing in the morning, because options are not liquid yet. Exactly why I am not sure. But don't place a market order to buy or sell during the market's opening, because you'll almost always be able to at a better price later during the day. This may sound like a small thing, but it's not. A sixteenth of a point here, an eighth there, and your option position might not recover, especially if you traded both ends of the deal (getting in *and* getting out of the same trade) during this time span.

Equally important, don't let a position get to the point where you have to sell or buy during the last 15 minutes of trading, because you're going to get hammered by the big boys.

These two timing tips can make or break you, so don't ignore them just because they sound simple.

**5.** Stocks go up and stocks go down, so why do almost all individual traders concern themselves only with rising prices? I could play amateur psychiatrist here, but why bother? The fact is that most investors are afraid of shorting the market (investing based on the belief that stock's price will go down), and that is probably costing them big money, especially for those who trade options. This is because put options are more often a better buy. I think this is because the investor psychology we just talked about causes a smaller market universe; they usually trade at a lower price. Your profit potential is as unlimited as with a call, but it will cost you less (normally) to control the 100 shares of stock.

Of course, you know by now that I believe it is imperative that individual investors learn how to make money in both a bull and a bear market. Unfortunately, most don't. Additionally, almost all newer entrants into the stock market don't for obvious reasons. Not knowing how to make money in both kinds of markets is a little like knowing how to drive but not bothering to learn how to back up, because 99.9 percent of the time you're going forward. That's okay until that one-tenth rears its ugly head and you have no choice but to back up. That's what is going to happen to the market, so learn what you need to do before you have no choice, because then it will, for most, be too late.

**6.** Watch the volume of the options you're considering. There are times when you may want to buy two, three, four options of one stock only to find that not one contract of the same has traded all day. Imagine what that is going to do to your strategy. Your broker can tell you how many contracts have traded during the day—always ask about volume before placing an order. You don't want to get into no-man's-land.

Here's a tip that almost always will solve this problem. Trade one of the other contracts on the same stock. The difference in time and cost often makes one option on a stock dormant while others on the same stock are aggressively trading.

**7.** Do not deviate from your plan, no matter what. We talked about greed earlier, but I want to mention it again. Remember, the greed issue with options is different from the greed issue with stocks (although the principle is the same), so go back and read that earlier section in this chapter.

**8.** Always get out prior to the expiration date. We are trading options, and we don't want to be forced actually to trade the stock (not only is this dangerous, but remember, that's one of the reasons we are trading options instead of the stock itself). Pick a date when you are going to close out your position (assuming you haven't reached your profit target—in which case you would be out already). Ensure that the date chosen gives you enough time to accomplish your profit objective. This date should be at least a month prior to the expiration date of the option. This is critical!

**9.** Options tend to be a little more stable in terms of price change than many stocks might be, which is why you can afford to follow this important recommendation. Although many option traders would disagree (but they're pros), don't trade options using market orders. Use limit orders. You may wish to give the broker an okay for a sixteenth or eighth of a point variation—that's up to you—but I strongly recommend staying away from market orders. Notwithstanding the relative stability of option costs, once things get moving they can happen fast, so fast that you may, by using a market order, end up buying a dead bang loser because your order was placed at the wrong time.

This strategy, however, shouldn't bother you, because you want, especially with options, to be in as much control as possible. You've already picked an option, you know your final exit date (assuming you aren't out prior), you've targeted your profit, and you've calculated your diversity considerations. Therefore, why take a chance—what could be a large chance—with a market order that could screw up everything?

**10.** Stay on top of your trades. Even when you place a limit order you can get hurt, and hurt bad, because the right option buy 30 minutes ago can be a terrible buy by the time it is executed. How? The stock heads in the wrong direction big time in the window of your option timing.

Let's say you have a limit order out for an option that is bid at $1\frac{7}{8}$, offered at 2. It takes your broker 20 minutes to execute the order. During this time the stock drops from $45 to $43.50. Your broker calls to tell you that your order was executed at $1\frac{7}{8}$, which was a good price at $45 but a terrible price with the stock at $43.50. In fact, you probably paid double what it should have cost at $43.50.

Obviously, then, since an option's value is based on stock price, you must, when executing a trade, be aware of both option and stock price. Stay on your broker or the Internet for real-time quotes until the trade is made. Any interim stock price movements have to be considered. It's possible that you will at least want to refigure your bid or perhaps cancel altogether.

By the way, consider, using this same scenario, making this trade using a market order. Many of you will say that if a market order had been used this would not have been a problem—no, it probably wouldn't have been. Still, by doing this you may be trading one problem for another. We've already discussed why you don't want to trade options with a market order. No, you can all but eliminate this problem by staying on top of the trade until executed. This is not the time or place to get lazy; there's too much at stake.

As I have said repeatedly, options are not for everyone. If they're not for you, this discussion has still been helpful in that I perhaps helped convince you they are not for you, and that's worth knowing. For the rest of you, you now know enough to consider the process. Again, I felt this worth a few words because it does fit with my TTS discovery, as the value of an option on a stock is predicated on the value of the stock and where—which direction—it is heading. My stock picking system answers those questions. You can let it go at that and stick with the stock, or take it to the next level—but remember this: The TTS is one thing, and picking options is another. If you don't master both sides of the equation, you may pick winning stock after winning stock and still lose money because your options were poorly bought and sold. On the other hand, since you now have the ability to pick winning stocks and you know the direction they're heading, then, assuming you master the options concept, you have the makings of substantial, perhaps huge, profits. Remember that with options, unlike stocks, if they are traded correctly you know the absolute worst that can happen to you (which never should happen if you follow my guidelines), while the upside potentially has no limits.

# CHAPTER 5

# Managing Your Portfolio

## Maximizing Portfolio Return

Every dollar that passes through your investment portfolio must be used to increase your income. Doing less is wasteful and foolish.

The best way to increase your return is to use one or more of the many money market accounts that pay interest instead of letting money, your money, just sit in a non–interest-bearing stock account.

Of course, you must also compare service fees on accounts, as some, while offering a fair market-competitive interest rate, take back that and more in account fees. Clearly, comparison shopping is called for in today's complicated financial marketplace.

### Working Your Money

Here are some additional tips that will help you squeeze every cent out of every dollar.

First, never accumulate idle cash. Don't let cash sit after selling securities, and don't delay in depositing checks into your money market account(s). The sooner you deposit them, the sooner you'll start earning interest.

And don't forget that dividends should start earning interest as soon as possible if they're not used to buy additional stock. Here, too, don't let them sit in a non–interest-bearing stock account.

Second, work your money. Find the accounts that are right for you, and combine them into a personal cash flow system that offers the best possible interest rate return.

If this sounds complicated, it's not. Actually, it's more time-consuming than complicated. Once you've decided on your account combination(s) (stock account, money market, etc.), even time isn't a problem as it's just a matter of a few minutes a week to maximize the use of your cash.

Depending on your financial particulars, you may be losing a substantial sum of money by misusing or underutilizing your cash. My estimate is that the average investor, by not working his or her money, loses $300 to $500 a year by not giving his or her cash the management it deserves.

That may not sound like much, but over the years it adds up, especially if you compound the savings. Let's use the lower estimate, $300, and see what it amounts to over a 40-year financial lifetime if reinvested. Three hundred dollars is an average of $25 per month. If we invest that added income every month for 40 years at an average return rate of just 5 percent, what balance do you think you will have? The answer is a most impressive $38,150.50.

Using the larger estimate of $500, you'd have a monthly deposit of $41.66. At the same average return and term, 5 percent over 40 years, you will have earned an almost unbelievable $63,574.

At 10 percent the $300 would return an account worth $158,101.99. Five hundred dollars of yearly reinvested savings would equal $263,461.15. This is a clear example of the principle that it's important to save money, but it's equally important to use those savings for a greater return. In the short run this may not amount to a hill of beans, but in the long run we're talking about a lot of beans.

Even if your financial lifetime is substantially less than 40 years, the added income will be worth the effort of maximizing your cash, thereby maximizing the return on your portfolio. It's a simple and profitable habit to get into.

Regardless of the return rates at any point in time, you can see that maximizing your cash is an integral part of any successful investment plan.

### Liquidity and Safety

Of course, we cannot forget liquidity, the ability immediately to get to and use your money. It allows the investor, due to a judicious balance of investments and cash, to make immediate changes as circumstances dictate. But your cash should provide more than instant liquidity. Cash management should add to the total portfolio return in the form of interest and/or other forms of return.

If you've read this far you know that I believe in reasonable safety for the invested funds. Following that line of reasoning, you might think that I would recommend that you put all your cash deposits in a federally insured financial institution. Right? Wrong!

This subject is important for two reasons: First, you must understand that many financial markets are not stable or backed by anything other than trust—the faith of investors in the market as opposed to, for example, anything of equal tangible value, such as gold or silver. Destroy the trust in the system and you have created conditions ripe for disaster. That's one reason why the crash of 1987 happened so rapidly on Black Monday. It didn't start because trust was destroyed, but once the market started to rapidly retreat, panic ensued because people had lost faith. The balloon had been punctured.

The same principle holds true with financial institutions. The safety of your local bank, regardless of its apparent stability, is highly suspect. Worse yet, your bank could have an unprofessional management team. The Federal Deposit Insurance Corporation

(FDIC) reports that many financial institutional closings are prompted by mismanagement or illegal insider actions by directors or officers. Additionally, the FDIC has only a small fraction in reserve for the deposits it insures, much like the stock market's value grossly exceeds its accounting worth (a company's assets divided by number of outstanding shares). Its fail-safe is that it's backed by the full faith and credit of the federal government. Unfortunately, the national debt is trillions of dollars, and, as the collapse of the Federal Savings and Loan Insurance Corporation (FSLIC) proved conclusively, when you rely on federally backed deposit insurance, you (as a taxpayer) are insuring yourself. I've expanded on this nuance not only to make the obvious point, but to show you that you have to take everything into consideration when making a financial decision; all things are not necessarily as they appear.

The corporate assets of most reputable investment firms are actually a far better "insurance policy" than what financial institutions offer. That brings us to the alternative to traditional cash savings vehicles: money market funds.

### Money Market Funds

Money market funds, as offered on the market by brokerage houses, historically pay more—in some cases a lot more—than traditional financial institutions. In the not-too-distant past their rates were almost double bank savings rates. Each share of the fund has a redemption value of one dollar. Some people use a money market fund as a semi or long-term savings account, which I don't recommend. You really shouldn't have a savings account at all. With the liquidity in the market, a standard type of savings account is basically foolish. We talked about this earlier. I do, however, recommend money market funds as a place to park your investment monies that are not working at any particular moment. In many cases you can write checks against your account as long as the check exceeds a certain minimum amount. A few examples of fund types:

- *Generic funds.* These funds invest your money in some government securities, bank certificates of deposit, and some good to excellent commercial paper.

- *Government securities funds.* These funds invest only in government securities. If you're nervous about bank CDs and commercial paper, these funds will give you peace of mind—however, as you might expect, because there is less risk, the returns are usually lower than those of other market vehicles.

- *Tax-exempt funds.* These funds purchase short-term obligations of municipalities. Their interest payments are nontaxable. For most of us this is a nonissue, because without the tax considerations the rates are below market. Only the wealthy should consider tax-exempts.

Reviewing: Money market funds can offer numerous possible benefits, such as the ability to write checks at no cost, immediate flexibility, statement accounting, and convenience for your investment plan. Every money market fund has nuances, so shop around for the best deal.

Money market funds should not be confused with a money market account, which was the banking industry's answer to the money market fund. The banks, because savings interest rates dropped so low, have lost so much money to Wall Street in the past 10 years that they have tried to repackage as many of their services in what I call Wall Streetese (like-sounding accounts that are actually very different). Be sure you're getting the account you want and not an account that sounds like what you want. Also, as new accounts are being introduced almost daily, ask the people at your brokerage house what they have to offer. Tell them that you don't want one dollar of your account(s) to ever sit without earning as much as possible, and you'd like to know what they recommend. This is how you create constant cash flow on every dollar. Remember, though, don't look for a little more interest and in the process sacrifice liquidity. We're investing in the stock market, not a savings account.

Having your stock account and money market fund account with the same brokerage house is quite convenient, and makes your plan even easier to manage. It allows you to work your cash with a phone call. Of course, when returns are low, you may have to look elsewhere, but that's not the issue. The point is, never let cash sit without spending a reasonable amount of time maximizing its worth regardless of market conditions.

Every money market fund is different, so understand what you are buying. Stick with institutions, houses, and corporations you know by name. Investigate. Know the firm(s) you are doing business with. Above all, remember that your trust is misplaced if you trust other people or institutions with your financial future. That's not to say you shouldn't use banks, brokerage houses, and so on; rather, it's an acknowledgment of the required perspective.

Obviously, based on the existence of this discussion, I believe most people don't use their cash correctly. They may agonize over their other investments (stocks, bonds, etc.), and then let thousands of dollars sit in an account earning virtually nothing. A gap of this kind in a financial plan can, as the earlier examples prove, be very costly.

Cash is an asset; treat it as such. Andrew Tobias says in *The Only Other Investment Guide You'll Ever Need*, "Cash is variously meant to mean cash, as in dollar bills, tens, and twenties, or 'cash equivalents'—things like money market funds or treasury bills that you could immediately turn into cash, but you have the added attraction of paying some interest until you do. To hold cash (of whichever variety) is to sit on the sidelines." So you tell me, what does anyone gain by sitting on the sidelines? Put it this way: You don't want a good view of the game; you want to *win* the game. Charles Givens says in *Wealth without Risk*, "To become a successful investor, you must be willing to move your money." Enough said.

## Protecting Your Earnings

I don't like the implications of this subject, but as the number of complaints filed against stockbrokers is large and growing, I have no choice but to review it. After all, what good is it to make a fortune employing the Trinity Trading System (TTS) and then lose it to an incompetent or dishonest broker? Tactics like churning (excessive trading of a customer's account by a broker), selling marginal securities, high-pressure selling, as well as criminal violations are commonplace.

The why of brokerage abuse is simple. It's profitable and there's seldom a penalty. The how of the abuse is also simple. It's the commission sales system, which pays brokers for what they sell as opposed to what they earn for their clients.

Full-commission brokers justify their fees by saying the fees are fair remuneration for their expert advice. Notwithstanding their rationalization, the vast majority of trade decisions are made solely by the consumer, and the broker is nothing more than a middleman. Millions of daily trades are charged for advice when none was asked for or was given. This is one of the reasons online trading has exploded like it has.

Brokers are paid a sizable percentage of the fees they generate, so the more trades, the larger their salaries. Of course, that's only part of the problem. For instance, your broker may withhold information that would allow the average investor to make an intelligent financial decision. Unknown to many investors, sponsors of some investments offer incentives for selling their products. Brokers encourage you and others to invest in vehicle A or tax shelter B without caring if it fits your wants and needs. All brokers care about are the free trips they'll earn if they can meet their quotas. In my opinion, brokers should be forced by law to reveal all potential conflicts of interest when they are selling an investment. But, until they are, you have to be on guard.

Brokers are highly regulated, yet broker abuses continue to escalate. Why? Although the regulations are more than adequate, they are seldom enforced. Add to that, brokers are constantly pressured by their houses to sell, sell, sell. If brokers don't meet their sales goals, they are soon without employment. It is easy to see why many forget that they are morally charged with the financial well-being of their clients. The reality of the industry is that sales come first.

Am I being unfair? I don't think so, and neither, apparently, does Thomas Saler, author of *Lies Your Broker Tells You* (1989), one of the best books on the subject of broker abuses. From the book:

> Buyer beware has never been more timely. Americans who believe in financial planning, who think the future can be secured through the valued advice of their trusted brokers, are in for a rude awakening. Most brokers are not investment experts; they are super salespeople. Un- or misinformed, their goal is to sell and make commissions. Inundated only with information, and unable to assess most of it, given its sheer volume, brokers sell themselves and the image of their brokerage firms. To make their money, aggressive brokers must snag clients whenever and wherever they can, using whatever means they have at their disposal. And those means have included high risk trading, fraud, misrepresentation of investment strategies, illegal transferal of a client's funds into a broker's personal account, theft, forgery, unauthorized trading, falsification of documents, and insider trading.

Mr. Saler, a former stockbroker, knows what he is talking about. After reading what he has to say I think you'll have to admit that I am not being an alarmist, and I am not being unfair.

### How to Avoid Problems

I recommend the following to avoid problems:

First, use a discount house or trade online. Doing so can save you as much as 75 percent on your trading costs. Truth is, if you need the advice of a full-service broker, you probably shouldn't be in the market.

Second, if you use a broker, consider the possibility that you may run into an incompetent or dishonest one. A quick test:

- Does your broker call you too often?
- Have most of your broker-initiated trades been losers and the winners don't come close to making up the loss?
- Does your broker use buzzwords like "can't miss," "will double in price," "have to buy now"?

If you recognize any of these habits, your broker, even if you ignore his or her advice, probably isn't your best choice for a market adviser. He or she is obviously incompetent. Too many brokers don't know what they're doing. Again, they're salespeople, and that's all they are. They simply push whatever stocks their bosses recommend or anything they think they can interest you in. Although there are exceptions, many have little personal market expertise.

Most investors allow their brokers to become the dominant players in the relationship. That's a huge mistake. Never forget, brokers work for you. Demand results. If they don't do exactly what you want done in a timely fashion, fire them. It's ironic that so many aggressive business professionals who wouldn't hesitate to fire an employee for one small mistake allow their brokers to cost them thousands of dollars without saying a word. Incompetence, delays in trades, trades not made, and so forth have to be dealt with immediately. The solution? Again, termination.

But the dishonest broker is another problem. Some readers may ask why this is so important. It's important because street-named stock allows the possibility that your broker may, for example, sell the stock and personally use the proceeds, pledge the stock for his or her personal borrowing, or leverage your stock for his or her purposes. That's why you have to check your statements carefully. Match their records with yours. Some brokers will tell you that theft isn't a problem because the Securities Investor Protection Corporation (SIPC) insures their clients' securities. That protection is often misunderstood. It protects against loss or theft only, not valuation. If, because of a broker's actions, your stock has but a fraction of its previous value when it's returned, the depreciation is not necessarily insured. Substantial loss could occur, insurance notwithstanding.

If your broker gives you excuses about statement irregularities, talk to his or her supervisor and write the Securities and Exchange Commission (SEC) immediately. I also suggest a letter to the National Association of Securities Dealers, Inc. (address given later in chapter).

Almost all investors have a broker relationship of some sort. That means you are vulnerable. An incompetent broker can cost you a small fortune. A dishonest broker can take it all.

### The System Protects the Broker at Your Expense

Since the entire securities industry is based on trust, one dishonest broker is too many. This has become an even more important issue since the Supreme Court and the SEC made it easier for the dishonest broker to defraud clients. In *Shearson/American Express vs. McMahon*, the court effectively took away the right of the investor to sue for fraud. No matter how large the loss or the severity of the violation, the only investor option is arbitration supervised by the securities industry. That doesn't sound fair, because it's not. Whenever you allow an industry to police itself, the consumer is at risk. Arbitration on these grounds allows for virtually no discovery, no depositions, no legal representation, or other aspects of a fraud investigation one might expect. In the end, it's your word against the broker's, and the winner will be decided by fellow industry brothers who have a vested interest in the outcome.

Even if you do win, the decision has no effect on future cases of the same kind, or even those involving the same broker. Since criminal charges have nothing to do with arbitration, the broker can be assured of being safe from punishment. Brokers that lose are required only to make restitution. If the brokerage house perpetrated the same fraud on others, no class action benefits accrue. This process not only ignores justice, it encourages fraud.

In case you feel that I am once again being an alarmist, pull out the account form(s) from your brokerage house. Find the section that waives your right to sue. Nearly all the new account forms have this clause. It states that no matter what happens, you will not sue the house or its representative(s). Strip away the legalese and it means if you want to play the game you have to play by their rules, once again proving beyond doubt that the stock market is not a level playing field. Of course, any sensible investor knew all along that the market had major flaws, but this is too much. Would you take your car to a garage that made you sign a waiver stating no matter how bad the repairs, even if they caused your family an accident, you wouldn't sue? Of course not. Yet, investors are asked to give a like all-inclusive waiver to their brokers. What can you do? Now more than ever, understand that your broker is a potential adversary. Any industry that wants the consumer to waive the right to sue for fraud must feel there is a good chance there might be cause for suit. Check your monthly reports and money market account. Ask where your stock is. Take nothing for granted. Your future may depend on you being responsible and aggressive.

### What to Do to Resolve a Problem

Fortunately, there are agencies to help wronged investors. Regardless of the offense, you have no recourse but to try to recover what monies were lost. Once you decide to pursue matters, and before getting involved with the arbitration process, here's where to turn:

1. Call your broker. If he or she isn't able or willing to arrange an outcome that meets with your satisfaction, address an officer of the house. State your complaint in writing. Outline the action you want the house to take to make things right. Make sure to keep copies of all correspondence.

Legitimate brokers and their firms don't want bad publicity, so you have leverage with your complaint. Most grievances are resolved in this manner.

2. File with the broker's trade agency: National Association of Securities Dealers (NASD), Surveillance Department, 1735 K Street, NW, Washington, DC 20006, (202) 728-8000.

3. File with the exchange's discipline committee. Write or call:

   New York Stock Exchange, 11 Wall Street, New York, NY 10005, (212) 656-3000.

   American Stock Exchange, 86 Trinity Place, New York, NY 10006, (212) 306-1000.

   Boston Stock Exchange, 1 Boston Place, Boston, MA 02108, (617) 723-9500.

   Cincinnati Stock Exchange, 205 Dixie Terminal, Cincinnati, OH 45202, (513) 621-1410.

   Midwest Stock Exchange, 440 S. LaSalle Street, Chicago, IL 60605, (312) 663-2222.

   Pacific Stock Exchange, 301 Pine Street, San Francisco, CA 94104, (415) 393-4000.

   Philadelphia Stock Exchange, 1900 Market Street, Philadelphia, PA 10103, (215) 496-5000.

4. Call your state securities officer. Most governmental actions against brokers are processed by this agency. To find the office in your state, write or call: The North American Securities Administration Association, 555 New Jersey Avenue, NW, Suite 750, Washington, DC 20001, (202) 737-0900. They will give you the number to call locally.

5. Make federal contact: The Securities and Exchange Commission (SEC) and the Commodity Futures Trading Commission (CFTC) are available depending on the nature of the difficulty. Write or call: SEC, Consumer Affairs, 450 15th Street, NW,

Washington, DC 20549, (202) 272-7440, or CFTC, Office of Public Information, 2033 K Street, NW, Washington, DC 20581, (202) 254-8630.

You cannot afford to let your broker, or anyone else for that matter, waste or steal your money. If the matter is questionable, pursue it anyway. Let the appropriate agency fix blame. Get in touch with as many agencies as possible, thereby increasing your chance of success. Don't forget nontraditional methods like radio, newspaper, and television action lines. Use every moral method conceivable prior to getting involved with the self-serving industry arbitration process that almost guarantees your money is lost.

Take action. You have no choice. That's the bad news. The good news is that an aggressive investor who understands the system can win almost any legitimate broker dispute.

Lastly, remember that your broker is not your friend. He or she wins with every trade (through commissions and fees); you don't. Most importantly, allow me to state once again—if you need a full-service broker you probably shouldn't be in the market. Fortunately, with the strategy contained in this book, you'll be able to avoid most of the problems associated with full-service "service." Notwithstanding, the issues of illegalities my strategy cannot resolve are the reason for this discourse. Simply stated, the TTS can make you wealthier then you ever dreamed possible—don't let your broker take that away from you and your family.

## What about Taxes?

There are literally hundreds of books on the subject of income taxes (e.g., how to lower them, how to file, and so on). In each and in almost every book on the stock market, there is a chapter on capital gains taxes—what you've generated when you sell a stock that has appreciated in value from when you purchased it. The authors of these books are very dedicated in dissecting the applicable tax law and advising this strategy or that. They'll explain the difference between long-term capital gains and short-term capital gains. The good ones even explain how you may be able to sell a losing stock and still squeeze a tax benefit from the loss. And they'll tell you about the new changes in the law that will give you a lower capital gains tax if you hold an investment at least five years. They'll go on to say, correctly so, that paying capital gains taxes is less expensive than paying the regular income tax and, therefore, the tax on dividends and interest. They are acknowledging that over the years the tax code has tried in its own twisted way to encourage investments.

### Tax Avoidance

It goes without saying that everyone should make every attempt legally to avoid paying taxes, and, as the government is advocating investing, especially for our retirement, we should use the tax code to our advantage. The affluent know this important money-saving truth: Tax evasion is illegal, but avoidance isn't. There is a fine line here, but one that is workable. Supreme Court Justice Felix Frankfurter said (I love this quote, especially the last two lines), "As to the astuteness of taxpayers in ordering their affairs as to minimize taxes, we have said that 'The very meaning of a line in the law is that you may intentionally go as close to it as you can if you do not pass it.' This is so because nobody owes any public duty to pay more than the law demands. Taxes are enforced extractions, not voluntary contributions."

Most of us never realize the distinction between tax evasion and avoidance. Let's use an analogy. Tax avoidance is like shopping at a discount grocery store. Tax evasion is like stealing groceries. The contrast is obvious. So are the consequences. Unfortunately, the Internal Revenue Service has us so intimidated that too few of us avoid what taxes we can. But on the subject of the stock market and taxes one has to have a slightly different perspective or goal. If not, you risk making poor investment choices.

There are, as you surely know, retirement accounts that will allow you to avoid paying tax on part of your income until such time as you retire and start accepting payments. These things are all well and good, but they give the average investor the wrong impression. In a broad sense, the stock market, unlike some investments, is not a good place to help you avoid paying income taxes.

Forget what your broker tells you. Forget what your accountant tells you. While they may have some strategies that in the short run may be beneficial, in the long run no one, in a generic sense, should invest with the primary consideration being avoiding taxes. There are two reasons: (1) The government can't be trusted, and (2) the market has volatility that makes it impossible for all things to remain equal. Let's explore this reasoning further.

### You Can't Trust the Tax Code or Congress

Why would anyone make a long-term investment commitment based on the present tax code? The tax code changes yearly. Your entire strategy that may be rock solid and golden this year may, because Congress once again changes the tax code, be the worst possible investment next year. No one, I repeat, no one, can keep up with the tax code. Forget euphemisms like "The Tax Simplification Act" (now, there's an oxymoron); no one, not even the IRS, can figure out the tax code. Someday when you have nothing better to do, call the IRS with a semicomplicated question. After receiving an answer, hang up and call again and again and again asking the same question. Chances are, no matter how many times you call you're going to get that many different answers from each new IRS employee you talk to. Well, that may be true, you say, but my accountant knows the right answers. Think again. Every year a major financial magazine gives a family's financial particulars to a number of highly qualified accounting firms to calculate the family's taxes. Again, as with IRS employees, they get as many different answers regarding taxes owed as the number of firms in the test-study. The point is, no one can figure out the tax code, and it keeps changing. It is impossible, then, to base any long-term investment strategy on the craziness of the IRS and Congress as it pertains to the tax code. Isn't investing hard enough without factoring in tax gobbledygook? It is for me, and besides, it doesn't, in the long term, guarantee you any more money in your pocket.

As to market volatility, I have seen many a good investment turn to garbage during the time the investor was holding on for tax purposes. For example, because of the taxes that would have to be paid this year they don't want to sell a stock that should be sold. So they hold on through the end of the year only to see the stock take a sharp reversal within days—and what happens? That profit/capital gains tax they were worried about is suddenly a loss. So they decide to hold on even longer in order to "get their money back," which ties up X amount of dollars for another year, which may or may not ever be recouped. There are a million stories like this and they all end the same way, badly. While you're trying to beat the IRS the market beats you. It happens all the time.

As any financial pro can tell you, probably the number one complaint among investors is taxes. I hear it so often that I am sick of it. If you don't like the tax code, vote for someone who will give us a system that is fair and equitable, one that has long-term stability we can rely on when we invest. In the meantime, quit complaining. More importantly, don't fall for the trap. You're not going to beat the system, so why try? We've reached my bottom line on this subject: Never make an investment decision (except immediate ones unaffected by a changing market or tax code) based on tax considerations. You're investing, so invest. That's where you're going to make your money. The IRS can't make a successful investor unsuccessful, nor can it make an unsuccessful investor successful.

Again, don't confuse this advice with the many logical investment decisions that must be made with an eye toward taxes. Specifically, transactions that have a tax impact now, right this minute (year-end comes to mind), or investments that are planned long-term for your retirement. Acknowledging that Social Security isn't going to be able to provide what it promised for most of us makes it wise to make other plans. And, although I don't trust Congress on this subject, what choice do you have? Do you really think, however, that 20 years from now when there may be trillions of dollars in IRAs and other tax-deferred accounts, that Congress won't be tempted to tax your monthly payments at a rate that may completely offset your tax savings to date? I think it's highly likely that Congress will do just that and more. Remember, there was no financial need/"means" testing for Social Security in the government's contract with taxpayers, but politicians are talking about it now.

Every time Congress needs more money it turns to the people who have been wise enough to make provisions for themselves and then calls them "greedy" when they protest. It's like two farmers who are wiped out because of a flood. One had the foresight to buy flood insurance, while the other didn't. What does the government do in situations like this? Out of "compassion" (read: reelection politics) it comes to the rescue of the farmer without flood insurance. It doesn't have to help the farmer who purchased insurance, so everything works out okay, right? Not hardly. The farmer who bought insurance paid a price (premium costs) that the other farmer didn't, for the same end result. That's what the government always does—it turns things upside down to "make things right."

I ask rhetorically, 20, 30 years from now when you have a secure retirement nest egg, isn't it just possible that the government will change the tax code so your retirement bails out those who made no provisions whatsoever? This is another reason I question the sanity of those who base long-term investment decisions on the tax code. How many more times will the government have to break a covenant with the American people before people wake up? Deal with the here and now. Don't find out the hard way that you would have been better off paying a tax rate you know about today than relying on paying some unknown tax rate later.

Again, we should all strive to pay lower taxes. Of course, with my simple approach to things, it once again occurs to me that we should elect people who keep their hands out of our pockets, but that's the stuff of another book.

The stock market is not a good place to be playing games with taxes. In his article entitled "Stocks versus Taxes and Inflation," Peter Brimelow wrote in *Forbes* magazine, "In other words, stocks can help you beat inflation; they aren't so good at beating taxation." He's right. Stocks, because they are generally affected by inflation, have a built-in mechanism that often offsets its pressure. On the other hand, taxes have a negative effect regardless of rate. To the investor, taxes are always a bane to whatever degree (rate) they affect a specific portfolio.

Let me take one more shot at brokers and brokerage firms while we are on this subject. Many brokers who work on commission will call their clients or make cold calls to prospects claiming to have an investment with big tax advantages. Cable television, movie deals, and limited partnerships in almost anything—not only are many of these deals absolute dead bang investment losers, but, because there are high commission and management fees, your tax savings may never materialize in such an amount to cover the loss of real money. This is yet further proof that not all brokers and the houses they work for are to be trusted. It also proves once again that the playing field is not level. Where is the SEC? These kinds of unconscionable brokers are the equivalent of snake oil salesmen selling to little old ladies on their deathbeds, because under normal circumstances the only people who get involved in these supposedly tax-saving fliers are those who don't know any better. Fortunately, most brokers don't peddle these kinds of deals.

### The Basic Tax Consideration Fallacy

Back to specifics. The "tax consideration" thought process itself has always fascinated me for this reason: Let's assume you're in the 39.6

percent tax bracket. What does that mean to a one dollar deduction? Simply put, having spent one dollar you're going to "get back" 39.6 cents. Of course, this facet of the total investment equation has to be coupled with whatever income and dividends your portfolio generates. Having said that, it is fair to say that by itself, unless you're a multimillionaire with special tax features regarding your investments, your one dollar spent in consideration of taxes returns but a fraction of what you spent. Yes, a consideration of tax savings is important, but not by and of itself.

Again, my bottom line: Never make an investment decision (except immediate ones unaffected by a changing market or tax code) based on tax considerations.

## Trading Online

We've talked about full-service brokers. We've talked about discount brokers. It's time to talk about trading online, because it is the perfect adjunct to the trading system outlined in this book. Trading online goes hand in hand with the fact that you, employing the principles in this book, don't need a broker—in fact, as I've hinted throughout, it's probably best if you don't use a full-service broker unless absolutely necessary.

Online investing is exciting and a remarkable technological innovation. I wouldn't necessarily recommend it to everyone unless they are armed with the information contained in this book. That's not to say, of course, that thousands of online investors haven't done quite well by themselves, because they have. But, and I know this is true, almost all were sophisticated investors with a trading game plan— they aren't part-time players. Online trading can and will cause you difficulty without a game plan. But you have one now, so let's get to it!

One of the things that is critical to online investing is choosing which online broker you are going to use. This isn't an unimportant issue, so don't think you can look in the phone book and throw a dart—you need to do a little research on what the different houses offer and at what cost. To that end, the rest of this chapter will help you immeasurably.

Online trading isn't as complicated as you may think (even if you're a computer illiterate like myself). Recent developments have made online trading available to almost everyone. It's reliable. It's safe. Most houses have lowered their costs (and still are doing so) while offering more and more services every day.

### The Online Trading Phenomenon

Online trading is a populist revolution for trading stocks. You no longer need your guru broker type. You don't need your traditional brokerage house. You don't need anyone or anything except your computer to make a trade. You can buy or sell thousands of shares of stocks while sitting at home in your shorts. Online trading is a grass-roots movement that may completely change Wall Street and its closed environment that has not, because of the cost of trading and the necessity of a broker, been good for the individual investor.

Trading online is so simple and inexpensive that over five million investors are doing so as of this writing. It is estimated that at present one out of every four trades is made online. My guess is that this number will get larger and larger until online trading is the number one form of executing orders.

Of course, traditional brokers hated the idea of online trading when it was first introduced, which is one reason everyone should consider online trading; when an industry is that dead-set against something the consumer would be wise to investigate. How revealing that almost every house that originally condemned the online trading idea either now has an online subsidiary/spin-off or shortly will. That says something about the honesty of the industry, doesn't it? Big houses fought the idea for their own bottom-line considerations. When their bottom-line considerations were forced to change and they could no longer hold back the tide, so did their "unbiased" opinion regarding the service. Let's review the service a little closer.

Just how difficult is it to trade online? Want to buy 100 shares of Kmart? Log in to your broker's web site, go to the trading center/page, type in the ticker symbol for Kmart and how many shares you want, hit the "execute trade" symbol, and, in almost all cases, within a few seconds you'll receive confirmation that your trade has been executed. Compare that to calling your broker, waiting on hold, then having to listen to a sales pitch and other ramblings. Perhaps the best part is that online trading will cost you far less than a trade with a full-service broker and noticeably less than with even a discount broker.

As good as the price is for online trading, it's going to get better and better. This is because there is a mini price war going on and the consumer almost always wins when that happens. Since the inception of online trading, prices have gone from around $55 per average trade to about $16 per average trade today (many firms are substantially less than the average). Some houses charge nothing on certain trades. Actually they are still making money on the trade; it just doesn't come from the investor. The house receives a quasi-commission for what is called "payment for order flow." This means that the market makers, the people who maintain a market for a stock or stocks by buying and selling the stocks they represent, pay the broker(s) to ensure they receive the trades of the house regardless of whose trades they are. This, by the way, is another one of those examples that exposes the inbreeding of a system that is supposed to be neutral; but, in this case, it may be beneficial to your bottom line.

However, you need to understand the myriad of conflicts in the market, and this is yet another. At any rate, this payment for order flow means you may, depending on the house and your trade, execute the trade at no cost or a very, very low cost—at a full-service house the very same trade may have cost you $200 or $300.

Online trading is starting to come into focus. First, it's faster. And now we realize that it's substantially cheaper. Not a bad combination, especially when you realize that the system in this book has picked a stock for you that the insiders and market momentum have already preordained would become a winner. In short, we have taken a winning daily double and turned it into a winning trifecta.

There may be some of you who like the sound of online trading, but are somewhat wary and have doubts. I can assure you that after a few trades you'll wonder why you ever put up with the nonsense at your old traditional house. But even at that, some of you may wish for more services, especially when you first start trading the TTS. That's okay—there are firms that are a little more traditional, that offer research news, company reports, technical charts, and data. If you feel the need for such services you'll want to pick one of the firms that makes such information available from my list at the end of this chapter. If you're a long-term investor, some of the added services may help you or even just your emotional well-being. But I have to be honest: Most of you are going to be concerned about one thing and one thing only—price. How much does a trade cost? The point I am trying to make is that you'll want to spend a little time determining what kind of online broker you want and need. If you don't, you'll come to a point where you're disappointed in the broker, because you chose the wrong broker to begin with.

### Types of Online Brokers

To help you make your choice, online brokers fall into three basic categories:

First are houses that cater to retail customers who buy and sell stocks on a fairly regular basis. Most retail customers look for the lowest-cost commissions, although some retail firms offer a variety of extras that you may enjoy looking at—especially the overall market outlook information. But don't get enamored. You now possess a powerful trading system, so you no longer need to waste time and effort with outmoded financial double-talk from an outmoded and suspect system. Don't let the usual market claptrap dissuade you. Rather, dovetail the house's information with those decisions you've already made with a given stock.

The second group of online brokerage firms caters to investors that are active but not hyperkinetic in their trading. These investors are long-term thinkers who take fewer risks with their investments. They usually trade in the blue chip stocks. They are the ones probably more interested in house research, company reports, and other associated data. They don't take fliers.

Of course, houses that cater to these traders cost a little more per trade.

The last house type caters to the traditional investor, the person who invests and basically forgets it. They know they should invest for the future, but they don't necessarily like the concept or process. They'll trade online, but only if it feels like they are doing things the "right" way (i.e., the old-fashioned way). They want to have their hands held. They crave broker attention. They want to talk a trade to death before committing a dime—and there are houses that will meet their demands. As you might expect, this type of house will do the most damage to your commission bottom line. Frankly, if you're that old school, why trade online?

On the subject of cost, you must be aware that the lowest advertised per-trade cost may not be your best bet, because you could be comparing apples and oranges. For example, brokerage X advertises an online per-trade cost of $6, which beats what you're paying now—but unless you've done your homework you may have missed that the $6 per trade applies only to market orders. Perhaps the brokerage charges $15 for a limit order. And if your computer crashes and you have to call in your order, it may cost $30 to do so. All of a sudden you may realize that you should have stayed put. Here's another potentially costly error if you choose the wrong online broker: If your broker doesn't have numerous ways for you to contact him or her, you could, in an emergency, be out of luck at an important time—such as a market reversal or worse. At the very time you need to change the stops on your positions you may not be able to contact anyone (because of traffic) as you watch a portion of your portfolio that could have been saved disappear right in front of your eyes. I'm not trying to scare you. What I want you to realize is that failing to plan is planning to fail. You need to consider every possible contingency before it hits the fan, not after. Then it's too late.

### Types of Online Orders

Once you determine which house or houses you are going to use (and for some investors it might be a good idea to use more than one), you have to understand a web site's order screen. It may be confusing at first. It's not just placing an order and that's it.

For example, there are the various types of orders from which you must choose:

- *All or nothing order.* The broker either fills the whole order or it is canceled.
- *Day order.* This order to buy or sell is canceled if it cannot be executed within the day placed.
- *Do not reduce order.* The broker is ordered not to reduce your order on the ex dividend date, as on that date the share price may be reduced by the value of the dividend.
- *Good till canceled order.* Unless you cancel the order, the broker will continue to try to execute the order no matter how long it takes.
- *Limit order.* This order tells the broker to trade the stock at a price of $X or better. If such a price cannot be garnered, the trade is not made.
- *Market order.* The broker is directed to place the order as soon as able at the best price available at that time.

- *Partial fill order.* The broker is directed by the client to fill the order in a series of steps.

- *Stop order.* This is an order to sell a stock once it reaches a predetermined price set by you.

As I said, these orders can become confusing, especially if you're used to talking to your broker and having him or her execute an order per your instructions even if you didn't know or understand the technicalities—or even if you weren't sure of the name of the type of order you needed. When you trade online you need to know what you want and how to place it and under what name the transaction will be recognizable and thereby fillable.

Some brokerage Web pages have a demonstration tour. Make use of it if your choice of a firm has one. The more familiar you are with the system the less likely a system error will be made.

### Top Online Brokers Guide

Having made an issue of finding the right online brokerage house, the following list of brokerages will help you both locate and contact the one(s) best for you. I have rated them based on (1) the competitiveness of their cost per trade and/or any other account costs; (2) their Web pages—whether they have a quality test mode, how easy it is or isn't to understand the page and its directions, the quality of their research (how up-to-date and in-depth), how up-to-the-minute their quotes are, and how easy it is to place an order; (3) what contact alternatives they offer (such as 24-hour broker contact if desired or required); and (4) the responsiveness of their customer service. Please make special note of this last item, as without good to excellent customer service the previous three considerations may have little meaning; you must be able to receive an almost immediate response from customer service, especially when there are problems in the market or with your account. Any house listed without a comment on customer service had a good to excellent rating, but things

change, which is why I recommend that you test the kind of re-
sponses you get about once a month. Ask a question, then see how
long it takes someone to get back to you. Are you satisfied with the
answer? If not, change houses before you find out the hard way that
the service has slipped.

These are the top online brokers and their services as of this
writing:

*Ameritrade:* www.ameritrade.com—800-454-9272—trade $8—
real-time quotes—free, but limited research—customer service is fair—trading page is average—24-hour live broker not
available.

*Charles Schwab:* www.schwab.com—800-435-4000—trade $29.95
—real-time quotes—decent research—almost 300 branch offices
means convenience—but the commissions are way too high for
the online industry—24-hour live broker available.

*Datek Online:* www.datek.com—888-454-2835—trade $9.99—real-
time quotes—decent, but limited research—low prices combined with fast order execution—additional nontrade services
are, at present, substandard—24-hour live broker not available.

*Discover Brokerage Direct:* www.discoverbrokerage.com—800-
584-6837—trade $14.95—real-time quotes—research is good,
but sometimes a little behind—good Web page, easy to understand—24-hour live broker available.

*DLJdirect:* www.dljdirect.com—800-825-5732—trade $20—real-
time quotes—good research—good Web page—trade costs too
high—24-hour live broker not available.

*E\*Trade:* www.etrade.com—800-786-2572—trade $14.95—real-
time quotes—research is a little slow—decent Web page—24-
hour live broker not available.

*Fidelity:* www.fidelity.com—800-544-7272—trade $14.95—real-
time quotes—weak research—decent service—charges for
some research—24-hour live broker available.

*National Discount Brokers:* www.ndb.com—800-888-3999—
trade $14.95—real-time quotes—some pages load slowly—good
trading page—24-hour live broker not available.

*Quick & Reilly:* www.quickway.net—800-837-7220—trade $19.95—
real-time quotes—decent research—no minimum balance requirement—24-hour live broker not available—Web page may
confuse some new traders.

*Sure Trade:* www.suretrade.com—800-566-2031—trade $7.95—
real-time quotes—at these prices, as you might expect, service
is at a minimum—however, research appears to be good to excellent—24-hour live broker not available.

*Waterhouse:* www.waterhouse.com—800-934-4410—trade $12—
real-time quotes—more traditional house; that is, they will walk
you through almost anything you need—decent research—24-
hour live broker available.

*Web Street Securities:* www.webstreetsecurities.com—800-932-
8723—trade $14.95—real-time quotes—fast site—some trades
(as noted earlier in general reference) are free of charge—decent research—24-hour live broker available.

The services offered by the online trading industry are changing
daily, so I encourage you to call each house listed and talk to someone, preferably a broker, to get the latest services being offered and
at what cost. Then, too, more houses are going online, so you want to
ensure that you check out new entrants.

You know, it's almost like online trading was invented for the stock
strategy revealed in this book. It goes hand in glove with the fact that
once you master the strategy (and let's face it, that's only going to
take a few minutes) you don't need the usual trappings associated
with the market. You have virtually no reason to need or talk to a broker. In fact, a broker, certainly the typical broker, is a hindrance,
wasting your time when you already know what you want and how
many shares you want to buy. My strategy and online trading elimi-

nate the need for unwanted broker sales calls (don't you just hate those?), sales calls that, if you listen, almost always cost you money—and even the occasional winner touted by your broker is almost always offset by his or her numerous losers. But that's all history now. Now, you, armed with the TTS and the ability to trade online, don't need anyone to make a fortune.

# CHAPTER 6

# Conclusion

This book contains an extremely powerful and most unique stock market investment discovery.

Understanding resistance barrier breakthroughs and what they actually represent—and then trading on those signals—eliminates human error and investment frailties. It protects your investment(s), while maximizing profits. It provides winning trade after winning trade regardless of market direction. In short, if you follow the plan you will be rewarded beyond what most could produce in even the best possible market conditions. And you can do so without being a market genius. In fact, as proved herein, you have to know very little about the stock market and virtually nothing about the stocks you buy and sell.

Information contained in this book not specifically devoted to picking winning stocks consists of principles that maximize the profit of your stock picks. At that point the plan is an account maintenance technique. Armed with its guidelines, your stock choices and account decisions are easy to determine.

Within reason, the plan doesn't depend on investment knowledge. Of course, if you pick a losing stock and don't protect your position with a stop-loss order, you're on your own. And if you don't let your winners ride via a rolling stop-loss, you're on your own there, too. On the other hand, if you follow the rules the plan will produce, and produce, and produce. The fine-tuning, as outlined, will make the plan work even better. If you see a swing when the market is changing direction, you may wish to get out of a position prior to the time originally planned. It's not necessary, but if the move is timed right all the better.

Follow the trends, signs, and benchmarks I've outlined. You must comprehend the entire gestalt as, over the long run, even though you might guess right occasionally, the plan will produce more than pure intuition could.

The most important element of the Trinity Trading System (TTS) is the offering of totally objective, unbelievably well researched stock picks and account management with just a few minutes of effort on your part per day. Over time, and with very little money to start, the system can make you wealthy. This isn't one of those plans that offers wealth as long as you have substantial capital to get started. You can begin with as little as a few hundred dollars, and add to it along the way.

The strategy has no bounds, it requires no market expert to help you, and it doesn't depend on a tremendously strong market for results. In fact, you're going to make money, big money, in all market conditions.

Again, don't let my strategy's simplicity fool you. Yes, it will take only a few minutes a day to produce extraordinary profits. Why? Because you're tapping into inside information you're not supposed to have. For the first time in your investing life, you are going to have the same head start on the market in general and individual stocks in particular as some of the world's richest and most powerful investors. That's why you and this strategy can do in minutes what most investors cannot do in hours, days, months, or years. I believe you will look back one day and realize that your decision to purchase this book and follow its advice was the best investment decision you ever made.

I have spent much time explaining why I believe there will be a crash of sorts down the line. I did so not to warn you of the crash itself, although I am, but rather to inform you of the reason why there will be a crash. It's the reason that's illuminating. The market will crash, if it hasn't already, because the market is not what most people think it is. It is no longer a reflection of a truly free market. Instead, it was designed by and for insiders and people with huge amounts of money—anyone who, through whatever means, has the capacity, legally or otherwise, to influence the market or individual stocks. You must understand this fact of life. I hope I have convinced you. I would hate for you to learn this the hard way.

I also tried to make clear that the economy that has driven the market upsurge (coupled with overselling/overvaluation) isn't as strong as everyone would have you believe. There are no federal surpluses (how can you have a surplus when you're many trillions of dollars in debt?), personal bankruptcies continue at a record pace, many banks are now starting to show weakness in their lending portfolios, credit card delinquencies are skyrocketing, and the world economy that we're depending on in the next century looks weaker by the day. Japan still has problems. Russia has problems. Much of South America has problems, and on and on. But there is another problem, the problem of economic cycles.

The following is from *Money, Greed and Risk* (1999), by Charles R. Morris:

In the end, of course, there is no magic formula that will sweep away all the issues raised by the uncertainties of capitalism. Perhaps because so much chance is hard-wired into the human condition, most adults, despite the rush that may accompany high-stakes activity, understand that it is foolish to take unnecessary risks with regard to personal safety or economic well-being. In fact, economists have thoroughly documented the pervasiveness of risk-averse behavior: The average individual, according to this research, actually takes fewer risks than he or she should (should, that is, according to the economists). Still, it seems true that Americans tolerate a greater degree of market risk than do many other wealthy societies. They do so not because they are exceptionally reckless, but rather they place a high value on the positive results of a relatively unfettered free market. Given that reality about our nation, the importance of a better understanding of how financial crises happen is obvious. . . .

The story of finance is therefore one of innovation, crisis, and consolidation. Industrial, commercial, or technological change calls forth an innovation—paper trade credits, private company stocks and bonds, retail stock markets, junk bonds, collateralized mortgage obligations, derivative instruments. In every case, the innovation solves an immediate problem—expanding trade, financing railroads, restructuring companies, stabilizing pension portfolios—and also triggers a period of greatly increased risk and instability, until institutions catch up. The cycles are as apparent today as they were two hundred years ago. Even many of the instruments are the same.

The old saying that "There's nothing new under the sun" comes to mind. Cycles are cycles, and while specifics may change, certain events are repeated. Sometimes, as I believe is happening now, there is nothing fundamentally wrong with the system per se; it's the abuse (overselling/overvaluation) of the system that is going to trigger a series of negative events that will adversely affect those who are unprepared. Regardless, it is clear that Morris is saying that financial crises are created in any financial environment; it's the nature of the beast. I agree. So for those of you who think that the good times will never end, think again. They will because it is preordained. I believe it may be exceptionally bad this time because the market has been so badly prostituted—this coupled with a normally expected cycle reversal could be devastating.

I have to comment on the bull run of these many years. I can assure you that you would have done even better using the TTS despite any success you may have had during that time. I want you to know that. My discovery will produce extraordinary profit in any market condition for one reason and one reason only—it is based/grounded in the market's one true constant: Market insiders and big-money investors strongly influence the market. That's the way it's been from day one (of course, to a lesser degree), that's the way it is now, and that's the way it always will be. And it will be this way in all market conditions.

Not many market strategies offer extraordinary profits in all conditions. Most head for the hills when the bear returns. They are nowhere to be found in a severe market reversal. I, on the other hand, am telling you my system works, period.

Let's review the bidding, so to speak.

- All economies are cyclical. While it may appear to some that the United States has broken that truth, it hasn't. The fact that a crash has temporarily been artificially avoided has postponed the inevitable, and that has created additional stress that will exacerbate the explosion when it happens.

- The stock market is grossly overvalued and oversold. I am trusting that I have convinced you of that by now. If you can't believe me, look again at the comments of Alan Greenspan mentioned earlier. Look again at the historical chart of the stock market.

- The world economy that we are depending on for our future is in shambles. The world market hasn't laid a good foundation (at this point) for the United States; it has, because everything is upside down, added weight to our own inherent financial weaknesses.

Now, why does any of this matter? What does this have to do with the stock market system outlined in this book? It's important because so many of you reading this book have entered the market during this amazing bull run, meaning you know only one thing—a market that keeps going up and up. That reference is dangerous beyond my ability to relate, because when it changes, and it surely will, those investors are going to be blindsided. They may lose their entire portfolios. They may lose most or all of their retirement funds. That's why this subject is important. You must understand that there are bull and bear markets, even though you may never have met the bear. That's why you must be prepared and invest your logic in a system, my system, that gives you a winning answer in all market conditions. The one-sided game you've been playing just won't cut it when the cycle makes its way around again.

So there's a lot going on here. The market you once knew will be gone at some point (if it's not already). Then there is the bastardization of the market by the insiders and big-money players. The convergence of these two events, coupled with an economy that is being portrayed as something it is not, portends disaster.

In closing, I want to note an important thought you may have—and probably did—miss to this point. I love the stock market! I love what it does. I love what it stands for (or what it stood for). I think it is the greatest place for the average investor to make money, big money. I am probably one of the market's biggest cheerleaders. Hard to believe, especially after all the negatives I've written, right? Wrong. I have said nothing bad about the stock market—my negative comments have all been centered around and pointed at the abuses of the stock market. I abhor the lies, the misrepresentations, the manipulation, the insider deals. The stock market was, and hopefully will be again, a pure financial transaction. But until it is, watch out. You're dealing with people who would financially ruin your family for life if they felt it was in their best interests to do so. That doesn't mean you shouldn't invest in the market, because I highly recommend that. All I am trying to say is watch yourself. This is not a level playing field. Find a system (and mine is the only one I know of) that understands the true nature of the market and trades based on the inequity therein. If that sounds harsh, it's not—it's simply the unvarnished truth.

# Appendix

## Mutual Funds

I hope by now that some of you are saying to yourselves, "What about mutual funds?" Good question—what about mutual funds? Won't they do much if not all that my system promises? Before answering that, let's review what conventional wisdom says about mutual funds.

### The Myths

- *Mutual funds are low-risk.* Mutual funds are highly regulated. They provide safety within the confines of an investment; a health service mutual fund, for example, may get out of Company X because it has problems. If you were invested in that stock, as opposed to the fund that had a portion of its money in the company, you would more than likely lose money, whereas the fund will cushion or negate the reversal. Risk is further decreased as fund managers don't last long with bad results, which means they have a vested interest in the results, not just sales commissions.

- *Mutual funds offer diversification.* This is especially helpful to the smaller investor. A fund can give you access to a number of stocks that by yourself you might not be able to afford. Currently, a fund cannot have more than 5 percent of its assets in any one company, which forces diversification and added safety.

- *Mutual funds are low- or no-load (low or no service fees).* Mutual fund shares have the commission included in the shares, or they have no fee whatsoever. They also allow for fractional shares, which, again for the smaller investor, is important.

- *Mutual funds are liquid.* They are almost as liquid as cash. Certainly they are more liquid than a bank certificate of deposit, and in fact can be turned around faster than many stock transactions.

- *Mutual funds have low minimums to invest.* Most funds allow entry for as little as $100. That's a compelling reason to consider funds, as seldom can you invest with these kinds of returns and so little to start.

- *Mutual funds are professionally managed.* As mentioned earlier, you have to be a professional or employ one. A mutual fund relationship provides necessary financial expertise.

- *Mutual funds are flexible.* Most funds have a parallel money market account for customers—meaning, as circumstances dictate a return to a cash position, all you have to do is make a phone call (usually toll free), and transfer what you think prudent. Mutual fund money market interest rates are very competitive and usually exceed what the financial institution industry is offering.

- *Mutual funds can produce profits in bull or bear markets.* Most mutual funds have a number of different funds that offer varying specialties. That means you can shift from yesterday's hot stock(s) to what's hot now.

So if all of this is true, why do you need my strategy? It sounds like all you have to do to get rich is start buying a mutual fund or funds and all of the considerations I seem to be concerned with just go away. Not true. As I said, this description of mutual funds is the conventional wisdom. Let's look at some unflattering truths.

### The Reality

First of all, mutual funds are not investments. Ric Edelman writes in *The Truth about Money* (1996), in the section entitled "Mutual Funds Are Not Investments":

> Rather, mutual funds simply are a method through which people invest. People call my firm all the time asking, "What are your mutual funds paying?" The truth is that mutual funds don't pay anything!
>
> A mutual fund, in fact, is merely a mirror—a reflection of something else. Thus if you own a mutual fund that invests in stocks, you own stocks, and you are as likely to make or lose money as any other person who invests in stock.

You can buy a mutual fund that invests in almost anything (bonds, real estate, government issues, etc.), but whatever the investment, Mr. Edelman, is correct: The safety factor is no better or worse for you than for anyone else investing in the same commodity. But there's more.

Are you aware that a fund is required to invest only 65 percent of its funds according to the strategy as outlined in its prospectus? While you're feeling secure knowing that fund X is investing in a genre of stocks you believe in, the truth is it may be doing a lot of investing you wouldn't be the least bit comfortable with if you were aware of it.

Of course, as a fund is always trying to glorify its image, the fund's name may be very misleading. For instance, some "income funds" make very little income, but it sure sounds good, doesn't it?

Churning, as explained earlier, has always been a problem with stockbrokers. It became a semiscandal a few years back, and, in somewhat of a defense of the industry, many houses guilty of the practice have cleaned up their acts, although it is still done with a regularity I find disturbing. What does this have to do with mutual funds? Everything, as mutual funds are a vehicle where it is easier to hide the practice of churning accounts because commissions are not easily discerned by the abused investor(s). The end result is more fees assessed and perhaps, depending on the trades, more capital gains taxes for trades that should not have been made. This is a real problem for mutual fund owners. Of course, because of a fund's volume, it can be a very lucrative practice—for the fund.

If you were going under the knife for open-heart surgery, wouldn't you want to know who the head surgeon is? Wouldn't you like to meet the man or woman who is going to prepare your personal and sole ownership business tax returns? Wouldn't you like to meet your daughter's fourth-grade teacher? You know, there are so many relationships that we rightfully demand accountability from by knowing who is in charge and what they think about X or Y; certainly we'd like to know their records in their fields of expertise. Yet, when we invest in most mutual funds we more often than not don't have the slightest idea of who's at the helm, what the person's strategy is, what his or her record of performance is, and so on.

The reason for this is that many funds, in order not to let any one person become a media star and therefore acquire too much power and leave for greener pastures, have instituted a group concept for their funds. But this presents problems. For instance, who is the lead dog? If the group has 10 players, are there 10 different strategies all being played within the fund itself? Are their 10 different people investing? What is the experience of each group member? What is the record of each? It is becoming harder and harder to know who has control of your money—and that is dangerous.

When you buy mutual funds, unknown to you, your financial future may be at the mercy of foreign markets as opposed to the U.S. stock market. There are many funds, now that this has become an issue, that state in their prospectuses that they have imposed a cap of, for instance, 10 percent of the fund being in foreign stocks. With only 10 percent of your fund being in foreign stocks it doesn't seem like there is much to worry about. Ten percent is, after all, a small portion of a fund, yet it can represent a great deal of money. At any rate, 10 percent seems about right, right?

Have you ever heard of American Depositary Receipts (ADRs)? I doubt it; it's one of the market's little secrets that insiders would rather you know nothing about. ADRs are listings of foreign companies on our exchanges that are purchased and sold much like general stock. While this isn't necessarily bad, as some ADRs are good investments, there is an element of deception that may cause you to rethink certain funds that advertise self-imposed foreign stock caps of X percent, when in reality, through ADRs, they may have considerably more of the fund invested in foreign companies.

Insiders argue that technically their advertisements are accurate, as ADRs are not foreign stocks; but, let's face it, if that foreign company has difficulties or even goes under, its stock and ADRs are going to get hurt. Frankly, perhaps more than the added exposure to foreign risk (although I think some funds are too heavily invested in foreign stocks and foreign markets) that investors may be buying into with some funds, I object strongly to the deception of ADRs. I'm 55 years old and have learned a lot over the years, especially about financial markets, and I'll tell you something—if a fund lies or tries to deceive you with bogus foreign stock caps, I can guarantee you it is lying or deceiving you on far more important issues.

And while we are on the subject of deception, many funds, like companies do with their prospectuses and year-end reports, try to put the best face forward on their performance. Regulatory agencies have pretty much put a stop recently to the more egregious false sales presentations, but they still exist. But before we get to what is still going on, I want to point out that you should be concerned with the fact that you may be investing in a mutual fund that up until just recently was routinely making misrepresentations to potential and present investors. You should take little comfort in the fact that the Securities and Exchange Commission had to step in and force the truth out of these people. And when you remember what a paper tiger the SEC is and its desire to protect insiders at all costs, you'll quickly realize how bad this situation had gotten for the SEC to do something it didn't want to do—come down on certain funds for their advertising. Now, before you get all warm and fuzzy inside, feeling that since the SEC fixed things there is nothing to worry about, many of the people who were front and center in an attempt to deceive are still around, most of them with the same funds. Knowing they can't be trusted makes you wonder what they're up to now.

But, as I said, even now many funds are trying to skirt the issue by, as opposed to outright lying, making a silk purse out of a sow's ear. For example, one real estate investment trust advertises an averaged return of X percent for the past four years. Later we find out in passing that the fund lost money last year—but, as we are reminded again, the fund has averaged X percent, a better than average return, over the past four years. The bad news is brushed over and made part of the good news. There's an old saying, "Figures don't lie, but liars always figure." This fund hasn't broken the law or SEC regulations, but you have to question its ethics. The real issue that investors have to be concerned with is that the fund lost money last year. Imagine, in a record bull run, this fund lost money. Want to trust it next year? How do you know that at the start of last year the old team didn't quit and it wasn't a completely new management group with one year's experience that let everything go to pieces? There are many questions to be asked. Frankly, because the fund shouldn't have lost money last year and the manager is trying to gloss over the fund's immediate record, I wouldn't give it any of my money.

Another problem with mutual funds is fees—their general fees, management fees of up to 1 percent of the fund's assets, and their sometimes hidden fees. For example, when you buy a closed-end mutual fund at its inception, you are paying an underwriting fee of approximately 6 to 7 percent. That's bad enough, but, as closed-end funds are then traded like stocks, you have to add in another cost because new funds normally trade at a discount. Take the underwriting fee, add to it the usual discount, and you're in the hole big time right out of the box. Did you know this? Was this clear in the prospectus or did any salesperson tell you about this? I doubt it, because their vested interest is to sell the offering and they couldn't do that very well by informing you that you could avoid all this costly nonsense by waiting to buy into the fund at a later date when the underwriting costs and discount have been "paid" by someone else. Here again, there is no violation of law or regulation, but is it ethical? And I have to ask again, why would you want to entrust your money to people who do business this way?

### Sometimes the Fund's Interests Are Not in Your Best Interest

Lastly, I want to warn you that, depending on the fund, you could lose money in it and still have to pay capital gains taxes. How does that sound, mutual fund investors? Remember, when you invest in a fund you have no control over your money (a violation of Rule 5 of the Ten Commandments of Stock Market Success); consequently, the fund's interest may conflict with yours. For example, for a variety of reasons a fund may sell out its position on a number of winning stocks while holding on to a number of year-end losers. This strategy may be perfectly logical and I am not implying that there's anything wrong with this scenario (but there could be). But, and this is the important point, because the fund has a different objective than you have, your interests might be subordinated to its, because the manager or group makes all the decisions. Bottom line? Your fund could lose money this year and you'll pay capital gains taxes anyway. No one should like this possibility, but it comes with the territory.

I'm going to stop this discussion now as it is not my objective to talk you out of mutual funds. All I want you to know is that, like much of the market, mutual funds may not be what you think they are. A fund may not be what you think it is. So why am I picking on mutual funds and not bonds and other investments? I am doing so because so many of the new individual market entrants of the past 10 years are heavily into mutual funds and, based on their experience due to the record bull run, they feel they can't lose, that their money is safe.

Here's the truth: Your fund can and, at some point probably will, lose money, especially if the market tumbles. Assuming your fund invests in stocks, remember that it is no safer than most stocks as, after all, your fund is made up of stocks. Yes, they offer limited diversity, but when a genre of stocks or investments is hit, your fund will be, too. And, as I mentioned, your fund, without your knowledge, may have around a third of its money in perhaps risky foreign markets.

Mutual funds are okay for some people, but, since you bought this book, I doubt if they are right for you as you must be looking for something better. Regardless, everyone should have a little more knowledge about mutual funds, especially people who are trusting their futures to the concept.

Having explained that the supposed benefits of mutual funds are exaggerated and somewhat misleading, there is only one real bottom-line issue when determining whether to buy mutual funds or trade my system—return. It goes without saying that I believe that the TTS will return far, far more than whatever mutual fund you're invested in. Further, should the market hit the wall, you'll be better off with my system as it is likely you'll be out of the market prior to the worst happening. No, I'm not picking on mutual funds; I am simply saying that they are not what many people think they are, especially new investors.

No one should invest in mutual funds unless you simply are not able or capable of investing on your own—and with the TTS being as simple as it is, I don't know how that's possible. But, if that's where you're at, mutual funds are certainly far better than nothing or bungling along on your own or with your broker.

## Q and A with the Author

One of the things I do with my books is submit them to friends whose judgment I trust. I ask them to read the text and then ask questions they deem appropriate for my target audience. This helps me help my readers, since, as any writer will tell you, so many times you leave out things that others not familiar with your work or the subject at hand will simply not understand. To you it seems self-evident; to someone reading it cold it may not make any sense at all.

I was not surprised that I didn't receive the usual number of questions with this book as with some of my others, as this book is about as simple as it gets in terms of demystifying the stock market. Notwithstanding, these are the questions and my answers:

**Q:** Why should anyone believe that you're right and all the experts are wrong in reference to the strength of the market and the economy?

**A:** First of all, I do not stand alone. Remember Alan Greenspan's remarks when the market was approaching 7,000—he, like myself, knew back then that the market was overvalued and oversold. And he is not the only one. Others are starting to see the light, and, as of this writing, more and more cracks in the facade are starting to materialize.

Beyond that, I think, being a history buff, that reviewing some of the comments prior to the Crash of 1929 might help us see that the "experts" are often wrong. Respected economist Irving Fisher wrote just prior to the Crash, "Stock prices have reached what looks like a permanently high plateau." Does that sound familiar? Haven't many respected economists of today said basically the same thing?

John D. Rockefeller said at about the same time, "Believing that fundamental conditions of the country are sound, my son and I have for some days been purchasing sound common stocks." Shortly thereafter it all hit the fan.

The point I am trying to make is this—you can find an "expert" to swear to anything. For the right amount of money you can locate a professional witness who will testify to anything. Why, then, with far more at stake monetarily in the stock market, would you find it shocking to realize that stock market "experts" will say anything to keep the bulls running, because that's where the money is. While there is money to be made in a bear market, the number of investors usually dries up and the number of trades decreases according to the severity of the turnaround.

Of course my reasoning for even mentioning the overvaluation and overselling and the coming results of same is this—it sets the table for telling investors, especially new investors, that they need a reliable system or plan to be successful in the long run. Throwing darts at a board won't cut it anymore. The good news is that the TTS will, as advertised, make money during any market conditions, because under all market conditions insiders and big money influence (unduly) the price of stocks.

**Q:** What do you think of the Securities and Exchange Commission?

**A:** Not much. I don't mean to be flip, but the SEC is a lot like (excuse, once again, the bank reference) bank regulators (remember the savings and loan collapse)—lots of talk, lots of regulation, and no action.

I don't even know where to start on this subject. Only those that have been ripped off by a broker or a house know what a paper tiger the SEC really is.

Ask those that have been talked into the risky business of day trading. They know that the SEC has little real consumer or protection value.

Although I asked previously, look once again at your brokerage house agreement. Check out the arbitration clause and then tell me if the SEC is doing a good job protecting the consumer by ensuring fair and equal treatment in disputes between investors and brokers.

Let me quote the renowned Milton Friedman: "Private monopolies seldom last long unless they can get government assistance in preserving their monopolistic position. In the stock market, the SEC both provides that assistance and shelters the industry from antitrust action." What he was referring to at the time (late 1960s) was the fact that retail brokerage houses had the same fee structures and that the specialists (see Glossary) system was unfair and loaded with vested-interest conflicts. Regardless of the subject, his reference makes clear that he thought then that the SEC had suspect motives. I ask rhetorically, what, in principle, has changed? It is still insiders looking out for insiders.

**Q:** Aren't your Ten Commandments of Stock Market Success rather on the conservative side? All your portfolio guidance has the same conservative tint to it—for instance, you recommend not pyramiding. I know people who have made huge sums of money pyramiding.

**A:** You're right. The TTS, excluding its discovery at its base, is conservative, and it is so for a reason. The market, in a general sense, is not the place for the average investor to make a quick, large, "Gee, I can retire now" killing. You can, however, make what I consider a quick enough killing. Witness many of the charting examples reviewed earlier. Large sums of money were made in a few months to a few years. That window should be adequate for most investors. Those wishing to make it all tomorrow should try commodities; you'll lose your shirt (unless you're a pro), but at least you'll do it quickly.

Quick killings are not my thing, not that I wouldn't like to make one; but, in fact, quick killings in the market usually refer to the investor, not what he or she made.

Things like pyramiding can work well for some people, and you can make a lot of money quickly—if things go your way. If they don't and your timing is off, you'll lose big instead of winning at least something.

The strategy in this book will make you big money in a short amount of time, certainly quicker than if you were on your own or taking the advice of most brokers. And it will do so and still let you get a good night's sleep.

**Q:** You said you let a stock "sell itself." Is that the approach you always recommend?

**A:** Never say never and never say always.

My opinion is that letting a stock sell itself makes a lot of sense, eliminates human error, and allows your profit run to meet or exceed your expectations. There is, however, another recommendation that can be made. Let's say you buy 100 shares of stock at $10 and it goes to $20 (not an unusual scenario with my strategy—look again at the charts). You might want to sell 50 shares, thereby retrieving your original investment. At that point you'll still own 50 shares at $20, or the same original investment valuation as when you started, except now you are playing with "house money," so to speak. Of course it doesn't have to get right to a doubling situation, but you get the point. I know people who have used this strategy and built a rather impressive portfolio doing so. After awhile you may have acquired a rather broad-based ownership of a large number of shares while still being able to use your original investment monies plus whatever you add over the years to buy other opportunities.

I'm glad you brought this subject up, because it gives me the opportunity to tell readers that they should be tailoring my recommendations to their needs. Don't—I repeat, don't—tamper with the principle of my strategy, but feel free to discover what portfolio management techniques work best for you. I think mine are rock solid, but when you write a book like this you have to write in a general sense with the understanding that not everything you say, as much as you believe in it, as much as you've tested it, will be right for everyone. I encourage you to make the TTS better—for you.

What I just said is why you should watch all the experts and talking heads and read the financial columnists with a jaundiced eye. Almost all of them give generic investment advice, and generic investment advice is dangerous. One size does not fit all.

**Q:** Haven't you made a big deal out of your "system"? People seem to be doing pretty well without following any system, and, although I understand why yours works, is it really necessary to follow it religiously?

**A:** I have tried throughout the book to make clear that we have been existing in a very unusual market for an extended period of time, so, yes, some of what you say is true—people have done very well on their own. But it is also true that the bull run has to come to an end, and when it does, the average new investor who's been doing so well is likely to give it all back and more. Why? Because they don't know how to react in all market conditions, that's why. That's like knowing how to drive (here comes another driving analogy) except when it rains, when it snows, or when it's dark outside. Eventually, one's common sense says, a situation will come up when you must drive when it's snowing or raining or it's dark out, so wouldn't it be a good idea to be prepared for that eventuality? Of course, I also said earlier that even though many new investors have done quite well, they could have done better using the TTS. So what I offer isn't just a system that will work when we have a reversal; it works at its peak under all conditions. It does so because it taps into the driving force that moves a stock—and that doesn't change.

Going back to the concept of a system, I say whether you follow mine or not you'd better be following a trading system. It's the only way to avoid hunches, hot tips, and so on. When asked in an interview with *Kiplinger's*, "Do you know any successful investor whose stock picking methods are pure happenstance?" Don Yacktman, a highly respected money manager, answered, "No. And the more logical an investing strategy, the more likely it is to succeed."

There are two important points here. First, he is stating that buying stocks without a plan (happenstance) is a losing strategy. Remember that the next time you get a "hot tip." Secondly, and equally important, he says that the more logical a strategy is the more likelihood of success. The TTS is logic boiled down to its lowest common denominator—and that's why it works.

**Q:** Almost every stock market system is tied into the theory of "buy low, sell high." Yours, on the other hand, seems to have gone in a completely different direction. Why?

**A:** Because my system works.

I didn't try to discover how I could tap into insider/big money information with any preconceived conceptions, meaning that I followed the statistics regardless of where they led. The facts started speaking loud and clear. Some interests influence, sometimes unduly, the stock market and individual stocks, and I wanted part of the action.

Then, too, "buy low, sell high" is an absurdity if taken literally. Of course we all want to buy low and sell high, but who knows what low is? Who knows what high is? We talked about this earlier. If you're looking for a bottom, you're basically guessing. If you're looking for a top, you're also guessing. If you use the TTS you're not guessing at all. With my system you clearly know the direction a stock is heading and—and this is extremely important—you know why and who is forcing the action. There's no guessing here.

The same holds true if you follow my "let the stock sell itself" strategy, as the stock will run out of steam and come back to you when it no longer has the strength you want to be investing in.

I'll tell you this—more people have lost big money trying to "buy low, sell high" than perhaps any strategy ever devised. Further, because the public has bought into the absurdity, insiders use that against them. That's why brokers call with stocks that you can get into "on the ground floor." They know that will ring a bell in the heads of many investors who are looking to "buy low, sell high."

**Q:** Can the TTS really be counted on in all market conditions?

**A:** Absolutely. That's one of the reasons it's special. As I said earlier, it always works because it relies on the one market constant (I hate to keep repeating this, but it's important); the market and specific stocks are influenced by insiders and big-monied investors. That's true in the best of times; that's true in the worst of times. Couple this with the force of the market and the momentum of the stock and you have a clear indication of movement and strength.

**Q:** If you really think the stock market is going to turn around, substantially turn around, how can people following your strategy know when to get out of the market? Aren't they going to get hurt just as badly as everyone else?

**A:** No, they're not. Not because of my system of picking winning stocks, but because they hopefully will have taken to heart my method of portfolio management as explained throughout. Specifically, depending on how fast the crash happens (and remember, I said it may take days or years), everyone will lose some money. The question is, how much? If investors have judiciously applied my rolling stop-loss strategy they will experience very little loss.

Of course, if you're following the other signs along the way, as pointed out in "Market Direction" in Chapter 4, you may not want to wait until it hits the fan. You may decide to get out of the market early and not return until the dust settles. And that wouldn't necessarily be a bad idea, as sometimes the best investment strategy is grab your money and go home.

I worry about people who think they always have to be in the market.

**Q:** Aren't you in contradiction with yourself? On one hand you say the stock market is overvalued and oversold and all the while your strategy/trading system must have been recommending many of those same stocks.

**A:** True enough, it has recommended many of them. But so what? Again, do not confuse a warning about the market with my trading system. The two are only intertwined because I had to tell investors, especially new investors, that this bull run isn't normal, so don't expect a continued win/win situation. They have to know that they need a trading system, or soon will need a trading system.

As for overvaluation, of course stocks are overvalued. Can anyone actually dispute that? But, because the TTS invests in what moves the market or a stock, we don't care if it's overvalued. All we care about is how strong the stock's momentum is. When it breaks through a 52-week price barrier three times within 24 days, it's strong, real strong. When we receive a buy signal using this criterion, I don't care if the stock is overvalued. It is irrelevant. That statement says a lot, by the way—if the market was a true reflection of free-market considerations, it would matter, really matter, if a stock was overvalued; but as the past several years have proven, it doesn't. Overvaluation is critical, of course, as it pertains to the market in general, but we discussed that earlier.

As I also suggested earlier, look at present-day stocks like the pet rock of yesterday. I've forgotten, but I think pet rocks sold for about three or four dollars. Actually it wouldn't matter what they sold for, because in real life they were worthless. But good marketing made them salable. You might even say they were "overvalued and oversold." Did that matter to those who were selling them hand over fist and making a fortune in the process? Of course not. All they cared about was whether there was a market for their product. Likewise, all you should care about is whether there's a market for your stock pick(s). A three-barrier breakthrough in 24 calendar days says there is.

Again, don't misunderstand. You should care that the market is poised for a fall; you should have, assuming you're following my strategy, little concern about individual stocks you've invested in.

**Q:** You said that you weren't sure why a period of 24 calendar days was the benchmark for barrier breakthroughs. I think you said it just worked out that way. How about the breakthroughs themselves? Why is three a buy signal? Why not one or two?

**A:** I can't give you a definitive answer, because the "why" of this strategy in terms of numbers and timing doesn't interest me per se. I can, however, speculate that three seems to be the winnowing-out number when coupled with the number of days (24).

It seems from my research that one or even two breakthroughs could be a false sign perhaps influenced by, for instance, a strong market run. In effect, a stock can be influenced to a new 52-week high by simply being available—a high tide raises all boats kind of thing. Of course, if the tide (run) is strong enough, a stock can be swept up to three new highs within 24 days when under other circumstances it would not have, but if that's the case, so what? Strength, whether market or individual stock (or both), says the stock is a good buy.

I found that a few stocks make as little as one breakthrough and go straight up. The same holds true with two breakthroughs. But, too many of those that don't make three breakthroughs retreat rather rapidly. Again, the winnowing-out process. One or two breakthroughs just isn't enough indication of true strength. Three is.

For those who may have said to themselves that if you buy the stock with one breakthrough you would make more money, that's not true on average. Sure, if a stock goes straight to the moon after its first breakthrough you would have made more by buying then, but remember this: You dramatically increase your odds of a profitable trade when a stock makes three breakthroughs. And even if a stock does go straight up after one breakthrough, how much did you really lose by not buying on the first breakthrough? Very little—all you will lose is the price differential between the first and third break-throughs, which is usually relatively small.

**Q:** Why do you recommend online trading?

**A:** Because with my system you don't need even a discount broker, much less a full-service one. And if you don't need one, why pay for one?

But even online you have to be careful and choose a broker that will meet your needs. That's why I included the phone numbers of the top online houses—so you could shop around. I think one of the most important features I would want in an online account is the ability to talk to a broker 24 hours a day, seven days a week if I have to. Computer systems crash, and if that happens in the middle of an important trade you want to be able to protect your position(s) via the phone to a real, live human being.

As I said in Chapter 5 in the section about online trading, it seems to me to be a perfect fit with a system like mine that all but eliminates the need for a traditional broker and brokerage house, research, and so on. It's simple, fast, and costs less.

**Q:** I don't know that I am comfortable with not reading a prospectus, year-end reports, research, and so forth. Why do you apparently think everyone else is wrong about the need to research prior to a trade?

**A:** I never said that a company's prospectus, year-end report, or anything else it offers shouldn't be read—I said they shouldn't be read by you. You see, this question points up the need to somewhat repeat what I said in the text regarding picking winning stocks.

All the things one would normally do regarding stocks are being done by others who are far better qualified to do so than you or I. On top of that, as I also said earlier, who has the time to read everything that should be read concerning the stocks that interest you? The pros do, only the pros. That's the point of my whole argument regarding research. I'm not saying it's a waste of time; I'm saying it's a complete waste of time for you to attempt. Even if you could, would it make much difference? Remember what I said regarding how these things are written. They are often presented in the best possible light without committing fraud. So you have a number of things working against you. There's not enough time to read everything, and even if you could you wouldn't understand it. But, and here's the bottom line, the pros do, and after they have done so they place their bets on certain stocks. Trusting their knowledge and inside track, I want to invest in the same stocks.

**Q:** Haven't you overdone your harping on the "insiders"?

**A:** No, if anything I've soft-peddled the issue. I think if the average investor really knew what went on behind the scenes in the market there would be a march on Wall Street by investors who have suddenly realized that they, regardless of their present-day success, have been had and earned less than they should/could have, because the system is unfair.

Let's use specialists as an example. A specialist has to have a lot of money and be chosen by the board of the exchange to be the center of all trading for a given stock or stocks. They, as it says in the Glossary, are supposed to ensure a stable market for the stock(s). For this service they receive a cut from every trade in that stock or stocks. You can imagine with present volume that specialists make an ungodly sum for doing nothing other than becoming a middleman in a transaction that actually needs no middleman. It's almost like a legal protection racket: If you want to trade a certain stock you're going to pay the "godfather" of that stock or stocks for the privilege—even if you're not aware the specialist is receiving a fee, or cut of a fee, at your expense.

One thing you need to know is this: Specialists, who basically just match up buyers and sellers, can and do trade their own stocks. Gee, do you think there is the possibility of a conflict of interest under these circumstances?

Because specialists are supposed to ensure a stable market, you'd think in a time of crisis they would jump to the rescue of their stock(s), but that's not always the case. For instance, when President Kennedy was shot the market nose-dived. It was only natural that it did, and it was only natural to believe that it would right itself almost as fast, or at least that's what common sense dictated. So what did the specialists do? Did they jump in as their lofty and valuable position of authority required by providing a "price support"? No, they allowed most prices to free-fall. It wasn't until the next day when the reversal started that the specialists stepped in and bought huge amounts of shares at rock-bottom prices only to see them rise in price almost immediately. Bottom line: Some specialists made small fortunes. They exploited their positions of trust for personal gain. This has happened on more than one occasion.

Is this a big deal? No, it's not, but it is important for investors to understand what the stock market really is, and then, too, this is just one more example of why you need to tap into what the insiders are doing. They have power, enormous power. Power that they turn into enormous amounts of money. You can do the same thing by following their lead.

**Q:** Are you saying that the only reason a stock's price rises or falls is because of insider pressure?

**A:** No. I am suggesting, however, that insider/big money pressure, combined with other market considerations, is often the impetus that makes a sizable move occur.

Having said that, it's important to note that, assuming an isolated stock's movement is not the direct result of insider/big money pressure, the movement/momentum is there nonetheless. In that case, although the why may be in doubt, the movement will not be; the stock will have had at least three barrier breakthroughs within 24 calendar days, and that's all we really care about.

Surely there are stocks that fall into the category of my example. Internet stocks, for instance. It wasn't so much the insiders that made the phenomenon happen, but rather an investor hysteria based on preissue hype (manufactured by insiders). These things, like Internet stocks, take on a life of their own for no apparent reason, but that doesn't mean we shouldn't ride, if appropriate, the profit to be made from others' hysterical mistakes.

**Q:** Just how valid is the resistance barrier theory?

**A:** Remember, I "discovered" (by reading the works of others) the barrier theory in commodities before I applied it to the stock market, so I have to go to the commodity market for your answer.

Virtually all commodity experts use some form of a price barrier breakthrough in their trading system, because they know that once a breakthrough of price barriers occurs that the price line tends to continue in that direction for an extended period of time—in short, something significant has happened. You might say, using a physics analogy, that a body (commodity/stock) in motion tends to stay in motion in the same linear direction.

I then found that a stock's 52-week highs and lows provide an excellent reference point to chart a stock with. It was easy to do (just look in the *Wall Street Journal*) and, because it was based on a one-year "study," I was eliminating any false, not based in hard facts, signals. This, coupled with the important nuance of three breakthroughs (as opposed to the one most commodity experts use) started to fine-tune my theory. As it became more applicable to the market (the theory of barrier breakthroughs) there was still something missing, a timing mechanism. As I explained in Chapter 3, "Picking Winning Stocks," I readily admit I backed into the answer by working in reverse; that is, I checked successful stock breakthroughs and looked for a common denominator. It took me longer than I want to admit to find the right number of days, not because it was complicated, but because the process was time-consuming.

The barrier breakthrough is valid in almost all situations where patterns are discernible, as there are patterns that, once revealed, can be enormously profitable. The stock picking strategy in this book is based in large part on the theory of an order in the stock market (even during times of chaos), coupled with established commodity trading techniques, coupled with my knowledge of the inside workings of the market, with a large dash of portfolio management that adds up to being something worthwhile at the bottom line.

**Q:** How come you have only four trends to follow in the section on market direction in Chapter 4? I know the government and most economists track many, many more.

**A:** For what we're trying to accomplish, in this case getting a head start on where the market is heading, the four I recommended are more than adequate.

It's also important to point out once again that the people you refer to are wrong much of the time. Remember, in many cases, these are the same people that "found" a trillion dollars of "surplus" they missed in their previous report of about a month earlier. These are the same guys that said the S&L crisis wouldn't cost the taxpayer a dime. They missed by billions and billions of dollars.

The point I'm trying to make is this: Most economists are good, hardworking people who try their best to give answers to financial questions. Judging by their track records, they aren't terribly successful. That's why last year's financial genius is often next year's financial fool. It's not them per se; it's one of the things you can depend on in financial markets—change. And, because human nature doesn't allow most of us to change easily, when the economic trappings change, those that don't change with them are toast.

By the way, the TTS does just that (makes necessary changes), because it reports what is happening in real time without clinging to any point of view, so when you trade this system you're not relying on me and my possible undiscovered or undisclosed financial failures, you're buying into tangible market momentum.

**Q:** While not necessarily germain to your strategy I'm curious about something. You've quoted Alan Greenspan repeatedly. Are you a fan?

**A:** I have no respect for the chairman of the Federal Reserve. I have, however, the highest respect for Mr. Greenspan, who is an intelligent man who understands the nation's economy. There's no conflict in my answer, as while I admire Mr. Greenspan, I have no respect for the position of chairman of the Federal Reserve. However, Mr. Greenspan and I often disagree. For example, I find hypocrisy in his railings about the stock market being overvalued when the overvaluation was fueled in part by the Fed's and other U.S. monetary authorities' recent policy of massive monetary expansion.

As for the Federal Reserve itself, in what I believe to be clear violation of Article 1, Section 8, Clause 5 of the Constitution, in 1913 Congress passed the Federal Reserve Act and in doing so gave the power to regulate our money to a handful of unelected bankers. Beyond that, as the constitutional violation is now, by the passage of time, moot, the Federal Reserve is not what most Americans think it is. It is not an agency of the federal government. It is a bank owned completely by its member commercial banks. No one in government has authority over the Fed once appointments have been made. In fact, the president, or any other elected government official for that matter, cannot even sit in on a Fed meeting without the permission of the Fed itself.

I object to an institution, a nongovernmental institution, having that much influence on the economy of our nation that is supposed to be a free market representative. If Mr. Greenspan wakes up tomorrow and decides to raise interest rates (he can raise only the Federal Reserve interest rate, with agreement from other voting Fed members— but then commercial banks always follow suit), every family in the United States with an affected adjustable rate mortgage (ARM) will be paying more for their homes, and others will be paying more for their new car loans, personal loans, and so on. Commercial rates will go up while the stock market goes down. No one or group of unelected people representing not the citizens, but rather commercial banks, should have that kind of power—which is the why of my answer.

You're right, your question doesn't pertain to my stock system per se; but it is another example of things not being what they seem, another example of a few people wielding unbelievable power to influence financial markets. Without exaggerating to make the point, the Federal Reserve—again, an institution owned solely by its member commercial banks—has more raw monetary power than the president, his entire administration, Congress, and the Supreme Court put together. Does that sound like a free market to you?

**Q:** Aren't you treating taxes rather cavalierly?

**A:** I take taxes as seriously as a heart attack, as do most thinking Americans. But, as an adjunct to any system of investing in the stock market it would be a mistake to give them too much credence, unless, as noted, there is an immediate impact that cannot be later lost due to investment reversal or tax law change.

The only point I was trying to make is that investing is investing—taxes are taxes. People shouldn't, as a general rule, let one influence the other.

Try to limit your tax obligation, hire a tax accountant if necessary, but don't make the mistake of letting tax law dictate to you when to buy or sell stock. Those who do are almost always sorry they did. Of course, this book isn't dedicated to tax advice; however, the subject had to be addressed because the TTS can be hurt by those who start playing the tax game.

**Q:** Your discussion of saving—was it really necessary? I mean, aren't most people in the stock market sophisticated enough to know the necessity of saving?

**A:** Apparently not, which is why I broached the subject. Then, too, I wanted to readjust the reader's thinking regarding saving. As I said, most people, when they think of saving, think of a savings account, but they are two different things. Saving is a principle, not an account.

And I know this: Once a person or family gets into the habit of paying themselves first and investing same in the stock market or other investment plan of their choosing, they will always do so, because, although it may take awhile, those savings and what they produce in income will grow to an amazing amount. That's why I included the savings charts—to convince people that what looks like nothing from week to week turns into something big, really big, down the line, which is why you shouldn't get discouraged and not bother.

For those in the stock market, savings are just as necessary. That little amount added to your investments each week or month will add up, but you must save out of every paycheck. It's like serious exercising. You can't just do it when you feel like it or when it's convenient, because you won't achieve the results you're looking for.

Saving gives you the funds to meet your financial objectives.

**Q:** I just can't see that looking after every dollar, working it, and so on, is worth the effort you say it is in the section about maximizing portfolio return.

**A:** The answer to your statement is somewhat contained in the answer right before this one. What seems like a small amount becomes a large amount when added to other savings and then applied to your investments.

I have to admit I have a hard time convincing many people on this important point that you should count every dollar because every dollar counts.

Maybe if I go back to my banking career I can make you understand. Banks are big business. In almost every major city the biggest buildings belong to the banks. They make millions or billions depending on their size. And how do they do that? By squeezing every dollar for all it's worth. An example: Why do you think your bank has a minimum balance requirement on checking accounts of X dollars? How do you think it arrived at that amount? I'll tell you. It surveyed the account base and determined what amount it can charge that will force the most accounts to pay a fee and still be competitive in its market. The bank wants every last dollar out of every last account.

The same holds true for all bank fees, interest rates, and so on. They aren't set arbitrarily. They are set to maximize the bank's return on your money. Banks know that a dollar here, a dollar there, and before you know it you're doing business in the biggest building in town.

Take the government as another example. Why do we have estate taxes? You would think that after a lifetime of paying Social Security taxes, federal income taxes, sales taxes, luxury taxes, user fee taxes, gas taxes, state taxes, real estate taxes, ad infinitum that the government would be satisfied that you paid your fair share. Not so. It wants one more pass at you when you die—it wants one more chance to maximize its return on your money.

See a pattern here? Everybody wants to maximize their return on your money. It only makes sense for you to do the same.

**Q:** Is there an overall philosophy you have regarding investing?

**A:** Philosophy? Not really, but I do have a thought that might be best expressed by the Nike slogan, "Just Do It!"

Dave Chilton said in *The Wealthy Barber*, "The number one enemy of personal finance is procrastination." He, based on my consulting, is right. Sometimes things are that simple. In *Invest in Yourself: Six Secrets to a Rich Life* (1998), authors Marc Eisenson, Gerri Detweiler, and Nancy Castleman write, "The way to wealth is straightforward and simple. Spend less than you earn, avoid debt, and then save and invest for growth." If you think about it, that's pretty much what I've been saying throughout, especially that save and invest part.

I think it is sad that we've gotten so used to believing those who profit by misleading, who say that investing, the market, stocks, bonds, and so on are so complicated that you can't really be successful on your own. Of course, having read this far, you know I believe that no one is going to make you rich except you. Don't get bogged down with financial doublespeak. Don't get bogged down by putting the process of investing off until tomorrow. Don't get bogged down by complicated systems and formulas that take up far more time than what they produce. Plain and simple, don't get bogged down. "Just Do It!"

**Q:** Have you cut out too much of the risk aspect of investing and in doing so cut the potential rewards? The saying "no pain, no gain" comes to mind.

**A:** Yes, my system reduces the element of risk, but not at the cost of potential profit. Quite the contrary: I would argue that the TTS does something exceptional and unique—it reduces risk while increasing the potential for gain because you are riding a proven winner, not just a stock with potential. Potential is great in a minor league pitching prospect; it's not that hot when you're investing.

I would also ask you to reread the chapter on options, which takes my system's gain potential to even greater heights.

Sorry for another sports analogy, but my system gives you the choice of picking 2:1 favorites or 50:1 long shots—with the potential of return being exactly the same. No, in the stock market, with my money, my family's future, I don't like risk. If I could eliminate it completely I would, but while that's impossible, I believe my system all but eliminates undue risk, especially if one uses my portfolio management techniques and pays close, very close, attention to their stop-loss orders.

**Q:** How important is it to follow the purchase price stock limitations you refer to?

**A:** I think this principle needs to be explained further. Let's say you had $500 and purchased a stock at $100 per share. If the stock doubled and went to $200 per share you would have made $500. On the other hand, you could have taken the same $500 and bought 50 shares of stock valued at $10 per share. If that stock doubled and went to $20 per share you would have made $500. There is, of course, no difference between the two returns because money offers a return based on percentages, not share volume. Simply put, $500 invested anywhere will return in profit $500 if it doubles. So profit potential is irrelevant in this decision.

The same holds true for stop-loss percentages. You, when buying a stock, will be willing to lose 10 percent of the trade. It doesn't matter if the stock is valued at $100 or $10 per share; all you're willing to lose is 10 percent, or, in these examples. $10 or $1 per share. Percentages here, too, make the number of shares, and therefore the price, irrelevant. But, and this is the issue, movement of stocks is often predicated on value/purchase price. The lower the price, the seemingly better chance of a quicker return. You follow the market—how many stocks at, let's say, $150 double quickly? How many at $6? What we're talking about is the likely time that a stock takes to produce growth. Of course, this is an averaged observation; there are exceptions.

Using this logic, does that mean we should all be buying penny stocks? Of course not. With penny stocks the element of risk is escalated beyond prudence. No, all I am trying to do is get you to see that there is a benchmark for the price of stocks in your range. It is a good idea to have stocks priced in your price range or below if for no other reason than to ensure your continued market perspective.

By the way, you'll find, again on average, more lower-priced stocks in the new highs category and higher-priced stocks in the new lows category. When you think about it, that only makes sense.

Again, don't be confused here; $500 is $500. A 100 percent return is a 100 percent return. A 10 percent loss is a 10 percent loss. What we're trying to do is build a balanced portfolio. Here again, perhaps this is too simple, but let me ask a rhetorical question. Does it sound right that a $10,000 portfolio should be buying stock at $200 a share? Let me put it yet another way. As you could see from the charts I presented, some of the stocks doubled, split, split again, and so on. If you had a stock at $20 and it doubled in value four times, it would be worth $320. If a $200 stock did the same thing you would have a stock valued at $3,200. Check the *Wall Street Journal*—I ask facetiously, how many listed stocks are selling for $3,200 a share?

You should also note that stock price is often affected by the length of time a company has been in existence. If a company is long-standing and has, for the most part, been profitable to some degree, it will take something substantial to make its probably high-priced stock move substantially—perhaps a new product like Viagra or something else that marketable and/or dramatic. But a newer company that is on the way up hasn't reached its status quo in the marketplace yet. Stocks are like water; they seek their own level and once having reached that level they aren't easily moved. Long-standing companies have reached their level (within parameters); newer entries have not. Both, of course, will be affected by the market itself, economic conditions, and so on; but there is an unknown potential with newer, less aged companies that for obvious reasons have lower-priced stocks.

So in the end we are talking perspective, portfolio management, and potential plus or minus. That is why I recommend buying stocks in your price range.

**Q:** In the chapter on options you repeatedly mentioned leverage. Could you give another example that might help me understand this principle?

**A:** Many people don't understand leverage, because, on its face, it doesn't seem to make sense. Somehow you end up controlling an asset for far less money than you could have purchased it outright for, and that seems wrong.

The example I always like to use is an option to buy real estate. Let's say you believe that your city's greatest potential for growth is west of town where there is a lot of vacant land. You go out and look at the area and believe that one 10-acre parcel might be ideally located for a major outlet store. Instead of trying to buy the property, getting a mortgage (if you could), and then trying to sell the property, you could approach the owner and ask if he or she would sell you the 10 acres for $10,000 an acre sometime within the next year and for the privilege of having a year to complete the deal you'll pay $1,000. Notwithstanding that I am just making up figures, deals like this happen all the time. If the seller thinks $10,000 an acre is a good deal and would like to make a quick $1,000 that he or she gets to keep no matter what, you have a deal. So you spent $1,000 instead of all the costs associated with a $100,000 mortgage (again, if you could get one) and you now have one year to sell the property. The mortgage route would have cost you closing costs and points of about $3,000 and the interest for a year of about $9,000 for a total of $12,000. Let's say you sell the property in a year at $15,000 an acre for a profit of $50,000. Your net with the option is a cool $49,000. Your net the normal way would have been only $38,000. You improved your return by 28.9 percent. Of course, if the property doesn't sell within a year, you lose your $1,000, or 100 percent of your investment. (This doesn't have to be the case with stock options.) Such is the nature of options. This principle works the same way with stocks. You can control and receive the profit from a stock for far less than it would have cost to buy it outright—you can do that because, like our land example, you have the same unknown considerations of a normal stock purchase, but they are crammed into a short period of time that, more than the stock value itself, may dictate your success or failure.

**Q:** What is the main advantage of your trading system over the many that are advertised nationally on TV or via direct mail?

**A:** Simplicity. There are new trading systems introduced every year and they all have one thing in common—they are complicated. If you need a seminar, book, trading manual, or videotape to trade a system (which most require), you are not going to be successful, because, unless you quit your job and trade full-time, the system, regardless of its validity, will eat you alive. It's too complicated to be functional. These trading systems have one strategy if X happens, another if Y happens, and you fall back and punt if Z happens. I tell you the truth: Just because a system is complicated doesn't mean it's good—it just means it's complicated; and that, at some point, is going to cause you trouble, big trouble.

Couple the simplicity of the TTS with its bottom-line results and you have a trading system that meets the criteria everyone should look for when looking to trade a system.

**Q:** Haven't you been exceptionally hard on stockbrokers in terms of their stock market knowledge?

**A:** Let me answer your question with a question. If your stockbrokers are so good at what they do, why are they still working?

Think about that. Here are people who work maybe 10 hours or more a day, making cold calls, listening to clients complain, arguing with people on the floor, taking guff from their bosses, and so on, telling you that they know the market so well that they are going to make you rich. Now, why would anyone work as hard as they do putting up with all sorts of garbage if they really had the key to wealth? Would you? Let's see, I can make myself rich and spend the rest of my life playing golf, taking vacations, or whatever else I want to do, or I can put myself into an early grave working for brokerage house X. Gee, I just don't know what to do.

I want to go on record here that while I have seemingly been somewhat hard on brokers, I know that most of them are hardworking, decent people who are just trying to make an honest living. Truth is, unless they are personally dishonest, they receive my criticism mainly because they are part of a system that has gone astray. Consequently, it's not personal. It is unfortunate that they have to take the brunt because they are the ones up front in the public's eye. It's like I used to tell all my staff at the bank: When customers come in the front door and you wait on them, you, in their eyes, are the bank. The same is true of brokers. They, for many investors, are the stock market, even though they are but a small cog in a gigantic wheel.

**Q:** I assume that the Trinity Trading System also works with Nasdaq—correct?

**A:** Yes, it does. I used the New York Stock Exchange listing as my example in Chapter 3, "Picking Winning Stocks," for obvious reasons, not the least of which was the fact that I primarily focused on the NYSE when I was bringing stocks to the attention of my newsletter readers—but the *Wall Street Journal* charts highs and lows not only for the NYSE, but for the Nasdaq National Market issues as well under the heading "NMS Highs/Lows." I found no difference in charting stocks from either exchange. The three breakthroughs are the same and the 24 calendar days are the same, because the high/low chart is based on the same 52-week criterion and the influences that move stocks in both exchanges are the same.

**Q:** What is your opinion of buying stocks on margin?

**A:** The average investor should never buy stocks on margin. While I know doing so is popular, especially now, and some people have made money doing so, the truth is that margin buying is dangerous. Having read this far all readers must know that I like the concept of leverage, which is what margin buying is in its simplest form; you use a portion of your money, coupled with monies borrowed from your broker (usually at below-market rates), to buy stocks. Example: You buy $2,000 worth of stock using $1,000 of your money and $1,000 of borrowed margin account monies. The stock increases in value to $3,000—which means you made $1,000 with an investment of $1,000 plus the low cost of the interest. Not bad!

Here's the other side of the coin: If the stock goes down "only" 50 percent in value you could lose 100 percent of your investment and owe the interest, too. But—and here is where the real problem lies with this type of leverage buying—if the market and/or your stock(s) decline sufficiently, and, therefore no longer represent the necessary percentages required by the account, your broker will call and tell you that you have to immediately increase the value of your account or sell your stock. Meaning, if you don't have the cash to do so, you will not be able to ride out a perhaps temporary positional loss that you believe will turn around. You'll have to take a loss, perhaps a huge loss, to settle your margin call, and unless you have other funds to deposit in your account to make up the difference, the matter is out of your hands. You have lost control of your stocks, and that violates Rule 5 of our Ten Commandments of Stock Market Success.

**Q:** Why hasn't someone invented or discovered your trading system before now? The theory of resistance barriers has been around a long time and *Wall Street Journal* has been publishing the highs and lows of stocks for an equally long time. It seems like someone should have put two and two together before now, especially if your system has merit.

**A:** I don't doubt for a moment that many investors use the highs and lows of a stock to determine or help determine whether they buy or sell stock. I also don't doubt that someone somewhere has devised a stock version of the commodity-based barrier breakthrough system. Nevertheless, to my knowledge, no one has ever put it all together in the simple manner I have and then broadened the technique to a complete trading system that includes market direction, portfolio management, rolling stop-losses, and so on. Further, I went the extra mile to maximize the potential return generated by such a system by researching how many breakthroughs generate the best and most reliable returns while reducing the potential for loss. I then fine-tuned further by researching how quickly the breakthroughs need to occur to, once again, maximize return while reducing risk. Yes, I would imagine that some people are utilizing portions of the TTS without even realizing it, but no one, again to my knowledge, has even come close to putting it all together. I also have to note this: I see things differently than most people. That doesn't make me right and them wrong; it just means I see things differently. I look hard and long to understand that which many people don't even see. I like to make things better, refine them. I love helping people, especially people I think are being taken advantage of in one form or another. Actually, that was a principal motivational factor in designing the TTS. I wanted to level the playing field so the small investor has the same chance of success as those with more money, power, and influence. I believe I have done what I set out to do.

**Q:** What do you think will be the reaction of the stock market community to your book and its criticism?

**A:** In fairness, it must be noted that any criticism was not gratuitous. It was required to give contextual meaning to the necessity of my system and what makes it tick.

However, unlike my other books that have been reviewed and accepted in a most positive light (one was named one of the "Best Books for Wise and Inquiring Consumers," by the *Library Journal*; others were chosen by numerous book clubs—McGraw-Hill, Rodale, Macmillan, Executive, *Fortune*, Book-of-the-Month, *Money*—and/or were published in audio format and featured in many national publications), I expect this book to be reviled, because I have, albeit necessarily, stepped on too many toes. Stock market books are reviewed by "market professionals" (read, insiders) that are part of the system and therefore often part of the problem, so it is to be expected, after exposing the market as an unlevel playing field, questioning the ethics of some brokers and their houses, bringing to light the conflict of interest of many market writers and TV talking heads, and the like, that there will be repercussions.

More important to my mind, the reaction of those that use the TTS will be beyond positive, because they will be interested in only one thing—what it produces, and in that context I will do quite well, because they're going to do quite well.

# Glossary

Stock-marketese causes confusion for many investors. This glossary will assist you in understanding your choices and opportunities.

**adjusted book value** The value of a company based on current market values instead of the cost minus depreciation standard.

**annual report** All publicly traded companies must issue a yearly report that includes certain financial information. Of course, management tries to paint a rosy picture in the text, regardless of how unfavorable the statistics may be.

**arbitrage** The nearly same-time sale of an asset purchased. The arbitrageur's profit margin is the difference between the buy and sell prices. In effect the arbitrageur simply acts as a middleman.

**asking price** The price at which a seller of an asset offers to sell.

**asset** Anything of value.

**balance sheet** A corporate statement showing a company's assets, liabilities, and capital.

**bankruptcy**   A condition whereby a company cannot pay its debts, and liabilities exceed assets. Bankruptcy can be either personal or corporate.

**bear market**   A period of time when the price trend of stocks and other investment vehicles is in a strong pattern of downward movement.

**bearer instrument**   Any negotiable instrument, stock, bond, check, and so on, that isn't made payable to a specifically named person or entity. Whoever has it in one's possession is considered the owner.

**bearish**   Believing that a bear market is coming or is here.

**bid price**   The price a buyer is willing to pay for a purchase.

**bond**   A certificate that represents a loan to a company or organization.

**book value**   The value of a company's stock, arrived at by taking company equity and dividing it by the total number of outstanding shares.

**broker**   A middleman for the stock market who buys and sells securities for investors.

**brokerage firm/house**   You generally purchase stocks through such a firm, as it's a member of the exchange where your stock is traded.

**bull market**   A period of time when the price trend of stocks, bonds, and so on is in a strong pattern of upward movement.

**bullish**   Believing a bull market is coming or is here.

**ball option**   The right to purchase a set quantity of stock or commodities at a given price if done before a certain agreed-upon date.

**capital**   The net assets of any corporation or person.

**capital gain**   A profit made from the sale of an investment.

**carrying charges**   The storing and/or interest charges on an investment.

**cash**   A medium of exchange.

**cash level**   The amount of liquid assets a company has on hand.

**cash value**   The value of a company using the cash (liquidity) minus liabilities method of accounting.

**certificate of deposit (CD)**   A contract for a deposit of a certain amount of money for a certain amount of time.

**churning**   Excessive trading in a customer's account that has as its sole purpose generating extra income (commissions) for the broker and his or her house.

**closed-end investment company**   A company that invests its shareholders' monies in other companies, usually through the purchase of shares.

**cold call**   A sales technique whereby the customer, without his or her permission, gets solicited via the phone for a stock account or specific sales. Stockbrokers buy lists from list brokers of people who, for whatever reason, are thought to be hot prospects.

**commission**   A fee (usually a percentage of a transaction) charged by brokerage houses for buying and selling securities for investors.

**common stock**   A certificate representing ownership, which is usually last in line in case of corporate liquidation.

**consumer price index (CPI)**   The consumer price index measures average changes in the prices of goods and services. It is based on the average prices of approximately 400 items that are selected to represent the movement of all goods and services. This is done across the nation on a monthly basis.

**contrarian**   An investor or market "expert" who is constantly doing the opposite of what the rest of the market is doing. His or her entire trading strategy may be based on doing what others might think irrational.

**convertible currency**   A currency that can be exchanged for an established commodity, usually a precious metal. The United States uses fiat money (money based on faith), which is not convertible.

**convertible security**   A security that can be exchanged for another known security or commodity at the order of the owner.

**corporation**   An entity that has received government approval to sell stock to investors.

**credit**   As a liability, obtaining borrowed money. As an asset, a deposit to your account(s).

**currency**   Government-issued money.

**current ratio**   A company's current (today's) assets divided by its current liabilities.

**custodial account**   Any account whereby one holds the assets of another.

**cycle**   Used in market terms, the recurring pattern of events.

**dealer**   Like a broker, the dealer buys and sells for others. But, unlike a broker, the dealer also buys and sells for his or her own account.

**debit**   Any form of withdrawal from your accounts.

**debt to equity ratio**   The amount of debt of a company expressed as a percentage of its entire capitalization.

**deflation**   A decrease in general prices, usually caused by a reduction in the money supply.

**deposit account**   Any account that is paid interest.

**depression**   An economic upheaval whereby the standard of living is greatly reduced for the general population.

**devaluation**   Lowering the redemption value of an asset. In general terms, this is normally done by governments with their currencies.

**discount**   The amount that an asset is sold for below its value or sale price.

**discount broker**   A firm just like all other brokerage houses, but its fees and commissions are substantially less—as much as 75 percent less.

**discount rate**   The interest rate charged commercial banks by the Federal Reserve for the privilege of borrowing money.

**discretion**   Allowing a broker to trade your account without getting your permission on each and every transaction.

**disinflation**   A time span when the inflation rate is declining.

**diversification**   Having a variety of stocks in your portfolio instead of just a few.

**dividend**   A payment to shareholders of record that represents a proportionate share of company profits.

**Dow Jones Industrial Average**   The market index that tracks the performance of 30 large U.S. companies that reflect the state of the national economy.

**downside risk**   The real possible monetary decline risk of an asset decreasing in value.

**earned income**   Your salary, wages, and so forth.

**earnings**   The profit of a company.

**earnings growth**   The growth of a company's earnings.

**economic cycle**   A pattern in an economy that alternates prosperity and financial retreat/recession/depression. It is an important and significant facet of a capitalist system; business and commodity prices do not remain constant, but, rather, are affected by various repeating events, such as seasonal variations, wars, depressions in other markets, union strikes, inflation, and so on.

**economics**   The study of how people and countries use resources.

**equity**   The net value of an asset (i.e., its value minus its liabilities).

**exchange rate**   The value of one currency expressed in the value of another currency.

**face value**   The value promised to a bondholder when the bond has matured.

**Federal Reserve**   Owned entirely by its member commercial banks; Fed policy (like the setting of interest rates) greatly impacts the stock market.

**fiduciary**   The act of holding the assets of another, for example, your stock or bank accounts.

**fluctuation**   The changing worth, up or down, of an asset.

**forward contract**   A contract agreement to deliver goods at a future date for a specific price agreed upon now.

**forward price**   The price of goods contained in a forward contract.

**401(k)**   Usually coupled with some kind of profit-sharing plan, this salary reduction retirement plan is funded by employee pretax and employer contributions.

**free market**  A market unencumbered by government. In real terms, no such market exists.

**fundamental analysis**  A technical analysis of a company's strength or weakness based solely on the numbers—for example, debt to equity ratio, earnings per share, and so on.

**futures contract**  A forward contract for buying and selling commodities (gold, wheat, cattle, copper, etc.).

**gap**  A price range that occasionally happens when no stock of a certain company is traded. For example, if the lowest price for stock X is $10 on Tuesday, when on Monday the highest the stock traded was $8, you have a $2 gap where no shares were sold or changed hands.

**hedge**  A side investment purchased to offset conceivable losses in another investment.

**incorporation**  The process whereby a company receives government approval to sell corporate stock.

**index**  There are hundreds of stock indexes that track the performances of certain types of stocks (e.g., the Standard & Poor's 500 and the Russell 2000).

**inflation**  Too much money chasing too few goods. Caused by government, not the private sector.

**initial public offering (IPO)**  To raise money, corporations issue certificates of ownership that they say have a value of, for example, $200 million. The company sells the certificates to a securities dealer/broker, who in turn sells them on the open market through stockbrokers. This is called the first market for the stock, as this is the first time these certificates have been made available to the general public. The entire process is called an initial public offering (IPO).

**insider trading**   Using secret information to buy and sell stocks for profit.

**interest**   The cost of renting money.

**interest rate differential**   The difference between two rates of interest. Example: Banks pay less than 5 percent interest on regular savings accounts while charging two, three, four, or more times that loaning the same monies to others.

**investment club**   A group of people who pool their funds and investment talents to buy and sell stocks.

**investment company**   A company that invests its shareholders' monies in investments, normally the stock market, of the company's choosing.

**investment vehicle**   Any form of investment; for example, mutual funds, certificates of deposit, real estate, investment coins, stocks, bonds, and so on.

**investor**   Someone who buys and sells stock in anticipation of profit.

**IPO**   Acronym for initial public offering.

**IRA**   An individual retirement account.

**junk bonds**   Bonds (unsecured loans) issued by a company for the sole purpose of trying to buy other companies. They have a high return and a high default rate—hence the name junk bonds.

**Keogh plan**   Self-employed retirement account—yearly contributions are free from taxes.

**leverage**   Leveraged transactions involve a degree of speculation; basically, one traded on equity or a portion thereof. Options are a perfect example of leverage.

**liability**   A financial obligation.

**limit order**   Offering to buy if the price falls below a certain price or to sell if it rises above a certain price.

**limited partnership**   Investors (the limited partners) have no say in the daily management of the company. The limited partners cannot lose any more than their investment should the company fail.

**liquidation**   The sale of assets.

**liquidity**   The ability to turn an asset into immediate cash. Real estate is not liquid. Mutual funds are.

**long-term debt**   Company debt that comes due after one year from today's date.

**long-term government debt**   Issues of the federal government that have a fixed rate of interest and maturity from 15 to 30 years.

**low-load mutual fund**   Mutual fund that has a sales cost of 1 to 3 percent.

**margin**   The amount of equity an investor has, as expressed in a percentage of the value of a margin account/purchase.

**margin call**   A demand by the lender that a loan be reduced because the value of the assets pledged has been reduced.

**margin maintenance**   The margin required by a lender. If that margin is not maintained, the assets will be sold.

**margin sale**   Assets sold because a margin call was not met.

**market**   A like group of transactions.

**market maker**   Broker who specializes in a certain stock and agrees to buy or sell that stock at any time.

**market makers securities**   Securities that are sold from the portfolio of the brokerage house as opposed to from another investor.

**market order**   An order to buy X number of shares of Company X at the lowest current price available.

**market timing**   A stock strategy based on current/short-term market forecasts.

**marketable**   The salability of an asset.

**maturity**   The date when a contract comes due.

**monetary inflation**   An increase in the supply of money.

**money**   A medium of exchange that is readily accepted.

**money market fund**   A short-term mutual fund that invests only in interest-bearing securities.

**money supply**   In the United States, the total of our currency.

**moratorium**   A legal delay on the payment of an obligation.

**mutual fund**   A company that invests its stockholders' money in other investments. The important aspect of a mutual fund is that its shares have to be redeemed immediately upon request and at net value.

**negotiable instrument**   An asset, represented by a certificate, that can be readily sold.

**no-load mutual fund**   Mutual fund that has no sales or redemption costs.

**option**   A security, sold by an investor, that allows another to buy or sell at a known price for a certain period of time.

**OTC market**   A network of brokers who trade over-the-counter stocks not listed on a stock exchange.

**par**   The stated value.

**par value**   The face value of a currency or security.

**parking**   Buying shares in a false name so the real owners aren't identifiable.

**penny stocks**   Small companies often have cheap stocks, sometimes costing pennies (hence the name), especially when they're just starting out. Extremely risky investments.

**per share earnings**   The earnings of a company divided by the number of shares outstanding.

**portfolio**   The total investments of an individual or corporation.

**preferred stock**   Stock costing more than common stock because it is less risky and pays higher dividends.

**premium**   The amount that an asset is sold for above its value or sale price.

**price-earnings ratio**   The level of a company's stock price relative to its earnings per share. Most large corporations have P/Es of about 14 (14 times earnings).

**price fixing**   Controlling the price of a tradable/salable commodity by increasing or decreasing the supply. This is usually thought of in the sense of a commodity like gold, silver, diamonds, wheat, corn, and so on, but it can be done with stocks by forcing (through sales) a stock's price up or down.

**prime interest rate**   The loan rate banks charge their best commercial customers. This is the bankers' definition.

**profit sharing**   A plan (yearly or retirement) whereby the employer shares a portion of the company's earnings with the employees.

**purchasing power**   The value of money expressed by the value of the goods the money can purchase.

**put option**   The right to sell an asset at a predetermined price at any time before a certain agreed-upon date.

**pyramiding**   Using paper profits to buy additional positions.

**Quotron**   A program that immediately relates the price movement of stocks and bonds.

**redemption**   The repurchasing of a security by the issuer.

**reserve**   Money put aside for the possibility of paying future losses. In some cases, like a bank's loan loss reserve, a reserve is required by law or statute.

**resistance level**   A price level at which selling is anticipated.

**return indicator**   Any one of numerous methods of assessing the return on an investment.

**return on equity**   Company profit divided by the shareholders' equity.

**reverse stock split**   Reducing the number of shares while increasing the value of said shares.

**right**   A security that allows shareholders to buy additional company stock prior to it being offered to other investors.

**risk capital**   Money used for investing that one can afford to lose without changing one's standard of living or creating a hardship.

**risk/reward ratio**   The ratio of risk as compared to the potential for gain. Normally, high risk equals potentially high rewards and vice versa.

**round lot**   The minimum size of trading that does not incur special trading fees. Often refers to 100 shares of stock.

**Russell 2000**   This index tracks the performance of 2,000 smaller U.S. companies.

**safekeeping account**   An account where one stores the assets of another.

**security**   In an investment sense, a certificate representing money entrusted to another.

**SEP**   The Simplified Employee Pension plan is employer funded.

**share**   A single piece of company stock.

**shareholder**   Anyone owning a share of stock in a company.

**shareholder equity**   The amount of money in a company that belongs to the shareholders.

**short sale**   The selling of a borrowed security.

**specialist**   Responsible for maintaining stability in specific stocks, a specialist is a member of the exchange, owns a seat on the exchange, and is the focal point of trades in those stocks he or she handles.

**speculation**   An investment that involves a high probability of loss.

**spot price**   The price for an immediate sale of an asset.

**spread**   The difference between the asked and bid prices.

**Standard & Poor's 500**   This index tracks the performances of 500 major U.S. companies.

**stock**   A percentage of ownership represented by a paper certificate.

**stock exchange**   A place where stock is bought and sold.

**stock market**   A network of investors and companies that buy and sell stock.

**stock split**   Exchanging X number of shares of stock for X plus or minus shares of stock.

**stop-loss order**   The order to sell an asset if it drops to a certain price level.

**stop order to buy**   The order to buy an asset if it reaches a certain price level.

**strike or striking price**   The price at which a warrant holder may buy an asset.

**takeover**   A transaction whereby one company takes control of another by buying controlling interest (enough stock) in the target company.

**tax**   Money taken from its owner by some form of government. To get a true read on your portfolio return, you must calculate after-tax earnings.

**technician**   A trader who uses charting of a stock to determine when to buy or sell.

**term-to-maturity**   The length of time a bondholder must wait to be paid for the investment.

**trade balance**   A nation's exports minus imports. Balance of trade payments occur when imports exceed exports. Over the long term this can be dangerous to a country's economy.

**trading**   The buying and selling of assets.

**Treasury bills**   Obligations of the federal government that have a fixed rate of interest for a fixed amount of time.

**unearned income**   Nonsalary income; for example, interest, royalties, and dividends.

**upside potential**   The reasonable expectation of the increasing value of an asset.

**warrant**   An option to purchase an asset at a fixed price on a predetermined date.

**wealth**   A measure of usable resources.

# Index

# Contacting the Author

To reach me with any comments, questions, or consulting needs, write:

**Reliance Enterprises, Inc.**
**P.O. Box 413**
**Marengo, IL 60152**